T0099855

On Earth
As It Is In Heaven

Kristin Schneider

TRAFFORD

"David's words with Sibyl's blending"

from the Sequence for the Dead.

To our daughter

Order this book online at www.trafford.com
or email orders@trafford.com

Most Trafford titles are also available at major online book retailers.

© Copyright 2004, 2011 Kristin Schneider.
All rights reserved. No part of this publication may be reproduced, stored in a retrieval system, or transmitted, in any form or by any means, electronic, mechanical, photocopying, recording, or otherwise, without the written prior permission of the author.

Printed in the United States of America.

ISBN: 978-1-4269-7569-1 (sc)
ISBN: 978-1-4269-7570-7 (e)

Trafford rev. 07/11/2011

www.trafford.com

North America & International
toll-free: 1 888 232 4444 (USA & Canada)
phone: 250 383 6864 • fax: 812 355 4082
Trafford Catalogue #03-2721 www.trafford.com/robots/03-2721.html

℘ AUTHOR'S NOTE ☙

This is a work of fiction. The names Sibyl and David I chose for their symbolism in the stories of the ancient Sibyls and their visits to the underworld, and the prophecies of King David. However, Sibyl contains fragments of myself. My philosophy of life, including my visions and dreams, and the confirmations received are included as Sibyl's. The webpage of the book may be found at www.trafford.com/robots/03-2721.html from which copies may be purchased.

Kristin Schneider
Camberwell,
9 July 2011

ഇ ACKNOWLEDGEMENTS ര

My sincere thanks go to the following people. To Juliette Thornton, for encouragement and support for this book. To Pam Marshall, Marianne Josephson, Elza Deres, Barbara Wilson and Margaret Healy for their inspiration for 'Leah'. To Judy Burrell, Delfina Manor, Alison and Alan Murphy, LeAnn Flanigan and Anne Fenton for help with the manuscript. To Liz Johnson for work with the cover design and for her computing skills. To Lynda Robertson and Ray Abbott for assistance with the layout. To Trafford Publishing who arrived at the right moment . And finally to my family, the spiritual and physical, whom I love more each day as the remembrance of our oneness grows.

ꟿ CONTENTS ꟿ

ꕥ PART 1 ꕥ

COMING FORTH INTO MATTER

I reach into my heart and find love. I scatter it to the stars, and they twinkle it back to the earth. My soul hitches a lift, skimming on a pulse of light. I pass by men and women, harvesting grain, making bread. I see hearth fires and bedrooms. Glances acknowledge my journey. Sirius beams me strength and purpose. My beacon ahead, I fly through the veils of existence and alight in grace. Sirius, remember me so that I live.

HERE I AM STANDING in the midst of my panic. I look out of my eyes and everything is altered. The clock has just struck thirteen! Insanity hovers. The room undulates, the real is unreal, the unreal is distorted reality. The pale green walls sway and darken. The cheerful curtains patterned with Eucalyptus leaves become cracks into another more sinister world, foetid vapours swirl around my legs, entrapping me in the stench of the old and not quite forgotten. The mists of my mind return me to the terrified little girl, desperately clutching at her mother's skirts. Don't let her go away and leave me! The outside world threatens with the unknown, the only thing which still has the force to frighten me.

I thought I had beaten panic. I've had it all my life, on and off. I'd developed a different strategy for living through it every time it has appeared. And I thought I had finished with it. It hasn't bothered me for about twenty years, just in flashes, easily assimilated. I'd developed my latest way of dealing with it when living in Sweden. It used to sneak up on me, from the side behind my line of vision. I would begin by feeling uncomfortable, needled. I would be going about my daily chores in the community where I lived, frowning, screwing up my face, trying to shrug off something invisible, not quite in my mind yet. Then suddenly I would see it. I would gasp in surprise. "Oh this is just another one of these things!" I would say, and then I would look directly at it, this disturbance. "So where are we going with you today?" I would say, and immediately the feeling would change. The flap would be over, and the frown would smooth out, a smile would return to my face. So many times I went through that procedure, I thought I had the measure of panic.

But here it is rearing out of control again. It doesn't respond when I look at it and say "What are you up to this time?"

It just gets worse day by day. My honesty is leading me nowhere , it seems to skirt around the edges of a truth which I can't quite grasp.

I wake up in the mornings, my heart pounding, sweating, a tight band around my diaphragm, feeling I haven't slept at all. High blood pressure, death by stroke, or worse, paralysis and a long life. My body is healthy, and could live long. My nervous system is beleaguered, too tired to move. Meditation gives me the only relief, and that transient.

*

I am a woman who has lived more than half her allotted lifespan. I have been a lover, a mother and have lived a long time alone. My career when I followed it was successful but I abandoned it to search for something deeper, a more elusive truth about life. I abandoned my marriage and religion for much the same reason, but never my children. They are scattered over the earth now, finding their own success, but still close to my heart. I am not endowed with physical beauty, or many physical possessions, but my spirit self creates beauty around me, gives me a patience and tolerance, a calmness and generosity which comes from years of silence, meditation, a reverence for nature and the habit of caring for others. I have been ruthless with my beliefs, retaining only those which enhance my life experience, and discarding those which produce limitation and guilt. That is an ongoing process, as beliefs subtly reveal themselves through life's challenges, begging attention and dismantling in one's handling of situations. I have the ultimate respect for myself as a being, as it is through the consideration and love of the self that I can serve all others.

My spirit dances with the wind through the red gums, twining gracefully with the great spirits of nature. Here I am unshackled, reflecting flowers, bathing in their perfume. I see myself performing aerial gymnastics, leaping from tree to tree, faster than the insects, more sure-footed than the birds. Then I spring back into my physical body, back to the flatfoot existence here on earth, plodding about, confined.

My physical self likes to wear bright clothes, unusual creations, deep dark blues and purples, highlights of gold and turquoise. I love soft mohair and brushed wool, furlined boots and coats. Bright coloured stones in rings and necklaces. But on ordinary days I am indistinguishable in my T shirts and trousers. I have given away most of the possessions I had when my children lived with me. I like to live without clutter, simply. I meet my needs, and a bit more, but when possessions start to crowd me again, I take another load down to the op shop. I still enjoy the feel of my lips on my grandmother's fine china cups, each delicately painted. Strong pictures on the walls. The Swedish forest drawn in pencil is fairyland, an aboriginal print, again of a forest is my home territory. Music I play all day long, favouring the overpowering passion of the human voice. I am orderly, with photographs and fresh flowers around my desk, a routine to follow each day, and no scruples when I occasionally leave it all and go out. I am in my centre, viewing the world as it spins around me, and radiating love to all within my sphere.

There are other times of course when stress clouds my spirit and I become lost in a maze of panic and uncertainty. The flowers in their vases fade, and my joy with them. Then I crave company and diversion. My mind sets up an incessant chatter, trying to delve into my feelings from its own limited perspective, trying to find the source of the malaise, to lift the anguish. And all the time I know I am chasing in vain circles, searching through illusion, but I can't stop as the hunt gathers speed.

I've gathered many techniques for lifting myself out of panic. But it is a strange creature. Its heavy fog creeps over my body like a personoid, peering behind my ears, lifting my breasts, inspecting the crevices under my arms to see what is hidden there. I lie waiting for it, breathing deeply, watching its progress, accepting it into me, into the vast resources of the human spirit. Resistance is useless. Drugs merely cloud the issue. Acceptance and understanding the only tools. Panic swoops on every uncertainty and weaves its cocoon of false beliefs around them. It is a chameleon, changing its ways in harmony with its surroundings. It is never the same, and that is the reason my mind goes into the frenzied chase, searching out the new aspects of the current onslaught. It is the soul seeking expression. But the soul's answer can also be elusive, and I must wait for the right moment, for its revelation of the new path.

Then suddenly the panic lifts. I feel bathed in a sudden beam of sunlight, or greeted by a smile from a fascinating stranger. I am suddenly lifted out of the whirlpool of horrors, and am back in my serene self, whom I had never wished to leave, standing triumphantly at the start of a new journey.

*

I had returned from living seven years overseas, and wondered how to start a new life. I missed my friends from the community where I had held a responsible position. The life, the friends and the work, all my support systems had gone, as I entered a vacuum which didn't recognize me. Australia had changed so much since I left. September 11, with its terrorist attack on the USA was in the past and the people were uneasy in the face of world events, clutching at anything to bring security. The politicians, the issues, the TV programs were not only different, they had leapt up a cog in their development and I didn't recognize the direction they had taken. I hardly recognized the city streets, the attitudes even less. Everything had gone wrong for me, beginning at an airport en route to Australia where I was cheated out of $500 for excess baggage which I didn't have. Then the medical insurance office refused to reimburse me for visits to the doctor. My regular payment of the premiums during my absence simply didn't count. What had become of this country, Australia Fair? Now a "foreigner", I had to reimmigrate to my own land, provide documents of rental (I was staying with family), registration for unemployment (I was not looking for a job), severance agreements from my previous residence (I'd left them behind), documents relating to purchase of a car (I purchased it from my parents, and as "anyone can change a registration," that didn't count). The inhumanity of the market-place economy was leaving its traces through the fabric of society. But it was not only Australia which was making difficulties for me, there were brick walls everywhere. Money which should have been sent on to me from overseas didn't come. Even the rug my friends had given me in parting had not arrived. I wondered if I should have stayed. But it felt clear that that work was finished for me, I had to take a step forward now, into the unknown.

I reached Australia jetlagged, fuzzy in the head, lost, and as usual, went to stay with my mother and father. My parents are old now, father often ill, they enjoyed my company and could use some help, although they would never ask for it. But it took away my independence. I was always a child in this household. The years had changed me into a person different from my parents, saddening them and gladdening me. I had lived through my old religious beliefs and broadened them into a life unruled by laws or prohibitions, driven by the principal of love, but still muddied by the fears and uncertainties in the physical life. I felt responsible for my father's oblique comments about my religion, or lack of it. Australia was not welcoming me home, I who had come obedient to my inner voice ready to love them all.

I survived my anxiety by writing my diary, covering the paper with fear, trying to make some sense of it. The sunlight found its way around the curtains, bringing desperate glimpses of the tops of the trees and the red roofs of the city. My room in my parents' home was neat and airy, one timber wall hung with pictures of past loves, children, art evocative of tenderness, and the other walls pale green, the floor polished cork tile, with Persian scatter rugs. The birch tree outside my upstairs window waved cheerily, reminding me of my beloved northern forests. I heard my parents moving around downstairs, dreading that I would overhear them talking about me. "What's Sibyl doing?" in my father's voice, reminding me of years of strictness and impatience, was enough to bring on another surge of guilt.

In between the place where my spirit loves and accepts all, and my uneasy affection for my father on the surface, was a moat of fear and distrust, now fuelled by my father's frustration with his body, which spilt over to those in the house with him. This distrust was a legacy of war. Born in 1942, I didn't meet my father till 1945, as he was engaged in frightening our own soldiers to death with dentistry in Bougainville. When I did meet him, my contrary nature did not sit well with his authoritarianism, and so the chasm begun by distance, began to widen.

*

Panic accompanies change in the psyche. Massive change in life direction. All my life I had been a scientist, I'd worked best with computers and figures. Suddenly I couldn't do this work any more, my whole being shuddering at the thought of it. My dreams, the symbols, the parts of life that worked, even the parts that didn't work all told me the same thing

"Leave the left-brain work! Be creative, artistic, expand your horizons." I had always considered that science was my art form. I was not an arty person, I'm hopeless at drawing. But I can write, and had always enjoyed recording events and composing stories. Sitting in the quiet of the early morning, parents still sleeping, I meditated into my life. To compound the situation, yesterday I had received a card from my friend Leah, a sensitive.

"You have a treasure to share in the story of you and David and if you commit yourself to the idea of completing the book you will be surprised and delighted with all that happens. The reason that I have written this and not phoned is that 'they' want you to read that the story already has a presence in this world. The message seemed to come from a male. I have no idea who they are but they were really adamant that you got the message. I had to get up in the freezing cold and write this NOW!"

I had been considering writing such a book, but needed this push to get me started. I have no hesitation in obeying such directives, I have had them before, and although my obedience has led me along strange paths, they had always brought a positive outcome. I decided to give myself a chance to undergo this life change.

Then I dozed off and suddenly I was dreaming. I saw David my lover of 20 years ago. I had loved David more than anyone else in my life, but eventually we had separated. He had died a year ago. And here he was talking to me again, showing that through love we could maintain contact even after death. Now I could see David in a new light. As he had never said an angry or sarcastic word to me in our many years together, he was able to become the father I had never had. My childhood wounds had begun to heal in his warmth and generosity, and now in my dreamworld he promised to help me to leave my shadows and grow be the love that I am. This would enable me to build a sparkling rainbow bridge across the moat of despair and distrust. Spanning the chasm of duality which coloured all our lives here on earth. The love and fear, the black and white of every situation. To understand how terrorism arises, the result of not enough love. Perhaps abolishing the power of panic forever. Life is a mosaic, with different people filling different spaces, and so long as the spaces are filled, it doesn't matter who fills them. Parents, lovers, friends, children all taking a part in filling out the final picture. I accepted his help in this task, to continue the work we had begun together on earth. I would build my bridge into the oneness, the unity of body, mind and spirit, the place where only love rules.

I needed now to return to my centre. I'd waited too long in the city. So I decided to leave my parents in their uneasy health and move to the country, keeping an eye on them from a distance. I would tell my story about the panic which has tormented me for too long. I'd trace it to its source to learn how it began. I would explore how I came to be who I am, and how David taught me so many things about love and life. I shall start right at the beginning.

My imagination takes me on a journey. I was being born. The idyllic warm nest had started to contract, pushing and shoving my tiny body towards the chosen life. My plans were detailed, I could see my life path stretching out in front of me. It was almost a reward this life, a chance to enjoy myself whilst helping others, many challenges, and above all, many different forms of loving. I was happy in my spirit world, but also excited at the thought of the physical life again. Fully aware at this point, I imagined both worlds. The world of spirit stretched around me on all sides. It was so different from physical vision. To know a single object gave me a complete view of all sides of it at once, not at all like physical sight where the eyes see only what is facing the observer. Then I imagined too, the complete awareness of not only the physical objects, but the feelings and thoughts, the smiles and whispers, these nuances of existence. A single thought ripples through the rest of creation, and all its effects are seen in the world of spirit. I could not be happy to leave all that awareness for the forgetfulness of the physical life, which was also visible in its three dimensional limitation. But I was on the roller-coaster ride to life on earth, there was no turning back.

I didn't really want to leave the womb, didn't want to enter the world all alone. Each contraction of my mother's womb opened the gate to the external world, little by little the portals drew aside. Suddenly the end of my warm nest gave me a smart kick up the backside, forcing my head down through the tight exit doors. "Here I go" I thought, "I'd better make the best of it." I felt squeezed as my head rotated down the narrow tunnel. Another contraction came, pushing me further into the birth canal. Dreadfully uncomfortable, this birth process. I wanted to break through and scream my frustration. Then another more powerful contraction tried to push my head through the opening. Something around my neck was holding me back. I felt it tug at me, impeding my progress. "What's going on? I'm trying to get born here!" The next contraction tightened something around my neck, and at the same time pushed my head out into the world. "It's awful, I'm doing my best here, can't you just let me through?" I felt the blood welling in my head, felt in need of oxygen, but the cord bit into my neck, cutting off the circulation both to my head and to the rest of my body. Every contraction increased the discomfort and yet kept me immobile. My frustration became molten. I could feel hands groping about my neck. Please just let me out of here, stop harassing me! I'm squashed in here. I can't go forward or back.

Can't somebody disentangle me? I want to get out and live this life. I felt another push behind me. Stop pushing me, I'm stuck! I'm doing my best to get out of here. The hands grasped the cord, and pushed it down over my shoulders, as they too were born. The rest of me wriggled out into the cold air, disliking the clammy feel of my wet body, and taking the first gasping breath. The valves of my respiratory system and heart opened, the blood changed its course, and here I was breathing like a human being. At this moment a grey cloud blocked out my memory of the spirit world I had come from, and I was left with only the three dimensional consciousness of a human baby. The tearing panic entered at that moment.

I was stripped of everything familiar. Suddenly alone, the terror gripped me. I forgot my plan, the love, the service. I was separated even from my mother, who lay anaesthetised. I felt only rage and fear! I screamed as if my lungs would burst. And nobody acknowledged my fear. I yelled and kicked. Nobody took the slightest notice.

"I'm telling you, I'm telling you!" They weighed me, and wrapped me in a cloth. "I don't want to be alone here! Won't anybody listen?"

"You have a beautiful baby girl" they said to my mother, just now awakening from the anaesthetic.

"I'm not beautiful, I'm angry" I yelled "Please just listen to me". I was tired now, dispirited, "Oh just go away and leave me alone!" My sobs became less, I curled myself up into a ball and snuffled myself to sleep. The outrage tucked away, ready to torment me at a later date.

Life and Love, Fear and Death. Life bringing love, tempered always by the fear of death, the perceived cessation of joy, the tomb. Or we could say Life and Fear, Love and Death. In an expanded vision Death becomes a sinking into Love. Tristan and Isolde. Life a path strewn with obstacles. But Life can be expanded also, into the beingness of all things, its cohesiveness coming from Love. In this vision, both fear and death disappear.

Life has to be lived however, insights gained through experience. We are born in our forgetfulness, and spend our life remembering who we are, putting together the strands we were born with, and which hover around us, waiting for recognition and consciousness. Consciousness brings power, the place of our soul in our lives, the gentle art of speech with the intangible, its answer flowing swiftly to the physical world, harmonious, altering our strands, changing directions at the merest thought. Love and Life. But the journey to this point is arduous, Life and Fear.

Birth and childhood hold the keys to one's life patterns. Several things stand out from my birth, which I have dramatized from comments from my mother, and my own observations of human behaviour. Although I remember no pictures of my birth, the feelings are intact, and by every means at my disposal, I can trace them to these events. Above all stands the separation. Physically from my mother, but also from mother spirit, unknowable, only glimpsed in flashes through the imagination.

I see the universe and my own life as one. I might very well be angry, I can scream and shout, be heard, acknowledged. But if I am at one, it all comes back to myself. I was angry with myself. I had orchestrated my own birth, caught the cord around my own neck, and then resigned myself to not being heard. The blueprint of frustration is born. My frustration now creates my own high blood pressure. My birth brought the beginnings of my life patterns. The abject fear I can feel at living alone. The terror of the new which can leave me paralyzed and mute. My disappointment when others don't see what to me is obvious. My insistence at doing things my way. My intolerance of interference. The panic of bottled up emotion. The commitment to love and service whose light rays break through the discomfort of life. My patterns no less, simply requiring my acknowledgement.

I was born in 1942, in the days which marked the turn of the tide of war towards the allies. As my father was in the armed services, my mother and I returned to my mother's family home on a farm in the country, which became my paradise.

Babies are still a part of their mother, within their mother's being. The fierce mothering urge begins as baby nestles into her, she caressing, fondling the tiny fingers, tickling the toes. Kissing the top of the downy head. I learned from my mother's touch, the intimacy of nursing at the breast, smiling and burbling my first sounds. I have always had the strong connection to my mother, and as I have matured I have added a deep respect to my child's feelings. But my infancy was filled with many murmurs, which have left echoes into adulthood.

In my grandparents' house I was not entirely comfortable in my body. Griping pains came, a restlessness also which prevented me sleeping. Enjoying the attention so much, it was hard to settle down afterwards. I was a bit of a squawker and was rescued by an eminent paediatrician who explained to my mother that there were many babies then who suffered a similar malaise. Their fathers away in the war, their mothers anxious for their husband's safety, the babies had felt the anxiety and taken it into themselves. The doctor advised my mother that I should be left out under the trees to grow like a little cabbage. So I lay outside in my pram, watching the trees waving to me, blissfully content.

At this time my father was still in Australia, before being posted overseas, and occasionally my mother could visit him in an army camp. How I missed her, nothing can take the place of the familiar touch and smell of the mother. When she was away I was cared for by my favourite aunt, Paddy. She had long dark hair, which I wondered at every time I saw Paddy brush it, then wind it around and around, stick hairpins through it (what kept them from falling out?) and secure the bun in a hairnet. She wore colourful dresses, and sometimes pants if she was working in the garden. I was bonded to my mother as are all babies, but my passion for Paddy was a sunburst of soul, the first golden light in my life. I fell in love with smiling Paddy from my earliest times. I wondered if it was because I never saw my father, or due to my mother's absences that I had formed such a strong attachment with her. Paddy was never so strict as the others, and childish tears were allowed with her. She loved me fiercely, and I her. I could be myself with Paddy. She understood fear, and cuddled it away.

I was the eldest child of the eldest child, my mother the only married one from the family of four girls and two boys. The boys were enlisted in the air force and the younger girls were away in the city studying. The family owned a dairy farm, grandfather ruled his household benevolently, grandmother was a motherly woman and there were people hired to help in the gardens and the house. With the men away the farms ran with the minimum of help, the women doing much of the work. Many foods were rationed, and if ration coupons went missing a major crisis could be precipitated.

My forbears were all Catholics, and this is where my training started. Generations of middle class Irish on the one side, Swiss vinegrowers on the other side. The Irish Catholicism brought with it both warmth and restriction. Its constraint felt like a root of such persistence that would take all my strength to pull up and eradicate the plant. It was highly visible here in Australia, so many big families, so many Irish names. The Swiss variety I was not so familiar with, although my great grandmother married at the age of 14, and after bearing 13 children died of exhaustion at the age of 43. It seemed that the Swiss Catholicism did not seem to have anything to recommend it either, if one were to consider the comfort of women. The family was expert in intellectualising every feeling, no tears allowed, bad temper outlawed. Keep it all inside. No wonder I kept even my shit inside, spending hours on the potty chair in the high-ceilinged bathroom, the big bath with a metal shower screen standing on feet in one corner, the old gas lamps still attached to the wall.

During the war years the family ritual was to gather together and listen to the BBC news at seven o'clock every evening. Grandfather was kind but firm, strict silence during his sacred half hour, everyone sat about with anxious faces dreading an invasion from Hitler or the Japanese. Many of my beliefs about war and fear had come about from this time. They had started on the carpet of my grandparent's living room, where I had sat watching the grownups' faces listening to the horrors broadcast as the millions died. I didn't understand what war was, I was just born. I drank in fear with my mother's milk, mother so anxious for my father. I felt it rush in as the family crouched over the whistling radio to listen to the news from Britain, disaster piled upon disaster. I was a baby, crawling across the carpet on the floor. I felt its recurring floral patterns stalk the assembled people. Bad, bad, bad, bad. It marched to a regular beat. Thump, thump, thump, thump went my heart. Fear without understanding the cause, difficult to deal with. I carried their anxiety as a feeling of approaching doom for many years as I heard the fanfare preceding the news, until I recognised the reason behind it.

The house stood in the centre of acres of garden, vegetables in the back, and trees, shrubs and flower beds in the front, punctuated with graceful palm trees. There were hidden places for children to wander, take the kittens, or my favourite powder puff. Often at bedtime if the powder puff had gone missing, someone would be dispatched to the garden to search for it with a torch, as it was my total comforter. When I was older, Paddy and I might go for a walk up to the bridge and throw stones into the creek and watch the ripples spreading, or out into the forest, looking up into the grey-green gum trees, sometimes spotting a koala high up in the branches. One day the kitten followed Paddy and me to the garden and played amongst the flowers. Suddenly startled, it bolted up Paddy's wide trouser leg, climbed across her belly, and groped its way down the other side to the ground as I fell about with laughter and Paddy nursed her scratches. I was sometimes held on the back of a horse, played with the dogs or on the swing hanging from the shady plane tree in the back yard. There were two cocker spaniels which smelt bad, so I ignored them in favour of the aristocratic Burke, a big black retriever. What an ideal childhood, what bliss. The house was large and rambling, wide verandas unexpectedly placed, some of them enclosed with a trellis, where the women slept. There were family routines, Grandma's breakfast in bed, the same every day of her life. Half a grapefruit, a bowl of All Bran, toast and grapefruit marmalade, and coffee with hot milk. Then the women would make the beds, prepare meals in the big dining room with lace table mats, white serviettes, plates with green and pink flowers around the edge. We ate chicken, roast potatoes and two vegetables, and home-made coffee ice cream. Even though the grown-ups might complain about prices, taxes, or the government, we never did without.

Grandfather was an imaginative, experimental farmer. The main farming activity was the milking of cows, and the dispatch of cream to the butter factory. But Grandfather also had paddocks of daffodils, asparagus and gladioli which he would pick and send to the city in the train.

As the war progressed, Italian prisoners of war were engaged to help with food production. They were handsome and romantic, bringing an unfamiliar culture from so far away, and sometimes even falling in love. One day there was a commotion , one of the prisoners had been repairing the roof and had fallen off. The ambulance came and everyone looked solemn. Children were not confided in, but I caught the confusion, the anxious looks, the murmured voices. But he survived. Later in life I had the privilege to see letters written by this prisoner's mother in Italy to my own mother, and felt his mother's gratitude that her son was cared for in a foreign land.

Eventually the war was over and the men started to come home. My father came sometimes, but it would be a year yet until he was free from the army, and my mother and I moved to the city where we would live with him.

Somewhere along the lines I stopped trusting in life. My first conscious memory of adversity came as a four-year-old child when my baby brother was born, and my mother came home in the train. I clambered eagerly into the train to meet my mother and she had this baby she was fussing over, obviously devoted to him, not interested in me any more. The baby's white bonnet fell on the floor, and I jumped on it, and ground it into the dirt. I felt displaced and didn't understand it. My mother said, missing the point,

"Oh, you're treading on the baby's bonnet, pick it up dear", as rage flickered in my eyes. I still had Paddy though, and clung even harder to her, now that I felt deserted by my mother.

As I consider my childhood, now that my life has been filled with so many later events I wonder what has happened to the things which are forgotten? Did I remember things which are important to who I am? And for some strange reason I don't believe that. I actually think that I have remembered a caricature of myself. I see that the episodes that I have told here form strings on which the rest of my life has been built, for better or worse and if I really delve into the closed memory banks, I may discover things that will change the way I feel about myself.

That I was timid in some ways I do remember. Once when I was maybe four or five years old I was exploring on my grandparents farm. I went into a large shed which had been the stables before motor cars, old harness and saddles lined the dark walls, smelling of oil and leather. I may have been searching for a cat, or kittens, but what I came upon was a pile of dirty sacks in a corner, and noticed a curl of smoke insinuating itself from them. Apprehension leapt into me, I was suddenly terrified, and guilty, almost as if I had lit the sacks myself. I ran inside to my mother, and found her with the others sitting in the drawing room at afternoon tea. I pulled at her dress, hid my face in her neck and whispered urgently that there was a fire. Suddenly there was great consternation, everyone jumped up and ran outside to see what was going on. My mother looked very grave and said to me

"Was it you who were playing with fire?"

"No," I said, feeling as if I was to blame.

The others couldn't find the fire and had to ask me to come and show them where it was. I remember standing with my mother in the doorway of the shed, in my pink smocked dress, and pointing towards the smouldering corner. Then it was clear I was not capable of lighting the old sacking. I was praised for finding and reporting the fire. But I wonder why my guilt and why my terror. Who knows what a child's consciousness brings with it? Or was I already at that age unable to believe well of myself?

Another instance of my timidity was my terror of the dismembered pieces of engines, all black and glistening with grease, so that I would never go into a mechanic's shop or a garage with my mother, without clutching her skirts, quivering with fear. Was I afraid again of the ultimate abandonment in the black dirty world? Then one day when I was much older I allowed my father to take me into a garage, and looked about and found that after all it was quite safe. My mother wanted to know why I would go there with Dad, but not with her. But that I think was a part of growing up.

Looking back at the small Sibyl of my babyhood days, I see her surrounded by love, in almost an aura of safety. Why then was she unable to bring it in and enjoy it to the full? Where was her self confidence? Was she encouraged too much to be individual and independent, without being given the requisite support? And was the requisite support that she needed the ability to express how she felt? My relatives were wont to say

"Don't cry now, it didn't hurt" or "Pick yourself up and stop making all that noise!" so that I didn't dare to show any emotion. Was this why I was so afraid to tell Mother about the fire? And did the guilt come because I felt so many things that I dared not express?

Was I affected by the household itself, where I could remember so much love among its strictnesses? I have been told many times that I am over strict with myself, and yet I am almost blind to this behaviour. Did I copy those who brought me up?

When I was very young, maybe two years old, I wandered out to the big orchard and dived my tiny fist into a hive of bees swaying on a tree. What I remember is standing outside and above, watching the child wailing, while Mother and Paddy brushed away the angry bees, even finding some inside my singlet. The experience was depersonalised, and made bearable by my absence from my body. Was this my way of expressing emotion, splitting off a part of my personality so that I couldn't be held responsible for my crying? Shades of another Sibyl. It was also my first reminder that life exists also outside the body.

Paddy and I were out the back in the laundry, a big room in which there were high storage shelves, the copper in the corner, a row of cement sinks along one wall under the windows, and in the centre a huge ironing table. It was always untidy in there, sacks in the corner on which the cat lay with her kittens, heaps of clothes in various stages of cleanliness and repair, and work clothes hanging on hooks on the wall. A stack of firewood and chips lay beside the copper.

"What's a Paddy?" I asked her.

"It's a flooded field where people grow rice, but it can be a paddywhack" said Paddy, pretending to give me a smack which turned into a tickle and a hug. "But for me it is short for Patricia, which means a noble person, so you have to be respectful when I am here." Paddy's eyes twinkled as she folded up a basketful of clean linen. I was being allowed to iron the handkerchiefs at the ironing table. In the corner the copper was boiling up the dirty work trousers.

"What's a Sibyl then?" I asked

"Sibyl is the fairy queen, but in the old stories she is more than that." What could be more than the fairy queen I wondered ,

"Tell me?"

"Sibyl lived in a cave, and wandered between this world and the world where dead people live. She brought messages back from dead people."

"What is a dead person?"

"When we get old we get sick and die, then if we have been very good our soul goes to live with God in heaven."

"What if we're naughty?"

"Then our soul goes to hell, where there are fires that burn us up for ever and ever. But we don't want to go there."

I had to climb down from my chair to get some more hankies from the ironing basket. Paddy had the big wooden stick and was poking the trousers in the copper.

"How does she bring messages from the dead people?"

"She was a prophetess, and those people can hear what the dead say."

"Can I do that?"

"I don't know, can you?"

"But I don't know how to do it, how do you?"

"I'm sure I don't know. It was a long time ago, I don't think people do it these days."

"But I am Sibyl too" my logic was perfect. If there were a way to talk to the dead I would have to find out about it. In my intrigue about the departed I forgot the fairy princess.

"What do the dead people want to say?"

"I suppose they might want to tell their friends how they are, or warn them of floods or earthquakes."

"How do they know about those things if we don't?"

"It's different when you are dead. They are like ghosts, they can walk through walls, they can see the past, present and future. They are waiting for the last day, when everybody will rise from the dead."

I silently ironed some more hankies, folding up the men's ones into squares, and the women's ones into rectangles. I was thinking about being dead, about ghosts, and rising again. It was unfamiliar, and yet somewhere I remembered something. Paddy took out a basket of washing to hang on the line. I remembered the slater I had found two days ago, lying curled up on the floor. I had asked Paddy why it wasn't moving. "It's dead" she said. "Can we take it to the vet?" I'd asked. "No its too late for that" she had said laughing. Some of its legs had broken off. I squeezed it and it broke in half, so I threw it away. I wondered if the dead slater had messages. Then I thought about ghosts walking through walls. How much fun it would be to sneak up on people and surprise them by appearing suddenly, instead of coming in through the door. And what was this about ghosts waiting for the last day? Paddy came in again with the empty basket, and I asked

"When is the last day?"

"No one knows." I tried a different approach.

"Do you know any dead people?"

"Yes, my grandmother and grandfather. And our friend Paul, he died in an accident the day before you were born. And some of the men have been killed in the war. Some boys from the town."

I did a double take. Killing was something dreadful. I knew about fear and being killed. I'd seen the grownups faces when they talked of it, felt its grimness.

"Are dead people killed?"

"Yes"

"Does it hurt?"

"Sometimes." I didn't like to think about things that hurt. I thought about ghosts instead. Paddy was emptying the copper, baling out the water. I'd finished ironing the hankies and asked for some tea towels. Paddy placed a heap of them in front of me.

"Are there any ghosts here?"

"I haven't seen any, but there is a lady in town who saw one one day"

"Did she talk to it?"

"I don't know, why don't you ask her?"

"I want to talk to ghosts, I want to be a real Sibyl"

"You are really Sibyl, but maybe you will talk to ghosts, and maybe not."

I had reason to continue my thoughts about death the next week. An old lady associated with the church had died, and the whole family went to her requiem. I walked up the aisle holding my picture book about bible stories in one hand and Paddy's in the other. Up the top of the aisle stood the coffin, with three tall candles burning on either side. I hadn't seen such a thing before, and whispered loudly

"What's that thing?"

"That's the coffin, Mrs Johnson's body is in there. Now you must be quiet, Mass is about to start!"

I looked at the coffin, and wondered how it felt to be in there. Myriad questions formed in my head, and I looked up at Paddy, but she was reading her prayer book with a 'Not now' look on her face, so I looked around at the people in the church. I saw that most had their eyes down but some were greeting each other as if they hadn't met for a long time. Church was so boring. I couldn't talk or walk around. The pictures on the wall I knew by heart. I opened my own book. Later at the cemetery I watched them lower the box into the big hole in the ground, and burst out

"How will Mrs Johnson get out?"

"It's only her body that's in there, her soul is in heaven. She doesn't need her body any more."

"Is she a ghost?"

"Sort of"

"Can she walk through walls?"

"I suppose so, but now we're going to talk to her daughter so no more questions for a while."

Paddy and I went into the church hall, where the grownups were pouring cups of tea, and helping themselves to sandwiches and cakes from long trestle tables with white table cloths. This was an appropriate distraction from life beyond the grave, and I made a beeline for the cakes with icing. Paddy was talking to the grownups. I couldn't understand why they said such boring things. My mother had brought my little brother and people were crowded around looking at him. I reached for another tart.

I was watching the people. Mrs Johnson's daughter had red eyes, and every so often she wiped away a tear. But she was talking to people, not yelling like I sometimes did when I cried. I saw a little boy taking a cake, and decided to do the same. I went over to him and said hello. We went outside and sat on the step to wait for Paddy and the others.

"Mrs Johnson is a ghost now" I told him.

"My mum said the devil will have taken her to hell for being so mean" he replied.

"Who is the devil?"

"He's a bad angel" I had seen angels in my bible stories, big people with wings. I hadn't met any yet, and certainly no devils either.

"What does he look like?"

"He's black and he's got horns and a tail with an arrow on the end, and a pitchfork to throw people into hell"

"Yuk" I said. "Do you think Mrs Johnson has really gone with the devil? Paddy said she was in heaven."

"I don't know. I liked her, she used to give me lollies. But Mum said she did."

Paddy came out, rescuing me from further lurid details. I repeated the conversation to her, and she smiled and said not to worry about the devil, if I was good he wouldn't bother me.

The next day a song came on the radio. I was taken with the words. This must be a ghost song. I told Paddy

"I heard a ghost song on the wireless!"

"Ghosts don't have songs on the wireless."

"But I heard it!"

"What was it?"

"IIIII ain't got no booooody," I sang. I saw a quick smile on Paddy's face as she tried to smother a laugh, failed and picked me up, hugging me hard. She tried to explain something, but my mind was made up, and I continued to sing my bodyless song.

My first ideas of life beyond the grave had begun. I was excited to hear about this new world. I kept my eyes and ears open for ghosts. Perhaps they wanted to bring a message, and I, Sibyl, was the obvious one to receive it. I could bring warnings, to save people from floods and bushfires. My fantasies wove ghosts, the spirits and fairyland into an imaginary world, forming a maze of expectations and beliefs, rich with my suppositions and dreams.

My father was now free from the army and lived in the city, where my mother would go to stay with him. Occasionally he visited my grandparent's house. One day my mother told me that we would be going to live in the city. I didn't think much about it. Then she started to pack up our things. My father put all our suitcases in the car and we set off, my parents, my baby brother and I in the cream Ford Prefect. We drove about half way to the city when the truth dawned on me. Paddy was not with us! She whom I loved above all, who had kept the terror and blackness away from me. Now without her it all came in. My heart broke. I saw the road winding its way to the city, the trees grey and dull, the rain drizzling down from sombre clouds. Desolation and lovelessness choked me, rose up in my throat and strangled me. Inside I knew that this was no short separation. I left Paddy, the house, the grandparents, the Australian nature, and was suddenly confined in a flat in the big city, a tiny backyard, a strict and scary father whom I did not recognize, the baby brother who had usurped my position with my mother and horror of horrors, school. This time I had no panic, only grim depression which formed an underlay to my life for some years.

I was a shy child who was used to playing alone. School was enormous, no one I knew, a nun in a black and white habit. I sat in the big classroom surrounded by unknown faces and lifted the lid of the desk so nobody could see me cry. Mother had packed enough lunch for a trooper, I had the appetite of a sparrow, and left the lunch on a bench outside. Sister came into the classroom wanting to know who hadn't eaten their lunch. In my confusion one part of me didn't remember my lunch, but another more passive part of me knew what was going on. Sister took me to the long bench and encouraged me to eat a bit more. So I sat outside alone, looking at my fruit cake and milk again, but it stayed the same size. Again, a stressful situation caused a dislocation in my awareness.

The first Christmas holidays from the big city were spent at my Grandma's farm, many family members gathering together, a favourite uncle back from the war, younger aunts flitting in and out. On Christmas eve Paddy helped me to put up a pillow case for Father Christmas, and insisted that we leave him some biscuits and a bottle of beer for his journey. The bottle was left there drained the next morning, next to my sack of goodies. He had obviously needed the beer. I laughed because there was something naughty about beer, not completely understanding its fate. I unpacked my presents, a tea set, a new doll, a book, and down the end always a balloon. I spent the day treasuring them, packing and unpacking them, too new to play with yet. I was so happy to be back with Paddy, back in the aura of safety.

All too soon the holidays were over and we were sitting in the big black steam train as it puffed and chuffed its way back to the gloomy city. One year I had an unexpected reprieve, there was a fire in our kitchen and we were not able to return before the house was cleaned and repainted. The clouds rolled away, and life began to sparkle again. Mother, brother and I stayed on at Grandma's and I was sent to the local primary school half a mile up the road. In this school there was one teacher, and all the children played together, grades didn't matter. We saluted the flag on Mondays, and the teacher asked us if we had brushed our teeth. I was really happy in this school and made friends with all of the children, started to relax and feel at home. I walked home with two children who lived in the farm over the road, and often went to their place for tea. The boy was older than me, the girl in the same grade. They were devoted to each other. This was a new concept to me who still felt uneasy with my brother and the competition that I felt towards him. One day one of the cats followed me to school (with a bit of encouragement from me) and curled up sleeping in the teacher's chair. He thought it was funny. The school and I shared the secret of mutual acceptance. On the day I was to leave they gave me a party. After that I had tea with the boy and girl from the next farm. I was surprised to be found worthy of the attention, in my family children were seen and not heard.

In the city we lived in a two story brick dwelling on the corner of a main road. My father had his dentist's surgery on the ground floor and the family lived in the apartment upstairs. I often slept in the corner room with its window looking out to the tram track. The trams were devils who stormed down the track in the night time, rattling and whistling, exciting the light spooks who would dance around my room as I peeped out of the bedclothes, afraid to move. But I must move every night to the toilet or suffer a wet bed in the morning, the washing of bed linen and more importantly the embarrassment. So I would get up most nights, dodging the dark shapes on the carpet, my nightmares creating the dead who lay there decomposing on my floor till daybreak, and the grasping fingers who reached out from under my bed for my ankles. Sometimes I would dream I was sitting on the toilet, only to wake immediately, sodden, oh no, not that dream again! Once the night terrors were so severe that I abandoned my stoicism and called for my mother. I expected her to be angry for wakening her , I must have been threatened with 'be quiet or else' in the past. This time to my surprise she came, she brought comfort and cuddles, a glass of warm milk to help me sleep. I wonder now why I had been so reluctant to call her, when she was so clearly glad to be there for me.

The other children at school were a puzzle to me. I was not used to so many people at once, and tried to keep myself hidden from them. In preparatory grade I only remembered feeling inferior to the other pretty girls who had curly hair and clear skin. My hair had begun to darken to mouse and go straighter, and I had the dreaded freckles. Not a beauty. One of my aunts had reminded me of this, she showed me a photo taken of me playing in the sandpit, and said,

"There's an ugly mugly! No it's a mugly ugly, because they are much uglier than ugly muglies!"

I had squirmed.

However, I was good at lessons, and soon was labelled "a brain" at school. I guessed it didn't matter too much what my label was, it included me in some things and excluded me from others. I didn't spend more than a couple of months in Prep before an inspector came to the school, and he was asking questions around my class too. I had my hand up all the time to answer questions, but he hardly ever asked me. I felt disappointed as I liked to show off and answer. However, the next day Sister went around the class pointing at some of the children, and we were moved up to grade one in the next room. This was quite a change, two classes in the same room, about 30 children in each class, one teacher who shared her time between the two grades. We shared the recital of tables, but otherwise were given work to complete whilst Sister taught the other grade.

Of second grade I remembered little. The Hunter River at Maitland flooded, and the children were asked to pray for the nuns at the sister convent there. A newspaper article showed a picture of a flooded street and a white towel being waved out of an upstairs window. My ready imagination transported the event to my own street and I lay in bed fearful that a flood would carry us all away.

My father the dentist was strict on teeth hygiene, (I rarely brushed my teeth) and disapproved of me eating sweets, (I gratified my sweet tooth whenever possible). One day I, being smart at arithmetic, won a Violet Crumble bar for my excellence.

"But are you allowed to have it? Would your father approve?" asked Sister.

"Yes"

On the way home I bit on the bar and my front tooth fell out. Guilt no.1. Then Sister told my father about me winning the chocolate. Guilt no. 2 when he raised his eyebrows to a quaking Sibyl.

My father sometimes called me down to the surgery to check my teeth. He poked around in my tiny mouth, big fingers, prodding here and there, then took an enormous syringe and stuck the needle into my gum. The look of it hurt more than the feel. Then he took a whirring drill and vibrated in my teeth. If he didn't use the syringe then the drilling sometimes hurt, sudden sharp pain filling my head. Once the drilling was over it wasn't so bad, filling the tooth with the grey stuff, lots of washing and spitting to clean my mouth. The terror of this event was overwhelming, as upstairs I lived with this man who downstairs did such awful things. In the background was the dreadful possibility that he would remember my teeth, and the beckoning finger would summon me down into the underworld. What is it about dentistry that so many people dread? Is there a connection with incest, the rape of the mouth with the big fingers feeling around, unwelcome? I could only say that I would rather have gone to another dentist, and had my father as only my father.

When I was seven years old everything became too much for my small body. I had learnt to live in my city surroundings, but I never learnt to enjoy them. I constantly pined for Paddy and the life I had first known in the country. I responded with the classic choice, 'Am I in or am I out?' I contracted pneumonia, a well-known scenario for children at that age, either sharpen up your will, don a few protective garments and continue to live, or simply die. I came home from school one day, too tired to notice the people in the street, or the cloudy sky. I dragged my stumbling feet into the kitchen where my mother stood preparing the evening meal. She put her hand on my forehead, suspecting a fever, and put me straight to bed. A welcome snuggly place when I felt so deathly tired. My consciousness drifted in and out over the next days. I vaguely remembered the doctor coming and putting the cold thing on my chest every day, then I would drift off again. Everything was quiet, even the telephone had a dull sound. (I later learnt that my father had put a padding over the bell so it made a muted sound.) I ate nothing, drank little, slept much, wandering in the in-between world. Thanks to the newly released sulpha drugs, I was helped to live. The pink pills administered with palpable hope by my parents brought with them confidence in recovery. As the fever left me I lay for many days in bed, drawing pictures, my favourite a green train, reading stories and starting to eat again. I craved the company of someone who would just sit with me a while. I devised a plan, to ask Dad to read me the longest story in my book. Every night after work Dad would come up and I would be lying in my old-fashioned bed with the wooden slats behind my head. I would ask

"Read 'Jack the Giant Killer' Dad?"

Never mind I often fell asleep during it, never mind that Dad might be tired and wanting his dinner. I became a tyrant, demanding attention. My greater will was suspended, I had made the big choice to live, but I could not control where or with whom. I did the best I could and put on my protection from the difficulties of childhood. The protective veil fell upon me even more strongly, blunting my yearnings, filtering incoming influences, enclosing me against the world.

I started to adapt to the long sojourn in the city. Back at school I found I was behind in my work and became aware for the first time of competition between students as I hastened to catch up to them. I became more grounded in life, made friends, did well in my lessons. I ate my food hungrily in the evenings, searching the plate for another tasty piece of meat, disappointed when there was no more. I might procrastinate on a Monday morning.

"Ugh I don't want to go to school, I just want to have a day to myself, no work, no lessons, I'll pretend to be sick so I don't have to get up."

But as the clock ticked on I would eventually drag myself out of bed, eat some porridge and take my Vegemite sandwiches down to the tramstop for the ride to school. I grew to know my father, giving him an uneasy affection. I often followed him up the hill to morning Mass, and helped him plant potatoes in the back yard. But I never loved my Dad with the passion I felt for Paddy. I grew to enjoy schoolwork, because I could do it easily.

I never felt at home with a large group of people, but could be friends with other children if the teacher was with them. One Sister used to sit in the playground with us at lunchtime, supervising the whole playground. I liked to sit beside her, on a cold winter's day, pulling my long grey socks up over my knees, and we children would do puzzles and games taken from the Children's Encyclopaedia. At home I played school, and taught my brother to spell, we danced and gave concerts to visiting grandparents, made cubby houses out of blankets and chairs, helped Mother tidy up the kitchen.

I was not always kind, my competitive nature spilled over to my little brother. I never forgot how I had met him, how I felt he had tossed me out of my position close to my mother's heart. I was always ready to lord it over him, and make his life miserable. But family loyalty was extended to him also. One day we were out driving, Mother and Father in the front and my brother and I in the back. We were commanded to sit on two arm rests next to the back doors, and hang on to the straps which hung from the roof. We were dutifully sitting, and as we turned a corner the door behind my brother flew open, he was unbalanced, and swung back too. Without thought I grabbed the front of his shirt, pulled him back into the car, saving him serious injury. I had saved myself along with my brother. I was not as mean as I sometimes felt, as the war with him and its occasional battles lasted until my teenage years.

One day Mother went out and left notes for my brother and me, with lists of jobs to do. This was huge fun, and I entered into the excitement of responsibility, giving pleasure to others with my service, earning respect and sometimes even love by performing simple tasks. The life of the "eldest child" began with that note. I cleaned the sink, scrubbed the bench, emptied the smelly compost billy and discovered that even that could be cleaned and the smell of mouldy scraps abolished. I hung clothes on the line, took them in, folded them, and put them away. Sometimes mother was ill, and with the help of one of the nurses from Dad's surgery downstairs, I would try some experimental cooking. An aunt had given me a children's cookbook, and I decided to bake a queen pudding. I did each step as directed, until I came to the end of the page and the pudding was not finished. Puzzled I rang to the nurse, who came up and looked in the book and told me the next step. I did that and found that again I was stumped. I rang again. The nurse came up and told me what to do next.

"How do you know?" I asked.

"It's written up here" the nurse pointed to the top of the next page. Then I felt stupid for myself, couldn't I even think to turn a page? and stupid for the nurse, why couldn't she just show me where it was written? and now I wonder about a child's world confined on a page that can't be turned.

My powder puff had by now become a piece of rabbit fur, deliciously soft, and stroked and cuddled in bed. My bedtime activity was to make up stories, where all the people in the story were parts of me. Paddy was often in them if a comforter was needed. One day I came home from school and sat down on the concrete step, needing a rest and some private space. I looked up to the sky, and noticed the moon above, pale in the afternoon light. I was drawn into a fantasy.

Once upon a time there lived in a great city a little girl. She lived in an upstairs house with her Mother and Father, her younger brother and sister. Usually she was a happy child. One day after school she came home and sat down in the back yard. It was a sunny day, warm and welcoming. She looked up and saw the moon above. She thought, I will fly up to the moon and see what it is like up there. She began to think I don't know how to fly, and suddenly she felt herself tugged by the hand and looked down to see a rubber doll spinning and dancing.

"I will take you to the moon" said the rubber doll, in her flubbery voice, "I know how to fly, and we can go and see the man in the moon".

So they joined hands and flew directly to the moon. They were surprised by what they saw. They landed on the edge of a great forest, tall with pine trees, spruce and fir, just like it was in the Northern countries on earth. They walked around the edge of the trees. Here it was not good weather, different from our sunny days on earth. Clouds covered the sky, and it was dim and miserable. Soon they came to a ramshackle old building, and outside it was sitting an old man. He was dressed in rags, and was shivering with the cold. He had no food, and was very hungry.

The rubber doll and I rescued the man in the moon, built him a new house in meticulous detail, which I had learnt from watching my father working at cabinet making in the garage at night. I made up stories about all the characters in my favourite books. Mary Grant Bruce's Billabong books were my all time favourites, but Enid Blyton's Famous Five and the Anne books were popular, or serials from the radio. Anything in which I could find someone in terrible trouble and save them by love and practicality. I included as many practical details as possible to keep the suspense running before the final collapse into the luxury of passionate reunion. I fell in love with the more glamorous heroes and had them rescue me over and over again. But I was the central character in all the stories. Perhaps it was my way of learning to live on earth and to experience love here in the midst of my family where discipline ruled and love was not overtly shown. It is only now that I begin to understand the significance of rescue, how it is one of the codes written into my being. As the earth's purification by fire gathers pace, and Canberra and north eastern Victoria are ablaze I remember Sodom and Gomorrah. As I hear George Bush's plans for a war against Iraq escalating in inverse proportion to any perceived threat or reason for war, I remember Noah's Ark. And I pray for Ezekiel's chariots to return for our rescue.

I had occasion to think about death once more. A boy from my grade was run over after getting off a tram and we were told by nuns with sorrowful long faces. Then we went to the church and stood in long lines outside for what seemed like hours. We were hungry and thirsty, and were not allowed to move. At last the people came out of church and walked between our lines, which they called a guard of honour. We didn't see him again in school, because dead people couldn't go. Another day we were sent to church again and we walked inside. The church was packed with people, and we children had to kneel in the aisle down the back. There was a coffin further up the church, and we had been told we were there to pray for the soul of Father Moloney who had died. After kneeling for a time, we were motioned by our teacher to file forward, past the coffin. I looked in and saw a very still white face, eyes closed, hands folded, and cotton wool stuck in his nose. I looked away hurriedly, I did not want to see any more. I was sometimes haunted by the dead Father Moloney.

My father had told me about the death of Jesus on the cross, how he had died for love of all the people in the world, and had risen again on the third day. I was moved, I said

"Now tell me again!"

The teachings of Jesus gave me a beauty, a serenity about life, touching my heart with his grace and purpose. Some of his words brought me in close, 'I am the vine you are the branches'. Not I am the trunk and you are the branches, but a much closer relationship as if each of us was a part of the vine, who was God within. I readily believed everything I was taught, that Jesus was God, that heaven or hell awaited us after death. That we must treat others as we would like to be treated. I learnt to pray childishly, but I was gripped also by a sense of efficiency. The nuns had told us

"If you offer your day to God every morning, then every action, even every breath becomes a prayer!"

What a good idea, then nothing is wasted in the great points-scoring game of life.

The miracles of Jesus brought the aspect of magic, a great security in that he could raise people from the dead, even himself. Perhaps it was from this type of teaching that I received the impression that after death I would know everything.

But what I knew about the events in the grave, or when I became aware of decomposition and decay I cannot say. I listened to serials on the radio, read books, and had night fears about dead bodies, so the information was there. One day at Paddy's place when I was a bit older, we were walking across the paddocks, and came to the carcass of a sheep. It smelt horrible, and the organs were visible, along with the marching lines of the maggots, eating as if their last breakfast had arrived. This I looked at with interest, disgusting though it was, and I allowed myself to absorb the experience with some degree of composure. At Paddy's there was also the killing of sheep for meat, but this I didn't watch, it was too frightening. However, I often saw the dogs eating the offal, as I grimaced and averted my eyes.

*

When I was about nine years old, I went to bed as usual one night. By this time I had a room to myself, briefly, and could read in bed so long as I was not discovered late with the light on. There was a visitor for tea and Mother and Dad were sitting in the kitchen talking with him when I got up to go to the toilet. As I passed the sitting room door I peeped in, and saw the cake with cream and red and green icing decorating the top. It had been waiting for me all day, I had been longing to try the green icing, like jelly, shining, deep emerald. I stuck my finger in and stole a piece, licking my finger on the way back to bed. That night I became aware of my heart beating. Then as I changed my position in bed I didn't feel it beating any more. Perhaps it had stopped. I'd better feel it to make sure it was still going. I didn't want to die because of my heart stopping. Yes it was still beating. But wait, as the fear went through me, my heart jumped. What could that be? Not a physiologist yet, I wondered if my heart was going to stop, maybe because I had eaten the green icing. Perhaps it was poisoned. My apprehensions gyrated, I became almost paralysed with the fear that my heart would stop. Perhaps God was calling me to him early, as had happened to one child saint on her first communion day. I didn't want to go to God yet, no matter how good they said he was. The fear went on every night, interspersed with details of horrible pictures from the Saturday Evening Post, the frostbitten feet of some unfortunate person, bodies found decaying, bodies in war. Or my bedsheets would be covered with huge juicy, slimy snails, and I was lying on them and squashing them. I became terrified of death, and prayed

"Please God let me live just one more year" a child's prayer of wanting, destined to be answered as a continuation of want. I never understood what connection the green icing had had with my panic. Food colouring leading to hyperactivity? Or sneaking food? Or denying something deep inside?

When God's year was up I was not fearful any more. I remembered the pact and wondered if I would die, but was not surprised when the day went by and I was still alive.

About this time a dream recurred, there were white lines starting at the top of the page, and as they travelled down they became first an angry red and finally were gobbled up in black filth at the bottom of the page. The page of life, dramatised. I would awaken too hot, kick off the bedclothes, get cold, pull the bedclothes on and dream again.

As an adult I wondered what my dream had meant, and came back to my training in keeping emotion bottled up. 'Show a brave front', Mother's words, which are so destructive to the life of feeling. I realised my dream had spoken to me of my emotional life in trouble, because of grief, anger and frustration unexpressed, and above all, of the love imprisoned behind my veil, crying to be heard.

*

Another aspect of school which left its strong mark was the teaching of religion, and all its attitudes and nuances. There seemed to be a gap between the sublime truths taught by Jesus which went straight to my heart, and the rules and regulations of religion. Religion as taught seemed to link up with the discipline I had learned at my grandmother's place, above all, the suppression of feeling so that work could be accomplished without distraction. It never spoke about ghosts or messages from the dead, about which I longed to know more.

Catholic religion was a strong force throughout the entire family. An Irish Catholic religion, Mass every Sunday and holy days, no meat on Fridays, fasting every lent (but not for farm workers who were exempt due to the heavy work involved). First confession and holy communion at seven years old, confirmation at ten years old. The catechism which had to be memorized, (Who made the world? God made the world, as an insurance policy against life.) Nuns at school and priests for dinner on Sundays. Half an hour of religious instruction every morning in the first lesson (the most important subject, must be passed before all others). Hell for those who disobeyed, sighs and pitying looks for those who fell by the wayside, not going to Mass or perhaps going only at Christmas and Easter. An attitude of suspicion towards organizations outside the Catholic Church, secular bodies, non-Catholics in general. Praise for Catholic countries like Ireland and Spain (never mind their politics) praise for our Holy Father the Pope, infallibly sitting on the throne of Catholicism. Praise and monetary support for the local Catholic Church, the missions in countries like India. Many children, greatly loved, sprawling families, a kindness here.

Sometimes I stayed with Paddy for the holidays. There religion was not quite so strict as it was in the city. There were occasional excuses why one did not have to travel 30 miles to Mass, and in fact we only went when the priest came to the little wooden church standing in its bare paddock 15 miles away at Woodside. Maybe every second week. Likewise with meat on Friday, which was allowed for men doing heavy work.

I entered strongly into the spirit of the Catholic Church. I enjoyed the rules and the guarantees. I enjoyed school fetes and house parties, where I won on the spinning wheels and lucky numbers. I enjoyed my school friends, their houses, their mothers who gave me cake and sweets (these were banned at home because they were bad for the teeth). I read stories of martyrs, the gorier the better, and made up my own scenarios for martyrdom not understanding that what you give out you get back. My mother once said a martyr's death was the best because it guaranteed immediate entry into heaven. To me it felt like a waste of a life, and I was afraid of the pain of being killed, so I rejected that insurance. However I often won the prize for Religious Knowledge. I was seriously intellectual about Catholicism, did my best to discover its wisdom. Its rules made some boundaries to guard against the intrusion of the unknown.

I was a quiet, hard-working child, conflict avoidance my specialty. All throughout my school years the nuns thought I was perfect for them, a true candidate for the convent.

"You'd make a lovely nun, dear" they'd say.

I shrank from the idea, and said so. They answered, one and all

"Oh but if God wants you you can't escape!"

Vocations were illustrated in books, stories, the lives of saints. I felt a foreboding of something outside myself that I would not be able to control. I disliked the life of nuns, I wanted to get married and have lots of children like my mother, and have a husband who loved me. The fear of having a vocation started when I was eight or nine years old and continued till I was twenty. It was difficult to throw off. I had periods when I would feel an overwhelming dread that God would call me, and then I would stop thinking about it and go on normally until something would happen to remind me of the danger. This was the beginning of a new panic. For most of my childhood years I could fob myself off with

"Oh it's a long time yet, I'll worry about it when I'm older."

Paddy had married and lived on another farm, not so far from my grandparents. During the school holidays I was invited to stay. My affection for Paddy was recognized amongst my family, and no doubt my mother was glad to have fewer children in the house, as she was always either pregnant or nursing a newborn baby. At Paddy's I really had a holiday, maybe even removing my protective veil briefly. Just sitting looking at Paddy was enough for me, helping in the kitchen, cooking scones with her and drying the dishes were all extra delights. On Mondays Paddy lit the copper and boiled up water and we did the washing. Paddy and I doing the washing together had become almost a ritual. At first when I went to stay there, there was no electricity, so as well as the light of Paddy's smile, there were special lanterns for the living room and candles which threw spooky shadows around the bedroom. Later my uncle installed his own generator for 12 volt electricity, and Paddy bought some appliances. The toilet was a can out the back which was usually emptied by my uncle, sometimes by Paddy with my help. A big wood heap outside the back door, where the logs were split for the stove. The split wood was stored in a woodbox beside the kitchen, and sometimes a snake would venture in, and so Paddy disliked putting her hand in there in the dark. Her house had another excitement, it was riddled with white ants. The door lintels and window frames in some places were completely eaten out , we could stick our fingers through the paint and find space underneath. Nobody worried about it. Outside were a clutter of ramshackle sheds to explore, plus the well-kept wool shed and sheep yards and huge cypress trees in lines, originally planted as windbreaks, and wonderful to climb. I took up a rug and a book and lay reading high above the world, a view to the sea on one side, and to the hills on the other.

I started to read adult books at Paddy's place , I joined the Argonaut's Club on the radio, and listened to plays and serials at night with Paddy. Her husband was a kind man, and a good farmer, but also an alcoholic so he wasn't often at home. Paddy would light the fire in the sitting room and we would sit together listening to the Jack Davey show, Bob Dyer's 'Pick a Box' and radio plays. Paddy soon had her own children, whom I loved as fiercely as I loved Paddy.

When I was seven Father Christmas brought me a doll called Rosebud, who slept and woke, smiled prettily all day long, and endured countless privations and rescuings, operations and convalescences at the behest of her mother. Rosebud taught me how to play mother, before I came to try my skills on my younger brothers and cousins. I copied my mother and Paddy first with dolls and pets, kittens and puppies. I watched the hens gather their yellow soft chickens under their wings. Watching babies take early steps holding mother's hands. Reciting nursery rhymes with them. Jigging baby up and down on my foot "Ride a Cock Horse to Banbury Cross". Soft teddies cuddled in bed or wheeled around in a tiny pram.

I learned the value of coaxing and tickling, laughing and playing, to get the little ones on side. I played piggy toes and keeping secrets on the palms of the hands to capture attention, then read stories, acting the parts to involve my small audience. I was in demand as a baby-sitter, mainly for Paddy's children and my own brothers and sisters, and until I started to grow into a more individual life at about twelve, I threw my heart and soul into children's games.

The peak time of every sheep farmer's year is shearing, two and a half weeks of concentrated effort every September. In the house it meant ceaseless cooking as about ten extra men had to fed during the day and at least five extra would live in. This meant five cooked meals every day, breakfast, morning tea, lunch (a massive roast meal) afternoon tea, and tea at night. Breakfast and tea were also big cooked meals, and morning and afternoon tea consisted of generous sandwiches, scones and cake. The heavy work brought huge appetites, demanding lots of fuel. All this was cooked on a small wood stove by Paddy and another one or two women helpers. I loved the shearing, but Paddy hated it. Her day began at 5-30 am, when she got up before the dawn to light the fire in the kitchen, and started to cook breakfast of bacon and eggs, sausages and tomatoes, toast and tea. After breakfast the dishes were done by hand, in the one tiny sink. Then the cooking for the day started in earnest, all hands required. After lunch every day Paddy was down on her hands and knees scrubbing the kitchen floor, cleaning the ashes out of the grate in the dining room, more cooking, more sandwiches, more washing up. After tea Paddy would lie down early, exhausted.

There was only one tiny bathroom and the men had to queue to shave, and again to shower in the evenings, to take off the grimy lanolin and dust they had accumulated in the shed. Water was heated in pipes which ran through the wood stove, and there was little of it. It ran out suddenly and often. There was no chance for the family to wash until the men were safely in the shed or at the dinner table.

In the evenings, the men who stayed over would play cards or roulette, all betting small amounts of money, laughing and joking, swilling beer, telling yarns, teasing. I quickly learnt to play too, and this was my favourite time of the day, I was allowed to take money from a big jar of change for my bets, but unfortunately for the owners of the change, I never replaced it with my winnings.

All the farm labourers were involved in the shearing, plus a gang of three shearers, plus extra rouseabouts. A wool classer officiated at the big fleece table, pulling off the dags which were thrown in one direction, the bellies in another, and the final fleece was bundled up and placed in a high-walled bin, (a long, narrow room or space). When a bin was full I was allowed to help carry the fleeces to the press, and when both sides of the press were filled the presser jumped in and stamped it down. After the wool was miraculously pressed down into less than half the original volume I could help brand the bales.

Outside there were sheep to be mustered from the paddocks, bored wethers, petulant rams, and fussy mothers with lambs. The mothers' agitation grew as the lambs were drafted off, and put in a separate yard. When they were reunited after shearing it was a crazy scene of gaunt, white, unrecognizable mothers running around sniffing, snuffling, bleating, searching for their babies, who were by this time thirsty, crying in broken voices, scampering about bewildered, looking for a familiar grey woolly with a spare teat. Taking the wrong teat was always an unwelcome move, and was butted away, no Christian charity here. Eventually all were rematched successfully, and were escorted back to their home paddock, by a man on a big brown horse and a couple of dogs, a black and white border collie and a sleek black kelpie. Yard work was always a place where children could help out, and I made the most of it, calling out to the sheep,

"Push up there!"

Closing gates, waving arms, cutting off the ones who tried to escape.

This life was my first taste of farming. Paddy's family lived off the land to a great degree, killing a sheep for the kitchen, trapping or shooting rabbits, fishing in the sea, and sometimes shooting duck. They were in this way a hunter-gatherer society, and these were the ways one lived on the land in those days. Animals were to be eaten, ecology was not a consideration. Neighbours would gather for a foray down to the lakes where the wild duck lay, inside the sandy hummocks which kept the sea out. They would come back late with the birds, and stow them in the refrigerator. I was walking down by the lakes one day with my uncle, and we came across a boot stuck in the mud.

"That's Frank's boot" joked my uncle, "He gets a bit toey when he thinks the duck inspector is lurking in the bushes!"

One year at Paddy's place I noticed that nobody shut up the hens at night, there were no eggs to be brought in because nobody knew where they were being laid. The hens roosted in the cypress trees, cackling to themselves, safe from the prowling foxes. I decided to put this situation to rights. Every evening I would take some wheat and call the hens to their yard, and sprinkle the wheat on the ground there. The first night I got three hens to come, and so I locked them in till the next morning. Then I took out the kitchen scraps to the yard, and fed the imprisoned hens before opening the gates and letting them wander free. That night I repeated the procedure, and this time locked up half a dozen hens. Every night I locked up a few more hens, and every morning, I kept them in till lunch time. I was rewarded with one egg after a few days, and slowly the numbers built up until after a couple of weeks the hen house was restored to order, and a constant supply of eggs was being delivered to the kitchen. This was important to my self confidence at the time, showing myself that I could control life, and be productive.

Of course my heart broke again every time I returned to the city, but I managed to function, putting on my veil again to deal with city life.

*

Back at school in the city the other children in school continued to perplex me. The first friend I could remember was the boy who sat next to me in third grade , we walked home together after school, and chattered on about our school work, homework, families. But the next year this boy and some of the others moved on to another school, often the Christian Brothers, so again I had to find a friend.

One day a man came to the school to show us some of the wonders of the Great Barrier Reef. He showed us slides, and real stuffed crocodiles, along with coloured corals and shells. I was fascinated. He explained the life swarming there, in a paradise of blue water and golden sun.

Then a priest came to tell us about the Communist menace. At first I thought he would be as exciting as the Great Barrier Reef man. But this was another story. At school the fear of the teachers had intensified with the fall of each domino. The priest who had been expelled from China came into our classroom telling horrible stories. He reawakened the consciousness of fear and war that I had learned on the carpet of my grandfathers sitting room, so many years ago. He described what war was, terrible death, burnings, drownings, torture, martyrdom of the Catholic priests in China, shootings like my friend's father in Changi prison camp. Flesh rent in agony. The communists were on their way, would be here within five years they told us, bringing their bombs and their mutilation.

With limbs paralysed with fright, I left the lesson and walked to the playground. A zombie. My friends were there, eating their sandwiches. My mouth was so dry I almost couldn't swallow my lunch, had to force it down, threw most of it away. I looked up to the sky expecting to see enemy aircraft approaching. Every sound was menacing, every truck in the street was carrying weapons or men to the war. It was only a matter of time.

The fear from the old days at Grandfather's place as the adults crouched over the radio listening to the war news came back to me. I had to set about dismantling the dread, tile by tile and brick by brick. Life had to go on, people had to eat, wash, live, care for the babies, even if we would be incinerated within a few years. At home I still had to do my homework, still listened to the Argonauts' Club on the radio, and folded up the nappies for Mother. I started to read war stories, and understand how it was that ordinary people lived in war, what happened in their day, what was altered. An early story told of bombing in London, and although it was grim, it showed what really happened. I had asked my father to read it to me one day but he said no, it wasn't a suitable book. Actually it was helping me to join with the mass of humanity who had endured war, and survived it, surviving not only the bullets and fire, but the arch enemy, fear itself. By my early teens I started to read more widely, the Battle of Britain, the brave pilots, prisoner of war camps, women spies in France. Now I could put words on the fear, and times and places, particular wars for particular reasons. This helped me to gain a perspective. Perhaps it was just then that war had happened, perhaps we could avoid it if we were nicer to each other, tolerance started to trickle in. Understanding both sides in a war or in an argument. Finding a solution without all the killing. Although my panic about war began to be alleviated by these means, there would be more work to be done as I grew older.

*

Most days I caught a tram to school and would watch it coming over the big hill, stopping at Derby Street first, then snaking down the tracks to the stop before the railway line. There I saw someone get on every day, I wondered who it was. When the tram came to my stop there was an attractive, neat girl, hair tied back in plaits, looped behind her head. She was in my grade and we smiled at each other, and when we got off the tram, we walked down the road together. After school we played on the swings, devising wild competitive games, and became best friends. Anne had an ordered life. Some days it was all right for her to play after school, but on other days she had a music lesson, often belatedly remembered, suddenly fleeing from the swings to the tram stop yelling

"I've got to go, Mum will be waiting", whilst I disconsolately continued swinging.

We met every day for years, rode bikes on the weekends, walked down to school, sometimes accompanying the nuns who marched down in penguin pairs, from the convent to the primary school and back every day. We shared schoolwork, Anne was as clever as I was, and played in the same netball team. We stayed over at each other's houses. At Anne's house they ate different meals, often cooked in unfamiliar ways, sometimes cold meat, potatoes and cabbage, and a pudding, and she had three older sisters. Their perspective was different. In this household mother and father both worked, the older girls were involved in their own lives, but also affectionate to we younger ones.

If I fell into friendship suddenly, I also fell out suddenly. In my final year at primary school, Anne became friendly with someone else. I overreacted like a jilted lover. No one understood. Anne came to talk to me as usual, not realizing the depths of my wound. My pride was hurt. My heart had been deceived again. I couldn't trust anyone. I wouldn't speak to Anne, couldn't. The agony of unbearable rejection. On the other side what could I say, nothing made sense. I felt I was somehow responsible for this, but didn't understand quite why. I leapt into the all too familiar pattern , I was unwanted, not special any more. Nothing had worked before, rejection simply had to be endured. I knew how to endure things, so that is what I did, for the months which passed by till I left the primary school and started life in the girls' boarding school where my mother and aunts had been before me.

At boarding school life was different, going from the top of the pile back to square one again. An older girl was put in charge of me to show me around for the first few weeks. However, I made friends with the lawless young lady who slept opposite me in the dormitory, and it was she who took me by the hand and made the first weeks bearable. The convent school was an enormous four-story red brick building, staffed mainly by nuns, with some lay teachers, all women. A two-tier structure of nuns, the Mothers who were teachers, and the Sisters who did the housework. Most of the girls came from rich families, and knew the best cake shops in town. My father never got the chance to be rich, he told us he had to spend all his money educating his many offspring, and doing the teeth of the neighbouring nuns and priests for free. I received a thorough academic education at this school.

Every term there was a special holiday in honour of one of the most reverend of the reverend nuns. On that morning the girls were awakened by the older girls dressed in costume, racing through the dormitories with whoops and yells. Everyone ran downstairs to peer over the banisters, whilst the senior girls enacted a skit on some local or recent happening, singing songs with the words changed to tease. Organized mayhem. The audience yelled and clapped, threw sweets at the players, maybe sprinkled water on them from above. Then they would dress, attend Mass in the chapel, and then go outside for a breakfast of frankfurters and rolls served on the tennis courts. The day which followed was filled with games and puzzles, the special hide and seek game "Cache" where the school was divided into two camps. The whole gang had to hide then reach home without being tagged by one of the other team. After a specified "hiding time" two scouts could be sent out to locate the hiding team. If they were spotted, they could then move on and hide somewhere else. In the enormous grounds of the convent no place was too sacred to hide in, and my team dodged into the ditch behind the huge cypress trees, in a secluded corner of the kitchen garden. Excitement grew as a scout was spotted

"Did she see us?"

"Wait till she goes then we'll move".

Thirty-five girls to hide together and outwit the other team was a tall order. When the scout had disappeared, we crept around the convent building, taking the long way round, the opposite way that the scout had taken.

"We'll hope they go direct to where we were, then we'll sneak home behind them."

Yes it was working, we spotted a group of uniforms flashing through a gap in the trees.

"They've gone, now run for home!"

The girls streaked for home, the other team catching sight of us just as the last girl was in, just made it! Laughter, recriminations, teasing. And the end of the holiday, an Alfred Hitchcock film in the hall.

During my teen-age years I continued to go to Paddy's place, usually twice a year in September and January. Electricity had come at last, and with it the stimulus of the right of passage into adulthood. We were sometimes a gang of kids there, when other cousins and neighbour's children visited. We smoked our first cigarettes, out of adult view. We chased each other out amongst the cypress hedges, found old deserted nests of eggs, with which we pelted each other, ducking the explosions of rotten egg gas. Other days we sat in the kitchen and listened to the stories that the adults told. Stories of the old days in the bush, the characters who had lived there long ago, tales embroidered by distance, time and occasionally alcohol.

One day, a warm sunny summer day, Paddy and I looked out and saw some young men walking through the paddocks, coming from the direction of the sea. They were members of the RAAF and had been dropped off on a bush track a couple of miles away. This was part of a training exercise in which they had to find their way back to base some 30 miles in the other direction without being 'captured' by any of the locals or their own troops. At this time I was immersed in stories of the escapes of British airmen through Europe during World War II and fancied myself as a rescuer cum resistance worker. The young men were handsome and happy, rather than brave and noble as they would have been during war. They were however hungry, and lost. Paddy and I were inspired to enter into this game, and we took the lads in and fed them a huge lunch, roast beef and potatoes, carrots and peas, washed down with beer and tea. We gave them a packet of sandwiches to take with them, as they had a long way to walk, and directed them around the properties of any neighbours who would be likely to report them, as of course everyone had been requested to do. I felt singled out. The kindliness which I experienced in these encounters from Paddy, the friendliness with which it was received by the young men as they sat and swapped stories, formed a strong basis for later values. Friendliness and a smile could cut through any barrier, and a scowl or a sulk could bring instant retribution.

Bush fires were another excitement in which the whole community was involved. From the women's point of view, there were endless sandwiches to be made, to be taken to a house near the front of the fire, where other women would be working, dabbing at smoke-filled eyes, serving tea to the fire fighters coming in black dirty at all hours of the day and night. The day after the fire the people would walk over the burnt paddocks, inspecting and detecting smouldering vegetation, beating it out or reporting it to the men. The fighters would congregate, talking and talking, purging it all, the highpoints, the amusements, the teases, the fellow who had turned down the wrong track and been confronted by flames leaping the road, who had singled handedly fought the blaze until help had spontaneously arrived. These and other exaggerations flew back and forth, amongst the involved, strengthening their bonds to each other in the community, welcoming those who had come from further afield and sharing in the misfortune of loss of pasture, and maybe stock. Bringing spirit to life in the bushland.

Paddy was a good-hearted friend and would talk to me about things I was afraid to talk to my mother about. My first period started when I was there one holiday. I knew about periods, and had been eagerly awaiting my first one. Then it came and I had no equipment with me. I tried to pad my pants with wads of toilet paper, which didn't help much. The bleeding got heavier. No chance of hiding anything when one used a can toilet. Paddy asked me if I had periods.

"Yes" I exploded "It's my first one and I haven't got any things".

Paddy went to the cupboard and tore up rags, padded them with cotton wool, and gave me two pins. The used pads we burnt in the stove. I had come of age, I felt respected by Paddy and honoured in my womanhood.

Sometimes there were other kids to make friends with. On Paddy's property there lived an old man in a hut down near the beach. He lived by trapping rabbits, which he gathered every day, and hung on a screen between two trees out on the road for the rabbit collector. They were covered by a hessian curtain, and usually by maggots too, as the hessian was quite ineffective. He took his horse and buggy to the nearby town once a fortnight or so to buy food and a supply of the amber liquid, and arrived back rolling uncertainly. The first time I observed this strange behaviour I called urgently to Paddy to come because Bill was sick, but she just smiled and said he was only drunk. That fact was duly recorded and filed in my brain. Bill had two nephews who visited with their father sometimes. The boys and I went out for expeditions over the paddocks, indulging in a bit of youthful spirits and hilarity. One day the younger boy bet with his brother that he would swallow tadpoles, and put them in his mouth, intending to take them out later. The tadpoles were not so easily tamed and swam down his throat to their last resting place, accompanied by a startled look of helplessness on the boy's face.

And so I climbed through my teens.

The Catholic religion had its academic side, the philosophy of the great Catholic thinkers, the theology of mysticism, and this I enjoyed. The definition of the Blessed Trinity. The love of God for himself personifies his Son, their love for each other becomes the Holy Spirit. However the teachings in religious instruction classes stayed in my head whereas the kindness of some of my teachers went to my heart.

The tenor of Irish Catholicism is unlike the continental versions. The Irish version takes control of every thought, word and action. There is no leeway for the conscience, even though this is not admitted to. People born behind the Iron Curtain have kept their Christianity alive in their hearts and minds, admitting nothing to the authorities of their illegal thoughts. Their conscience takes control of their life, they are never separated from their innermost wishes. The Irish Catholicism seeks to do just that, to separate man from his conscience. It causes dreadful uneasiness. Its members have to struggle on the inside to be free, whereas those born into Communism struggle against an outer enemy. Different battles, neither easier nor harder to win.

We girls delighted in teenage pursuits, going to the movies, having crushes on film stars. We often wrote to film stars and requested autographed photographs. Such polite letters, "Dear so-an-so, I greatly admired your acting in … Please would you send me…." My favourite was the sultry Marlon Brando, the bad guy come good in 'Guys and Dolls', and I wrote the standard letter. The address? Marlon Brando, Hollywood, USA. Then I forgot about it. In the meantime my family moved house, to a larger block of land where my parents had built a modern mansion fitted out with all the conveniences to make large-scale child-rearing a breeze. So the answer when it came went to the old address where my father still had his dental surgery. Father, concerned for virtue of his teenage daughter, opened the letter and looked at the handsome face on the photograph. He kept it a while before giving it to me,

"It came some time ago, I want you to think about your morals" he said as he gave it to me.

I felt my privacy had been breached, not only had my letter been opened, but my crush had been discovered. My silent teenage soul cringed. I couldn't look at the photo, nor at myself, so invaded did I feel. As for voicing my thoughts to another, or to my father, that was impossible. These were the 1950's, children weren't that brave. I gave my photo to a friend.

Sexuality when it comes brings a revolution. Naturally I explored my body, and passed through the gates of pleasure. For me this had nothing to do with sex. In the Catholic school the girls had had frequent talks by holy priests to warn them against impurity in all its deadly forms. Fortunately I was naive and the priests' language so obtuse that I never connected impurity with my hands. Lucky me. I didn't make the connection until I was eighteen years old, and by then my adolescence was over. I was surprised

"Oh is that what sex is?"

The nuns were still trying to conscript me to become a nun, but I kept sweeping their advice under the carpet. In my later teenage years when sexuality became more pressing, I fantasized about a blissful marriage-night consummation, followed by years of guilt for having deserted my vocation to the convent. The issue of taking my own power and making my own decision was as yet unknown. This problem festered like a tubercular lesion, out of sight until the appropriate irritation would bring it floridly to the surface.

The Anne story repeated itself twice during my teens. After I had been separated from Anne III for some time, and had endured the agony yet again, I learned to grow up and alter my response. With Anne III I had become interested in boys, and in one glorious holiday at her place I had developed a crush on a young handsome male, one of Anne's acquaintances. We girls giggled and laid plans for hours, pored over his photograph, and never met him. After Anne III and I had endured our cooling off period, one day she caught my eye in the studyroom, and waved his photo at me. A fit of the giggles repaired the old damage, and we were friends again, but not in the same way. Just good friends. It was fashionable to have crushes on the older girls , the soul must have its outlets to passion. Crushes were accompanied with gossip, hero worship and giggling, fantasy but no touching. My friends had taken the place of lovers in a way, so close did we become. But now a corner was turned, and I experienced a new sort of friendship. I was ready to open myself to an interaction without dependency. I wanted to share fun and laughter, interest, studies. Netta was a tall quiet girl from Cumbalunga. Even the names, Netta and Cumbalunga made my classmates laugh good-naturedly. Netta and I became mates. She was an intelligent girl, but often felt an outsider. We walked and talked together, but as we were by now in our final years, it was a more mature friendship. We discussed our work, books, thoughts and aspirations. Travelling to the matriculation exams together in trams, drinking chocolate milkshakes with marshmallow before returning to school. She was the first of many friends to accompany me.

*

I walked into the library to seek information on my name. I was getting myself ready to leave school at the end of the year, wondering about University, courses, and my self. After all who was I? I was sixteen years old, I had taken on responsibilities, I was a prefect now, the sacristan and in the major societies of the school. My character was forming as I contemplated my wishes in the face of the great world outside. I was meticulous about performing tasks, good at my studies, a fast runner. But I liked to keep myself to myself. Preferred small gatherings, maybe one or two friends. Shyed away from parties, or crowds of people I didn't know. But I had no deep purpose, no goal alluring me. My memories, imaginings and fantasies wafted around me, forming unlikely scenarios. I read widely, stories of mystics and saints, commended highly by the nuns and catered for extensively in our library. I read of Sister Josefa, the little Spanish sister who earlier this century had visits from Jesus, and from the devil who retaliated by spreading sulphurous fumes throughout her convent for everyone to smell. There must be something in this talk of ghosts and spirits. My lessons on religion did not satisfy my craving for knowledge on the subject. Then I remembered Paddy's story of the Sibyl who brought messages from the dead, and again it stirred my imagination. I still found the idea intriguing. So today I planned to delve into Roman history and mythology, the origins of the Sibyl. The reference books were under the shelf on the far wall where there was a mural of Jesus walking on water towards his fearful apostles. What was it he had said in one of the gospels? 'These things you shall do and more?'

I burrowed through the old books. Sibyl was t he Goddess of Nature and Mother all living things. Her prophetic spirit inspired a series of priestesses in various places in the ancient world, including the sacred cave at Cumae, famed as an entrance to the after life. She conversed with the dead and brought back their predictions to the world. I read of their prophecies, written in the Sibylline Books, and how they had been rewritten by both Christians and Jews, to make it seem that Sibyl had prophesied the coming of Christ. How King Tarquin had wished to buy the nine Sibylline Books, but had found the price too high. The Sibyl at that time had thrown three of the books in the fire, and doubled the price of the remainder. When he still wouldn't buy them, she repeated the performance, until the king finally bought the remaining three books for four times the original price. And then a reference to the travels of Aeneas in the underworld with the Sibyl. Aeneas rang a bell, who was it who had written about him? I walked over to shelf where the classics were shelved. There I saw Virgil, 'The Aeneid', I took it down. A whole chapter on the visit to the underworld, here was largess. I sat in an armchair in the corner and started to read. I met the raving Sibyl, uttering truth draped in obscurity, granting Aeneas' plea to enter the underworld to meet his dear father just one more time. The breaking of the golden bough, Aeneas' talisman of protection. His subsequent journey with the Sibyl into the cavern towards the realms of the dead. The different groups amongst the dead impressed me, first with the evils, disease and poverty, then the tree of False Dreams, and strange beasts against whom Aeneas drew his sword until the Sibyl reassured him that they were mere shades, without substance. They passed a group of souls awaiting burial, who must either receive the rituals of death or wait one hundred years to be accepted by Charon the ferryman, to their eternal rest on the other side of the river Styx. And everywhere Aeneas met people he had known on earth, so understanding the stories of their deaths, he was able to appreciate the circumstances in which they now found themselves. They passed the turnoff which divided heaven from hell, by the tower in which souls atoned for their sins in torture and lamentation, and hurried onwards to the souls in bliss, and Aeneas' father. Heard his prophecies, and finally departed with the Sibyl through the Gate of Ivory, back to the physical world.

What could I take from this story for my own identity as Sibyl? What on earth could be relevant today? Sibyl showed Aeneas the way, she could move freely on both sides of the River of Death. It showed a certain comfort in life, if one could move into the realms beyond death and back again there was no need to fear dying. Death must be a more subtle change, not black and white as people often believed. The Catholic Church taught strongly of life after death, heaven and hell, and all the saints believed in it too. But Virgil had painted detailed pictures of how it could be, how one's behaviour led to certain consequences. He fleshed out the different scenes, imagined life into the bare teachings of the nuns. He helped me to draw aside veils in my understanding. But if I searched for a goal or a path for my life, I was disappointed.

*

My final exams were over, and true to my school which specialized in teaching the humanities, I received a Commonwealth scholarship on the basis of my good performance in French and German, but perversely went to study science. On the day I left school, I was surprised to see some of my classmates crying. I was exhilarated, leaving school at last was all I desired, my freedom to live my own life. I had sought advice from my local priest on how to combine Catholicism with my new life, but received only the priest's dry words,

"Do try and come to the Children of Mary meetings."

A memory of my mother's devotion, and her philosophy of child-bearing touched my heart, above all the words of priests and holy people,

"You just go on, trusting in the Will of God".

The young woman who stepped out of childhood was not conscious of how to solve the many conflicts in her life, even though she had begun to take correct paths to do this. The facing of troubles came instinctively, as she felt certain strategies working, alleviating discomfort. But she had no idea that an intellectual and an emotional life must be intertwined to produce a contented human being or even that they were separate and required different methods of handling. The conflicts within me would be addressed as one by one situations were created to show me the way through them, towards a greater balance.

*

Inside me was a dark chasm of uncertainty, as I wondered where I would find love. No intellectuality touched this point, it was immune to logical thought, impenetrable by parental affection, outside the realm of religion. The other side of the chasm was shrouded in a veil, penetrable only by love. Love was always difficult to find, so second best fantasy stepped in as man followed man through my attentions. Naturally, the chasm lay untouched, and just an occasional shaft of light sometimes filtered in through the veil.

The temple to my service had flung its doors open, candles were burning as desire flooded my soul. Dripping in temptation, drowning in the knowledge that one day the union with the beloved would occur. One day I would step over the chasm, tear away the veil and enter the rest of my life, however long it would take to happen. This message echoed throughout my soul.

℘ PART 2 ℘

FILLING MY SKIN

My skin is loose, unfilled with substance. I look about and see conflict, ambiguity and I feel distress. Nothing is as it seems. Eyes and lips speak contradictions. I am tearing apart, trying to amass experience, and yet unwilling to lay down the fat of what I see. Sirius, who am I, what am I doing here? Show me a way through. I create quiet within, expanding and making new. Society's rules and expectations flow through me, into my stillness. Sirius guides my conscience, making sense of opposites Slowly, slowly my skin fills with truth. In pain and joy I am becoming a person, rounded and full.

AT UNIVERSITY IN THE FIRST TERM I dressed like a dolly bird, tight skirts, high heels, and discomfort. I had some acquaintances from school, but they were studying arts or law and I was in a science course, one of four women in a class of seventy. I was terrified of the boys, but they paid no attention to us, being too busy drinking beer and chasing attractive nurses. They were partners in practical classes, and there I formed some tentative friendships with a few of them. I had a pictorial mind and had enormous difficulty in following words, so lectures and mathematical formulas flew over my head. Neither did I know how to study, how to translate the symbols into pictures which my mind could easily retain. My practical classes were my salvation, as they brought me into contact with experimental method, easily understood, and with the demonstrators who liked to answer questions. So I scrabbled for my existence in this new world, an alien environment.

In term two, I changed completely, dressed in slacks and jumpers, a comfortable uniform in the pre jeans era, and made my first friend, Leah. Leah had a boyfriend. I knew that Leah's first loyalty was always to him. Within those bounds we had a really long and mutually beneficial friendship. We talked for hours on the telephone, comparing our lives, building the bases of our characters together. Leah was another Catholic, interested in the issues of social justice, the new ALP, and the humanist world of university Catholics, embodied in the Newman Society. She was studying law/arts, and we met at daily Mass in the arts lecture theatre. The Church and sex were discussed at length. All of us subscribed to the Catholic pronouncements of no sex, not even masturbation, outside marriage. No divorce, no artificial birth control. The Catholic pill, "hold it firmly between the knees". The rhythm method of conception! Sympathy for those whose lives were spent in torment bound to a partner when the marriage wasn't working. Or, if one was brave enough to leave a partner, then a life spent in celibacy and some disapproval. And when that didn't work, then off to confession, but unfortunately confession didn't work unless the sinner vowed to give up the sin in question.

I wonder if people believe such things these days. It feels now as if the soul of mankind has broken free, and that few have had to take the tortuous path that I took to dissect away the regulations and find peace. Those who take their pleasures now seem to have the freedom to do so without the soul searching which we had to do. Perhaps it only takes a few people to follow the logic of thought backwards to its source, to dismantle the architecture of these concepts, reject it, and once done it is done for all.

Leah knew many of the boys from the Christian Brothers schools through her boyfriend, and soon I knew them too. They were easy to know, natural, undemanding, and easy to talk to. Not vaguely interesting boyfriend material for me, but just then it didn't matter. They often said to me, however,

"Do you know McGowan, he's in second year, up the country this year?"

"No" I would reply, feeling curious about him.

One day in the cafeteria, my friends called me over.

"Come and meet McGowan!" they shouted.

I was impressed. James McGowan was tall and slim, very good looking, with a wicked twinkle in his blue eyes, curly brown hair. The boys were drinking coffee, sitting around and joking. Good time guys. I joined them, we sparked off each other, laughing all the while, a friendship spawned, then we went our separate ways.

The months at university went by and study continued to be very uncertain during my first year. I struggled on with the many readjustments I had to make, coming from a regimented Catholic boarding school into university life where study was self-determined. Before the chemistry examination a friend came over to my place, and we revised together a question which I had no idea about. In pictorial form it took on a new life, I understood suddenly the molecular rearrangements which occurred as water changed phase between vapour, liquid and solid and how the parameters of pressure and temperature affected these changes. The ability to make molecular pictures brought a revolution in my consciousness of science, and as the question appeared verbatim on the examination, it came none too soon.

The examinations came and went and I scraped through. I had a knack with them, would often pick the right questions to study in advance, knowing just enough for a bare pass. Next year would be spent at college in the country.

In the early days of my year in the country, the last days of the cricket season were being played out, and the men who had been in last year's team came back for the finals. James returned, and he and I started to meet at the cricket, and to take long driving trips to various country towns, eating out together after the matches. This was definitely boyfriend material, and the letters flew between Leah and I, discussing every aspect of the liaison. Soon he had kissed me, the crossover point was reached, and we became a couple. Even if he swore to his friends that he would sooner bare his bum in Myer's window than be with me, he *was* with me. Done was done.

Now that I was James' girlfriend, my tubercular lesion concerning marriage vs the convent became suitably irritated and flared up. The panic grew, coming in waves, then departing for months at a time. I had no strategy but avoidance, pushing the whole question underground with all my force. The stronger I pushed it down, the worse it felt when it resurfaced. In my third university year, it started to attack me again. I was at home that day, miserably pacing up and down, upstairs and downstairs, kitchen to living room, outside in the garden, up and down, never resting, up and down, up and down. My mother was a keen observer of her children, saying little but remaining intimately connected with them. Eventually she corralled me in the hallway,

"What's the caged lion act about?"

"Nothing."

We each took a deep breath.

"It's not nothing when you have been pacing up and down all day, looking as miserable as a bandicoot!"

"I think I have to be a nun, and I don't want to, I want to get married" I exploded.

"Oh is that all!"

Her relief was almost solid. I wondered why. Did Mother think I was pregnant or something?

"That's not so bad, we'll talk to a priest about it, he'll tell you what to do. I have never had the idea you would be a good nun."

I was not too comforted by this, I well remembered the nuns saying they hadn't wanted to enter the convent either, but God had got them in the end. But I felt better to have shared my dread.

"Go and have a bath and go to bed with a book, you look worn out. I'll bring you something to eat" mother said.

The misery receded as a little comfort was allowed in. Later on in bed my father came to talk to me, was kind, supportive. They stood by me when I was in trouble, my parents. I wondered about priests. I remembered someone who had come to the University, to the Newman Society, and had given understandable, even amusing talks about sex. I could imagine that he might be a good one to talk to.

I sat in the bare hallway of the priests' headquarters at the Cathedral, waiting for my appointment. The ceilings were high, the walls cream, the woodwork dark. Draughts blew along the corridor stirring up the dust rats every time someone opened the front door. But it was early evening, there were not many people around. I had told James what had happened, afraid for his reaction as well as my own fate. Curiously he almost had not taken in what I had said. I had left him up at the University, to wait for my return. I wondered how I would be able to tell him, as I held out little hope that we would be able to marry after tonight's decision. The heavy door opposite me opened and the priest, a middle-aged man with a kindly smile beckoned me into the small interview room. I tumbled out my worries, saw them flooding over the desk towards him.

"Yes, this is a common worry of young girls" he said, stemming the flood with his experience, "They come out of the Catholic Schools believing that God has called them. But I think that once you have met a young man and fallen in love, that this is what you have chosen to do, so you can forget about the convent."

"You mean it is all right to get married?"

"This is how I see the situation."

I was astounded. How many years had I suffered this affliction, this hiding from my internal war, and so easily the whole conflagration was extinguished, the peace proclaimed? My scruples dissolved in logic. I was allowed to make a choice. I gave the priest a generous donation, and sped back to the University. There in the lounge lay James, sleeping soundly. I went to him, kissed him awake,

"It's all right, I'm free"

Free to make a different mistake? Or?

The psyche is a strange beast which takes much handling to bring into line. I found that it took a little time to get over the onslaught of the nuns. Firstly, the way of doom-thinking had become habitual, so I fell easily back into the old way of reasoning, the terrors reappeared, but not so vehemently. I contemplated another visit to the priest, but then the bout of fear would die down again, so eventually I didn't go. I doubted sometimes that I should accept someone else's glib solution. Could life really be so simple? But life itself brought the conclusion to this episode, by its continuance, by the work which had to be done and submitted, and which in its own quirky way ensured constant development.

The next development came from the persistence of my doom-thinking. The new peace was shattered by the dogs of war which had lain sleeping since my baby days. I knew now that after all I would not be able to marry because the Russian bombers were on their way to Australia, the last Domino in the world, and that fire and ruin faced me and the rest of my city. As I drove through the countryside I would look out over the green paddocks and dread that one day I would see them black, cratered from the bombs and burnt out.

This panic was not as difficult to deal with as the nuns, because now I was learning that confrontation was a tool I could use. I was often with James and the other friends at the University, and began tentatively to discuss politics with them. The black colour of the earth-globe started to change to a more optimistic landscape. I could identify the world's trouble spots and see that realistically they were not as large as I had imagined. There were pockets of trouble, bounded by the societies who warred.

Then I wondered "How does it feel to kill a man, how could they bear to hurt one another". Unthinkable images of holding a gun to another man's head, or stabbing into a ribcage floated around my head. The first world war, the trenches, bayonets. There I found a ray of hope. The soldiers did not hate one another, they were actually victims of a political decision. One Christmas, the Germans and the English had come out into No Man's Land and exchanged gifts and food. Extended the hands of friendship over the battle-ground. They had showed humanity. All was not lost. Perhaps it was the hatred I dreaded most.

After the war of course, there was the shell shock. People talked about shell shock with hushed voices, as if it should be normal to go to the war, kill men from afar or in hand to hand combat, see bits of bodies lying around, smelling the decay, and complete with undiminished courage and spirit, return to their homes in the same frame of mind in which they left. It was not acceptable to be shell-shocked. Close to mental illness and the madhouse. Back at home the men often took to the other spirit to deaden their outraged feelings. This also was lamented quietly. Or 'He wasn't any good after the war', was another saying to explain bachelors, living alone with only the bottle as companion, occasional visits to hospital and a too-early death. My Uncle Charlie was an exception, he took the last group of men out of Gallipoli in the great retreat, rode his horse at Beersheba, and was loved into an old age with his family. Strong in love he must have been.

But I was still only eighteen years old. I was still afraid of the seven o'clock news, but becoming more astute, I did some research, talked to my friends, read up on politics and began to join the real world. The fear gradually diminished as I dissolved the domino theory in my mind, and trusted with the rest of the world in America.

This panic was quite quickly dealt with, and taught me about success in confronting fears, and also about going back in time, to unravel the fear from its earliest beginnings, step by step to the present. It worked for that type of panic which started in the very real facts of the second world war, and continued, fed from other facts assembled incorrectly, until in the end the whole fear cloud was built on misinformation.

The next panic followed quickly, and again was simply dealt with in its beginning stages. But it had strings going into the past and the future which had to be played out over many years. This panic was the fear of madness, and was brought on by treating a running nose.

My family used many drugs, not opium or even nicotine, but the ordinary drugs from the pharmacy. They used them for the slightest sniffle, and encouraged me to do likewise. Antihistamines, used for the treatment of hay fever, work through the central nervous system. Sometimes they cause strange reactions in certain people. A high dosage can cause hallucination, restlessness and confusion. In me the drug produced a slight dislocation in my consciousness, I sat in the chair, feeling that I was unreal, not a part of the scene in the living room. I saw my father come in and sit down, saw my little brothers playing in the corner, and felt as if I were watching from a vantage point which had nothing to do with them. I wondered if this was how you felt when you went mad. I did not attribute it to the drug at first, just sitting in terror trying to grasp at my life and my consciousness. The next day I felt normal again. Later I told my mother about it, and she answered

"Yes those pills sometimes make me feel a bit queer".

I avoided them from then on. I was seriously terrified of madness, lunatics, mental hospitals, asylums, my fear springing straight from books of centuries past. This panic was a tremor of things to come, but in itself was dealt with in my understanding of the effect of the drug, and the beginning of my avoidance of all drugs.

As I came out of these panics, I went into hard study, under James' direction. He explained things to me, and as he was repeating the third year, we had many subjects in common. It was always clear to me that I relied heavily on his tuition, both for the subject material itself and for methods of study. We were rewarded for our efforts, and secured our degrees with a sprinkling of honours.

We had had a tempestuous relationship, but shared many interests, family background as well as fondness. My stubbornness in the face of slight family opposition ensured that we stayed together. We became engaged and soon we were married, seeking the love and affection to which we were so vulnerable. I stood beside my husband at the altar, reciting after the priest the responses.

"I Sibyl, take thee James for my lawful husband, to have and to hold, from this day forward, for better for worse, for richer for poorer, in sickness and in health until death do us part."

I was consequently surprised to hear in my head, a voice say

"Or some other time!"

Was this the fine print in my contract? Or a protection against making a vow which I would find impossible to keep? For many years James and I were faithful to each other, but I was at least prewarned of the way things would change. I had always been charmed by engaging men, and had thought that marriage and a sex life would put a stop to it, but found myself repeatedly attracted to other men. Puzzling. Life did not work as I had believed it would. However the good Catholic girl would not make love to other men, it was forbidden. I simply noted my feelings.

James was a man of many talents. He was tall, good-looking, friendly and out-going. It suited me well to be with him, as I was shy and liked to stay in the background. If he could break the ice for me I could feel more assured in large groups of people. James was a stirrer, and throughout his University years had often played pranks on authority, especially if they took themselves too seriously. He was intolerant of humbug, or of people who unjustly tried to impose their will upon him, and was brave enough to confront people with whom he disagreed. His parents were the archetypal battlers, his father was the gentlest policeman I have ever met, and his mother a primary school teacher, and a great reader of Australiana. I had enjoyed listening to stories of her years in schools and James' own childhood. I learned that he had been asthmatic as a child, heard how his parents had taken him out in the car as a last resort, opening the windows to literally blow the air into his gasping body.

James was clever, and had put himself through school and university by winning a succession of scholarships. He was known for his succession of girlfriends, his roving eye, and his quick tongue. He could be rude and funny, but he was also gentle and loving, not only to me, but within our circle of friends.

When we married I assumed that I would have children and that my career was virtually at an end. James and I agreed about Catholicism, and tried to make it a part of our lives. He readily took on the responsibility of providing for me and future children financially. But all in all, he was still a young man, rearing to go. He threw himself into his new work and friendships with new colleagues, his sport, cricket and baseball, and the time left over he spent with me. It was clear that I did not come first in this schedule, but before the children arrived it didn't matter. We tried to take on the impossibilities of the Catholic Church's attitudes to marriage, and again, before the children arrived that too seemed to work.

At first we lived close to the University where we both worked, and one evening a friend gave us a lift home. I was in the back of the car with a blue suitcase, and James and our friend in the front. Suddenly, as we passed a side street, a car beetled out and slammed into the left side of our car. I had been watching it come towards us, and in this split second my thoughts went slowly, wondering what it would feel like when it hit. I was tossed around inside the car, but no great damage was done. We prised ourselves out, I stood on the footpath beside my suitcase now with a big dent in it, whilst the men talked to the driver of the other car. An old couple came up to see if I was all right. And then an odd thing happened. I was suddenly above the scene, on the other side of the road almost, watching the old couple as they spoke to this young woman with the bent suitcase, and she was sobbing and sobbing. I, from the other side of the road shrugged my shoulders, not understanding my precise relationship to the scene below. A taxi came, the men and the young woman got in and were driven up the road to my house. I followed, keeping an eye on them. I saw my friends with whom we shared the house open the door, take the young woman upstairs, and put her to bed. I went too. They seemed genuinely concerned about her. Then they brought her a drink of hot chocolate, and Zap! I was back in my body to drink it.

"Are you all right?" my friend asked. She had been really worried.

"Yes I'm quite all right, thanks for the drink" I answered, wondering what the fuss was about. Of course I was all right! I remembered the accident, I hadn't been hurt only shaken up. I was hazy about how I had reached home, but remembered clearly my wish to drink the chocolate. At that time I was unaware that the spirit could leave the body in times of stress. I must have seemed like a zombie to my friends, it was no wonder that they were concerned for me, but it took many years before I understood what had happened. Eventually I read about astral travel, and saw it for myself in other people.

My grandmother, my mother and Paddy had lived as mothers of large families. My grandmother had been a nurse, but substituted community work for her profession when the children had grown up. Paddy told me that on leaving school she had been first cousin to a slave. She and my mother had left school during the depression. At this time the family estate was in financial difficulty. Two great aunts who owned large shares in the property had died within days of each other, and left their shares to each other, thus inflicting double probate expenses on the eventual recipient of their land, my grandfather. Money became short. So my mother had to stay at home and help with the running of the house and garden. Paddy, my mother and grandmother were my role models, they and countless other families of school friends. In our family there was a slight stigma attached to mothers who worked. A lowered glance, a murmuring voice, as if the normal speech could result in unwelcome contamination.

I had only these images. No other life but a copy of theirs was possible. All my schooling, my university degree would be laid aside, my husband would provide the money, and I would look after the house and children. Even the government approved of this stereotype. In the teaching profession, for example, women's wages were set lower than men's and if they were to marry, they lost their permanence. They could work on in temporary positions until they fell pregnant, when they would be required to leave. Rumblings of discontent with these restrictions were beginning to be heard around the university when I had been a student. A friend had married, and had related the difficulties which had suddenly arrived at her door. Her teaching bursary had been suspended consequent upon her marriage, despite her intention to continue her studies. The loss of livelihood had left the new couple destitute.

But this was not my situation. I had decided to adopt my parents' role model as my own. I even considered the idea of leaving work as soon as I married, but even my mother counselled against this. She, remembering the depression and her abhorrence of waste, advised me to use my new qualifications by working at least until the children arrived. So I found a job assisting in a research project in the school from which I had graduated. James, having reached his goal of first class honours, had received a research scholarship and had begun work for his doctorate. After a year I left work, to a speech made by the professor whose tangled thoughts flowed through suave lips.

"Sibyl is leaving to get married, and we wish her all the best for her future", was accompanied by laughing interjections

"And about time too" as I had been married a respectable year by then and was enormously pregnant.

I had my first wedding anniversary in the hospital with my beautiful baby Mia. All my training with my brothers and cousins, all my early childhood memories came back as I held this soft creature in my arms, and vowed to teach her to love as I loved. She was a happy child, vigorous, intelligent, and James and I were entranced with her. I was relaxed in my handling of her, and she rewarded us with smiles and chuckles.

I wished to keep a perfect house, having seen friends whose days were spent happily scrubbing baths and hand basins. This did not come automatically, I had had experience in helping mother and Paddy, but the discipline of cleaning, bedmaking, dishwashing, and especially cooking every day had to be learnt step by step. And other events intervened, so that my house was well kept but not polished. After Mia's birth I was occupied with caring for her, and the housework took second place. For all the good things about being a mother, the down sides were the baby blues, the isolation in the suburbs, and the cessation and lack of replacement for my career. I continued to study when I could, and actually decided for a while to do a Master's degree in Botany. I was unhappy that my studies now had to be brushed aside. I yearned for intellectual stimulation, for a balance between the enclosing life tending Mia with James' companionship, and a personal goal which would unfurl my wings and take me on unknown journeys.

It lifted after three months as I became pregnant again. I had landed into the life I had planned, but it was not working out as it had for my mother. She had never conceived while she was breast-feeding. This had the potential of doubling the number of children I would bear. Contraception in all its forms was banned by the Church, the Rhythm method may have to be attempted.

This year I received Betty Friedan's book, 'The Feminine Mystique' as a birthday gift. It arrived at the critical moment. Doors opened, the intellectual life reached in and beckoned me through.

Betty described the women in the USA, who had adopted the life in which I was engaged: professionless, without self confidence, bursting for involvement, but interred in the myth of happy housewife. She describes how this society discouraged aims for women above the satisfaction of the lowest needs of mankind, food, warmth, clothing and sexuality. Women were prisoners within their self-made walls of uninvolvement in a career, and encouraged to stay there by businesses who saw the advantage in having such excellent customers. Her words told me about my life. Explained how one could live in both worlds, and feel the better for it. How the whole family benefited from a woman's greater contentment. I adopted her thesis. I leapt into a new frame of mind. I vaulted over the obstacles which I had allowed my role models to place before me. Intellectually I started to live again.

But as I was pregnant, I was hauled back into the life of home and children. My mind was liberated however, and looked outwards once more, cherishing the idea that all was not lost. My emotional adaptation to these ideas was non existent. To give up the lifelong adherence to my family's principles, their beliefs and lifestyle, was not so easy as reading a book and adopting its arguments. While the new ideas were not being tested, life could continue as normal, but come a conflict between old and new, there would be trouble.

It was not only within the private walls of my home that the conflicts of role models began to be felt. Australia was supporting America in the Vietnam war at this time, conscription had been introduced, and the young men on reaching eighteen years were required to register for the national service ballot. Their birthdays would be drawn and those chosen were likely to find themselves at war with the Viet Cong, in a country whose ways they did not know, for a cause misrepresented by governments. Pacifism was not generally recognized as a defence in our society unless one was a Quaker. Some young men refused to register, but if caught, they were assured of conscription and subsequent service in Vietnam. Others were taken to court, and pleaded pacifism and were gaoled. The penalties were real and frightening. One of my brothers reached eighteen at this time, and refused to register. He spent years in fear of detection, which disrupted his life, and laid waste his ability to study.

I educated myself about the Vietnam war, and learned not to take sides too vehemently. I began to see the political arena in which I had been brought up as narrow and stifling. Anti-communism had formed the basis of a movement to which my parents had given their allegiance. In its early days it had had a real purpose, but these days its rationale had worn so thin that it seemed to tamper with the social conscience, to force an intervention in the internal affairs of other countries, on the pretext of defending the world against communism. Any regional dictator could be supported so long as he was anti-communist. I tried to see what Australia was defending, and what the Viet Cong were striving for. I could see no justification on either side for the anguish which the Vietnamese population was forced to bear. Or for the dehumanization of our young men, taught to kill.

Sam was born 13 months after Mia. This time the labour was quicker and more painful, and remembering the pain my body vowed it would be the last. Sam was a dear little boy, but he was not quite so easy going as Mia. He was bigger, slower and quieter than Mia had been, and extremely stubborn. This time the baby blues were banished by my return to a part-time teaching job in botany. It was the impetus that I needed at this time, and I was contented, working four afternoons a week for about four months of the year. The mental stimulation cleared my mind, and the children were well looked after by an elderly woman who became a close friend. She came to the house and even did some housework for me. I got to know my colleagues at work, and felt my life expand into a leisurely, but comfortable routine. The children were growing up healthy and bright-eyed. Everything in my life was expanding happily.

The next year I took another part time job teaching, to fill up some of the empty months. I was so confident that I decided to have another baby, and became pregnant again. So I was loaded up with responsibilities. James as usual was rather an absent figure, being caught up with his job as a research student entailing many nights after-hours work, his sport every weekend, and the mandatory Friday evenings in the pub with his friends. I was left to cope alone with the household, and met my social needs through my colleagues at work. I was stretched to my limit, and it was all right whilst things were going well.

But this year the tide of good fortune turned against me. To begin with Sam inherited his father's asthmatic constitution, and began to have colds, one after another.

The crash of my ordered existence came one day when I was about to leave for work. The babysitter had arrived, but Sam was in trouble again, had a heavy cold, his breathing was shallow, his asthma present as always. But the doctor had told me not to call it asthma. I was becoming confused as to the seriousness of his illness. Perhaps he wasn't as bad as I had thought , maybe he didn't need all this medicine. Every day for the last two weeks I had taken the train to the doctor's with the pram and my two babies, Sam had had his injection of penicillin, then we had trailed home again. Sometimes, if I had been at work, we would not begin the trek until the evening, in the dreary winter weather. I was tired from my third pregnancy, and desperately weary of Sam's illness. Nothing that I did helped very much. Did it really matter if I took him to the doctor's or not? I began to doubt my way of treating his illness. Perhaps if I let him go through a cold without all the medicine his immunity would be strengthened and he would become stronger. And now he had a cold again. So this morning, I resolved to go to work as usual, and trust that Sam would be all right with the baby sitter. I was split between my many conflicting responsibilities. I saw Sam sitting in his chair, sweaty, gasping and gave him his cough medicine. He didn't seem much worse than usual. But the babysitter was uneasy about him, perhaps being older and more experienced she saw more than I did. At her urging I took him to the doctor. The doctor, while not panicking, sent me directly to the Children's Hospital, where Sam was admitted. They put him in an oxygen tent, in a cot in a big airy room with other children. I remembered that when my sister had been in hospital twenty years ago, parents were not allowed to visit. I supposed it was the same now, the nurses would not want parents around, they would be looking after Sam now, and would need the ward to be quiet. I saw that Sam was settled in his bed, sat with him briefly and when he fell asleep I turned my attention to my other responsibilities. I called by my mother's and told her what had happened, called James at work to tell him. Then I went on to work. Soon the hospital contacted me saying that Sam was in intensive care now, would someone come to be there with him? I was surprised that they wanted me there, again remembering the olden days when parents were excluded, but I returned to the hospital. The nurses explained that they liked the parents to stay with the children, it helped them to recover, and I half heard what they said. Then I saw my baby in intensive care, drugged and unaware, a tube down his throat attached to the respirator, his chest heaving up and down, in the respirator's rhythm, and a drip inserted into a vein in his forehead. Suddenly I understood the gravity of his illness. I was swamped with horror, I had misunderstood the situation, he could die and it would be my fault. I became fully present, but at the same time was overwhelmed by an enormous shame. What sort of a mother was I, I hadn't stayed with him when he needed me? What sort of a scientist was I, I had not seen the seriousness of his condition? How could I admit such defeat and ever hold up my head again? And the child himself, lying there heaving, medicated with cortisone, the wonder drug for asthmatics, inert to everything except the machines. At least these doctors called it asthma. What was the little fellow doing in the machine-filled cot where he lay? I was aghast, I stood watching down over his blond hair damp with sweat. The staff were kind and matter of fact, but could not say that he would definitely survive. All my insides started to merge into one space, they became hot iron, so many conflicts all at once. I was helpless, wanted to leave but was clamped into the situation by my mind which allowed no deviation from a perceived duty. I stayed with Sam till early evening, and eventually James came in, bringing a friendly touch and a breath of sanity with him. I went home to the babysitter and Mia. Went home in another space, not touching earth, enclosed in a cage. I put Mia to bed, ate something, and sat in the kitchen. I wanted to pray to ask for Sam's recovery, but in those days I didn't believe in prayer. This was the time of the Vietnam war, and daily I saw frightful pictures of mothers and babies in deep distress on the television, bombed out, fleeing from napalm, soldiers carrying guns escorting them away from their menfolk, their burnt villages. How could I dare to ask for something for myself when the screamed petitions of the Vietnamese mothers went unheeded? And yet there was something in me, a desperation. If prayer could possibly work, help Sam to survive, I must try it. I dare not omit anything. I sat weeping, pushing through my own ordeal of humility, and asked that Sam should live, should come through his distress unscathed.

Everyone has their own contact with God, comparisons do not serve. God is the life which pulsates through people, is present in every heart.

"Thank you for the life of my son," the perfect prayer in the present, radiating strength and confidence. I did not know that then, I simply asked that he should live.

Worn out, I slept. James came home late saying that Sam was unchanged. First thing in the morning I rang the hospital, yes, Sam had been taken off the respirator, but was not responding to them. Yes, I should come in and spend time with him. My being had suffered a dislocation from the shock of everything that had happened the day before. The few tears that I had shed did very little to allow the realignment of my emotions with my mind and soul. I was so distraught that my feelings had begun to split off. But I pushed myself again to deal with the onslaught of the day.

Sam lay in a cot, totally inert, his eyes open but not seeing. There was no consciousness behind the eyes, no one at home. The doctor explained that his anoxia had been very severe, that brain damage could result. I put my emotions on hold again, splitting them further from the rest of my consciousness. It seemed that half of me stood listening, wondering

'Do they always tell parents that their children are vegetables in this offhand way? In the movies they give them a chair and a tranquillizer, or at least a cup of tea? ', whilst the other half of me spoke to the doctor.

I lifted Sam out of the cot and held him in my arms, stroked his forehead, rocked him gently. He lay motionless in my lap for hours and hours. Sometimes he slept, sometimes his eyes were open but there was no life behind them, just a body which breathed and ate through tubes. I talked to him, and felt his warmth against me. I laid him back in the cot and went to get a sandwich and take a breath of fresh air myself. Returning after lunch, James was briefly there. He told me that some friends working in the laboratory in the Children's Hospital had reported to him that they had had samples from a child whose oxygen levels were so low they were in the foetal range, and that he had found out that they were Sam's samples. This did nothing to reassure me. He went back to work, and I lifted Sam out of the cot and sat with him on my lap again. Suddenly his eyes were alive, he saw me and smiled, reached up to my face. I spoke to him, and smiled in return. Then he was gone again, back to being a lump lying there in my arms. I did not understand what was happening. As if his brain had come back and left again. But brains didn't behave like that. If they were damaged, the damage could not leave and suddenly return. I sat musing, still very split, not convinced of either the hopefulness or hopelessness of Sam's recovery. That afternoon he returned again briefly, then flew away again. I was wondering if hope was in order. As I began to hope, the split lessened a little.

The next day, I sat with Sam again on my knee. He returned almost immediately, stayed about five minutes before falling asleep. Awakened to lie inert for a brief while, then suddenly returned, smiling up at me, clutching my fingers. I called the doctor over.

"He's come back"

"Good, yes they do that, they sometimes take their time."

In later years I understood that the soul could leave the living body in times of great stress, returning when the danger was over. It seemed similar to what I had done after the car accident. This seemed to me to be the most likely explanation for Sam's behaviour. Together we joked about his "holiday" from his body in the years that followed. But at that time I had no way of understanding what I had seen.

As the days went by Sam returned to the way he had been before the illness. He was little the worse for wear. On the other hand, I had stored up my anxiety, my guilt, my feeling of overwhelming responsibility for another day, allowing it to fester in my system for a more painful draining later on.

Sam's asthma continued to plague the family, and there was added the onset of convulsive episodes. Epilepsy was less serious, and contained some moments which I could laugh about once my pain had subsided. Sam was just eighteen months old when it started, and it first manifested as infrequent momentary blackouts. I would accuse Mia who was a year older, of pushing him over. Daring eager Mia, not always innocent. One day I saw clearly that he had fallen on his own. He had crawled along towards me, then fell suddenly for no apparent reason, crashing his head on the wooden floor. When I picked him up he was already conscious again. I put him in his cot, and padded the sides to protect him from bumping himself. Gradually he became rigid, arching his head back, although he seemed fully conscious. When I picked him up he was smiling and talking to me as usual. What could this be? I took him to the doctor who promptly sent me without explanation to the Children's Hospital. Inside I was convinced that he must be dying. Otherwise the doctor would have explained it to me. My emotions split off again, there was no time for anything else. There was no one to call on for help or support. No way of crying my anguish. I had no faith in the ability of the medical profession to deal with neurological disturbances, having seen people with incurable nervous disorders. My job was simply to get the children into the car and drive them to the hospital. I wondered if Sam would be dead before we arrived at the hospital. I laid him on the floor behind the driver's seat, and kept feeling him with my hand as I drove along, and was surprised when he started to chuckle and play with my fingers. But I didn't dare to be relieved. I left Mia who had fallen asleep in the car-seat, and took Sam into the casualty department to await his death. I couldn't carry both children at once, and trusted that Mia would be all right for a while. I had rung James, and soon he came in and stood beside me. I felt supported, ever so slightly, and asked him to go out and get Mia. Soon he was back, Mia in his arms, smiling and talking. The hospital doctor examined Sam and when he said after a long examination and tests,

" I think we will admit him."

What was this banality when I had expected death?

"Isn't he going to die then?"

Which he answered with an explanation of the epilepsy, which as it happened was easily controlled.

Another dislocation had occurred within my personality, to join the previous ones, all stored up against another day. It may be like soldiers in war, they see their mates killed, attend the funeral, and are out fighting their next battle. Like them, I had absolutely no time for grieving or emotional expression. In addition, I had been brought up to think that the indulgence of emotions was weak behaviour, and that my responsibility was to keep on keeping on.

My pregnancy proceeded through all these trials , more visits to hospital and more asthma attacks. I was deathly tired, strung out to the last degree by the time I was ready to deliver. At Christmas time I gave birth to my daughter Esther. This baby, most like me, never fed well, was always thin. When the babies had been taken from the mothers after feeding I often heard one with a piercing, pained cry.

"I pity that poor mother," I thought.

It was my own baby, Esther, in too much pain to eat. Choking on the first few mouthfuls of milk, gushing from her mother, then coughing, crying, missing her feed, the milk stopping. Then hungry. If she was sleeping quietly, I knew it must soon be time for her to waken for her next feed, and the whole process would begin over again. This beautiful child, with her huge blue eyes and golden curls never learned to eat normally. She resembled her mother too closely, too exacting of the self. I wondered if the baby had been affected by the anxiety surrounding Sam's illness. I blamed myself for that too, adding another burden to my shoulders.

I battled through my next year, Sam's asthma manageable but continuous, the baby vomiting, Mia growing. James was still engrossed in his work, still absent many nights during the week and still involved in cricket practice and matches on the weekends. I saw little of him, wished it was otherwise, but again buttoned up my mouth to help to ensure his progress through his studies. It was an article of faith, that all post graduate students must work in their evenings, or they would not reach the coveted PhD. I ground down my needs, admitted to no emotions, but wondered sometimes why I cried so voluminously at the movies on television.

I was visiting a cousin, and from the next room heard a comment.

"What a thin, anxious-looking little thing Sibyl has become. She looks as if she is heading for a breakdown," followed by a murmured assent. I sat on the bed, too wretched to move. My shoulders shook, the tears rose, the tears which could have washed away the terrible anguish, but only a few squeezed their way through. That door was too frightening to open , I bolted it even more firmly closed.

I carried all the trauma from Sam and Esther, trying to keep going. I remembered the Vietnamese who were still suffering and bearing their grief, still not allowing myself to express my own. While I could go out to work, I could function, but at the end of the year the long Christmas holidays brought a four month stretch of unremitting child care. The panic and depression which came at this time was all engulfing. Being dislocated from my emotions no longer helped me, the feelings were on their way back, and would not be denied this time. I feared that something outside me would force me to kill myself. With this thought I was revisited by my terror of madness, my brain did not belong to me. 'Unhinged'. Knives, staircases, railway lines, poison, traffic, all became danger points. The supermarket was a place where panic could strike its most telling blows. Was this because of the abundance of choices to be made there, when all I cried out for was someone to tell me what to do, what was right for me, right for now, to lift even a corner of the responsibility which sat so heavily on me? The next panic had arrived in its many parts.

I had a friend with whom I worked whose husband was a psychiatrist at a research psychiatric hospital. They talked about the Unit, the new ideas for helping the mentally ill and I was fascinated, listening closely as we shared insights. Then with the progression of my own anguish, I decided I must confess my panic and seek help. Debased though I may become, interred for life in a Mental Asylum, in contact with the real crazies whom I dreaded, this was what was required of me. James took me to my friend's place one Saturday morning, a quivering mess. The husband took me into a modern brick building, treated me professionally, listened and gave me drugs for the weekend. The family and I went home, accompanied by James' lamentations that now he was late for the cricket. A part of me thought he could at least not complain that day. I lay on a rug in the back yard, feeling the drugs begin their grip. The tall trees, yellow box and long-leafed box receded from me. The grass was already brown, patches dead from the heat. No flowers in this season, late summer. Everything waited for the rain, and the resumption of the year's purpose. I too, had not worked in four months, the university teaching suspended for the summer. If only I could have held out two more weeks, I would have been able to distract myself in work. But this was not going to be allowed. Whatever plan I had agreed upon for my life, it did not include avoiding challenges. I tossed about on the rug, tried to sleep, but then got up and paced restlessly to and fro. The children had gone to their grandparents. As the drugs bit into my consciousness, my head became packed in cotton wool, dense and soft, impenetrable, longing for sleep, not sleep but rest, not rest but freedom, not freedom but absence. Absence from? Life? No! Never! I do not want to die! Glimpses of sharp blades, chisels in the shed, carving knives in the kitchen brought back the dread. Round and round the cycle went. Up and down went my pacing.

The drugs did not help me. By Monday I asked if I could be admitted to the hospital. Forced by something pushing from inside, I obeyed blindly. As I walked in through the door, I wondered if I would ever be allowed out. Again my insides had fused, the iron hot, strong but flowing in uncontrolled directions. My head did not belong on my shoulders , it was off on its own somewhere. I felt knives all around me, pointing their sharp blades at me. One false step and I would be impaled and die. I didn't understand death either. Desperately I clung to life, could not wish for death for an instant, was terrified to mention it for fear the unknown forces would take advantage of my lapse and cast me into unwelcome oblivion. The Sibyl who was interested in the plight of souls after death had no place in this anguish.

I had been fragmented into a thousand pieces, a smashed mirror. My childhood, its mixture of happiness and lost love, my adolescence in its birth of a person who could not draw together the ambiguities of feeling and obedience to her upbringing. My fledgling interest in my name, the Sibyl who brought comfort through her contact with the dead. The dislocation which had occurred more than once when feeling became too great and could not be denied. The duties of house and home, the lack of support, the too early extrusion from the womb of home to the arena of life had resulted in the complete disintegration of my personality. The major cause, my insistence in ignoring my emotions, casting them aside as unworthy adjuncts to a person of common sense. Something which people with work to do would not waste their time with. These pieces of my mirror flashed as they circled around, menacing me with their sharp edges. There was no further destruction which could be wreaked, save death. I was at my lowest ebb as I crawled through the doors of the hospital. And a lingering, decaying death was all I expected on the other side of those doors. I was without hope.

I sat in the waiting room to see the head doctor, completely split into terror on the one hand and on the other, false logic. I saw plants and dark furniture. The doctor asked me to come into his consulting room. Asked me how I felt. A voice came from my dry mouth and explained how it had been. It was only a part of me which answered, the feeling part was standing over by the door, looking at the tall ferns, wondering if this interview was safe. Safer to stand back a bit, even if it felt dislocated. The logical part was standing on razor blades.

"How long will I stay here?" I heard my voice ask, and was surprised to hear such a question.

"In cases like yours it is usually about two weeks"

You mean I shall leave here? It isn't permanent? One can actually recover? My self by the door was astounded. The razor blade Sibyl, just functioning, got up to go out with the nurse who had come to fetch her, and the feeling part followed after. I went to my room, and wondered if I should undress and get into bed and await my cure. But no, the nurse said

"There is a sitting room here, other patients you can talk to, lunch in the dining room at 12 noon, a meeting after lunch which you are expected to attend. And I am always around, if you want to talk, please come and see me."

I wandered out into the hallway, barely touching the floor, wondering what I could want to talk to the nurse about. A middle aged man walked along the passage towards me,

"Hello, I'm Gerald. You're new here are you?"

"Yes"

"What are you in for?"

"Ugh, I am afraid I will kill myself" I stammered, not at all used to answering such questions.

"I tried to kill myself too, but I was found and taken to the hospital. I left my watch to a friend, and he found it and guessed that something was wrong. It was he who came and called the ambulance."

I was surprised at the breezy way that Gerald could discuss his innermost secrets. I was flying about in distraction. He continued his story

"I came here after they had pumped me out and got me physically well again. Then my doctor put me on pills, and I came good in a couple of weeks. I can't really remember why I was so depressed. I'm going home in a few days, to see how I can cope with life again. Who is your doctor?"

"I just saw a friend who got me in here, and the chief doctor," my voice answered from far away.

"Everybody sees him first, then you have your own doctor," he explained. I was feeling puzzled. Where were the deranged morons, whom I had expected would be clawing at my knees as they dragged themselves around the floor? I had clearly got my ideas from the middle ages, and I had better have another look at the late 20th century. However the panic and dread were still gnawing at me. I felt like crying, or escaping or smashing something, anything to avoid its grasp. The sister who had admitted me came up and said

"The doctor will see you now Sibyl, come and I'll show you where his office is."

A good-looking young man was sitting behind the desk. He exuded charm and self possession. He smiled and introduced himself. I felt safer here in his office. And perhaps the treatment would start now, I allowed myself a smidgen of hope. I sat down, and he said,

"Tell me about yourself"

I thought wryly, the world opens before me. I began intellectually, keeping the feelings under tight control for fear he would think badly of me.

"I am a mother of three children, the second one is a boy, he gets asthma a lot, he has been very sick."

"How does that make you feel?" Invitation.

"Oh well, he wakes up most nights. He had a bad attack two years ago, he nearly died. I got a bad fright. It was my fault for not taking him to the doctor." No feeling!

"Did you eventually take him to the doctor?" Back to the drawing board.

"Yes, he would have died otherwise." Still no feeling!

"So why do you say you didn't take him to the doctor?" A second invitation.

"Because I wasn't going to, and the babysitter made me. I didn't think he was so bad." No, no, no!

I continued to explain my life to the doctor. And I continued to feel the panic. I asked

"What will my treatment be?" A peek through the shutters.

"We will continue to talk, I will prescribe you some tranquillisers, we will see how you get on." A gift.

"How will that help me?" Suspicious.

"It will help you to see yourself in a new way. But that's the end of the hour now, I'll see you again tomorrow". Goodbye now!

I stood up and walked out of the room, again an automaton. I walked towards my room, but the Sister came out and said,

"It's lunchtime, go down to the dining room, it's down the corridor on the right."

In the dining room were a host of people whom I hadn't met, and I was too timid to speak much to them. Some walked around with expressionless faces, little activity behind the eyes. What had haunted them out of existence? A young woman babbled on about the day she had put her head in the oven. My skin crawled with horror.

After lunch I was directed to go into the sitting room, where Sister and a doctor sat with us in a circle. One of the young men began to speak about how his parents had thrown him out of the house, how rejected he felt. Tears welled in his eyes.

"I can't help it, I just can't help who I like" he said.

It was not immediately obvious to me what the point of his story was, I who had come so recently. I was sorry for the lad , he was attractive and well educated.

"Do the pills help you?" asked Gerald, wanting to share his new-found cure.

"I don't take pills" answered the boy. He stared at the floor.

Another young man spoke

"Pills won't make my family accept me either. I am trying this new aversion therapy, but it doesn't make much difference." This man was older, more assertive.

The Sister looked around the group, catching my puzzled eyes in my wooden body.

"What are you feeling just no w Sibyl?" Another invitation.

"I am not used to talking about myself." Another rejection.

"This can be a way of getting to understand your illness" Why not?

"Yes I suppose so." Not today thanks.

I was still on the outside, still immersed in panic. It was an effort to answer at all, and impossible to get into the conversation of the group. But one of the young men had come from a farm near the school I had attended in the country. Even the thought of this peaceful, happy school brought a grain of comfort. After the group meeting I found myself standing beside him. I asked

"What is the aversion therapy that you have?"

"They show me pictures of men or women, and at the pictures of men I am given an electric shock."

I suddenly realized that these men were homosexual, and was appalled that their families should disown them for that. What can you do without your family I wondered? I didn't feel hopeful about aversion therapy either. I imagined my own free-ranging will, and couldn't see that it would brook any interference from electric shocks. It would simply cover my desires under a layer of fear.

But for myself there was still no hope. Although my mind was starting to appreciate the regime here, and lose the terror of the new, my soul was far away. Anguished at its separation from its chosen body, longing to come home and being prevented by my body, the very object of its desire, my body who in turn needed the return of soul to heal itself.

My mother came to visit me on my first afternoon there. She was greatly distressed that I was in the hospital. In an uncharacteristic revelation she told me that she had had the same feelings, that often when she had a new baby it had come upon her, and she had gone away for long holidays to Paddy's. I remembered these occasions, but had not understood them at the time. My mother said,

"It is only the adrenalin in your system, it doesn't mean that the world is really going to end. Nothing will happen to you!"

But although I appreciated her coming and saw her distress, the closeness between us took many years for me to register.

As I write this, she nears the end of her life. I see her more clearly now. There is irony there, that she who loved me and all her children so dearly, should have taught me so precisely her skills in emotional repression that I had to sit in a psychiatric hospital in panic.

But there is more that I missed. The love that I have sought since birth, through the terror of abandonment, the ceaseless chatter in my head as I scrabble about in my self-made cage, has beamed surely towards me every day of my life. But I, behind my protective screens, could not discern the love which she has for me. I have searched this way and that , I have writhed about facing the wrong direction, and have failed to appreciate the light which reaches me through the latticework of my screen. The love which in my terror and sadness I did not understand reaches me now as I see my mother's concern, her loyalty to each of us. But in the hospital, back in those dark times, I did not see.

After I had been there some days, and had had several interviews with my handsome young psychiatrist, I went out into the garden to sit under the trees on the seat, to be by myself and contemplate the day. As if by magic, the clouds rolled out of my mind, I felt clear in my head, happy even, normal. The part of me that had been standing outside suspiciously watching came inside again. It was safe to be back, at least for now. A glow filled me. What was this, it was so long since I had felt normal and happy? The handsome doctor had breathed life into me. Love entered my soul, and began to heal the smashed mirror that was me.

I began to I look forward to the sessions with my psychiatrist. The transference had begun. I was familiar with this occurrence and had been wary of it as one could never have any love relationship with the doctor. Clutching at appointments given in the cause of duty seemed to lead to only more longing. For now it was such a relief that I would put up with the down side. But as the panic subsided it was replaced by depression, chronically repressed grief, just as difficult and insidious to deal with as panic.

I had attended the group sessions every day and had begun to learn how they operated. I had begun to accept that patients might sit there weeping as they told their story. I had told my own story, but had told it without allowing one drop of emotion to be spilt. My eyes down, my voice low and repressed, I ground out my misery about Sam's illness, the difficulties looking after the children, James' absences at work. After I had been there for three weeks, the chief doctor turned up at the group meeting. The attention of the group was once more fastened on me.

"How do you feel about your husband, Sibyl?" asked the chief. He sat opposite and stared firmly at me.

"He is a good man, he works hard" I answered uncertainly.

"That is an opinion, not a feeling. How do you FEEL about him?"

I screwed up my face. Feel? I didn't feel anything. I thought for a while, everyone was silent.

"I love him, I suppose, I want him to be there."

"You say that he is hardly ever there. How does that feel?"

"Not good. But I have my responsibilities. I have to get things done." '*Please stop*' I was thinking.

"What do you do with your feeling that it is not go od for him to be away so much?" He was like a dog harrying a bone this doctor.

"I don't do anything with it."

"I think you turn it into panic and depression." I felt a cloud start to envelop me. I felt suffocated. I must fight it off. This man was insidiously attacking me. How could I get out of this cloud? How could I get him to stop?

"What *do* you feel Sibyl? How bad does it feel that you have to look after the children all day every day, without your husband's support? Don't *you* deserve to be cared for, don't *you* deserve a break? Some loving kindness?"

The cloud was choking me. I felt a band of tension mounting from my toes, up through my legs and hips, immobilizing me. My mind was working in slow motion. I saw my thoughts roll by at one mile an hour,
'By…the…time…this…tension…reaches…my…diaphragm…I… won't…be…able…to…breathe…and…I…will…die…I…must… find…a…way…to…release…this…tension…I…suppose...I… could…cry.'

Suddenly I was sobbing, my straight jacket opened. As the torrent of emotion burst through, the tension in the room released. It felt as if the whole room, not only the people in it sighed with relief. The meeting was almost over. The chief doctor said that my recovery had begun, but would take 'as long as it takes' to complete. The patients gathered around me and hugged me. For the first time I allowed myself to feel their kindnesses, instead of merely standing there and saying thank you, to enter more fully into the difficulties of their lives instead of sympathizing from the outside. My emotions had begun to be heard, and to integrate themselves into my life.

I grew to know the gentle boys, tormented by their inability either to conform in our society, or to accept the validity of their own homosexual experience. I chastely loved them all, and allowed them to comfort me. We conversed endlessly , I travelled with them in their misery, learning life by experience. I met the singer who had been a soldier in Northern Ireland, heard how his company platoon had mistakenly killed an old drunken priest, how he lived yet in his guilt. Met women like myself who loved their children but were caught in some sort of queer bind. Others told of their conversations with disembodied voices. The mental part of me, which was alive and well was able to take in what they were saying. The other part did not want to hear about people who had actually tried to kill themselves, it was still too frightening.

Home for the weekend with James and the children brought an immediate relapse, not as serious as before, but an awakening that the problems of my life now must be confronted, and that the peace of the hospital was merely a pause in my journey through the minefield. My insides contracted as I greeted the children. They had been staying with James' parents, who adored them. They were too young to understand what was going on in my mind, they were their usual selves, Mia teasing, Sam and Esther toddling, all needing food, baths, and cuddles. At the best of times their care needed 150% of my time and attention. The situation was precarious, but merciful time passed and with it slowly the misery. The university term began while I was in the hospital, so I brought my car in to the hospital, and drove over to the university for my classes. I stayed a total of three weeks at the hospital, then became an outpatient. I improved, became more stable and gradually addressed my life.

As I grew closer and closer to my doctor, so I felt better and better. Unbeknownst to me, the day of his transfer to another hospital was also coming closer and closer. When he left the path that I had been walking ended. The firm ground under my feet gave way, as I lost the love which had sustained me. I plummeted downwards again. This time it was the distress of bereavement. One day I stood in the kitchen in front of the stove weeping and grieving my desolation. Mia pushed aside the clothes that were drying there, and hugged me around the knees,

"Don't cry any more Mummy",

"My friend has gone away" I said, as I picked her up and held her.

Of course there was a new doctor. He began our first interview by reading out my first doctor's report of me. It ended with the words

"She is very lonely." I looked at him glumly.

"You felt safe with him, didn't you?"

"Yes"

"And I am new and unfamiliar?" His dark eyes watched me, trying to find me, skillfully hiding in there.

"I suppose so"

"It takes time to change over, it feels strange to me too". He seemed kind, but removed.

"Mmm"

"I'd like to give you some anti-depressant pills. They can have remarkable effects".

By this time I felt like crying, but I still didn't dare. I knew it was the way through, but it took more courage than I had that day. The doctor gave me a prescription and warned me about possible side effects, and anticipated the freedom from depression which they would bring.

"I'll see you next week then."

This new doctor was not at all like the first one. He was older, had been some time in general practice, and sent me in very different directions. He always made me talk about what I thought about him. He knew what I had felt for my first doctor. He was unconcerned that I should fall in love with him, but he insisted that I talk about it, so that I developed a very different relationship with this second doctor. I actually grew to trust him, and felt that with his help I started to lift myself out of the depression. I reached out and found pieces of the smashed mirror and began to integrate them into a much surer pattern, as a new person was born.

I began to make decisions for myself alone. The first was that I hated the antidepressant pills. The dry mouth, the confusion which interfered with my teaching, the recurrence of panic when I felt my teaching to be impaired started another trail of misery.

"Give them a chance to work, it can take up to six weeks for them to show their full effect."

The doctor was encouraging. I was skeptical. Then I started to suffer from derealization. This was the doctor's name for the feeling that I wasn't anywhere. I could see and feel, but perhaps I did not exist. Perhaps nothing that I saw existed. I would look in the mirror and wonder who was looking out at me. I would clutch at doorways and walls, to make sure they and I were there. The doctor's name for this condition told me that others had felt it too, but the feeling did not change. One day, as I walked over the university lawns to the bank, I felt I couldn't make it, to walk without a handrail or support of any kind, what would happen to me? I grabbed for the door as I entered the building, then kept my hand on the stanchions and the rope as I waited in the queue to be served. Barely managed to articulate my words to the teller. Trembling, I felt my way back to my classroom, and James. This episode decided me to abandon the drugs. The side effects vanished completely, including the derealization. In later years I wondered if derealization was another type of out of body experience. Was it similar to what I had felt after the car accident? Or the same as when Sam had been 'not at home' after his asthma attack? I had felt I was standing "beside myself" (has our language experienced it before?) not anchored in my body. I had perhaps experienced a shadow of it before when I had used the antihistamine drugs.

I stood at the crossroads, I had the opportunity to bring my life together now, but it would be hard toil. It would cause me pain to look at my feelings again, but I had no hesitation in doing so. I related to the doctor all about Sam's illness, and wept endless tears about my inabilities, my guilt and shame. After Sam had had his major illness, the hospital staff had thought he was retarded, and it became my worry too. Even before the illness he had been a slow learner, slow to sit, to stand, to walk. But he had done it all eventually. My psychiatrist's reaction was direct

"Bring him in, I'd like to meet him."

James by now was attending the psychiatrist's sessions with me. Although he tried to support me at times, there was no great change in our relationship. We brought Sam in, and watched while the doctor talked gently to him. He was a social child, smiling and happy, loved the attention, read his book for the doctor and performed intelligently.

"No problems there" said the doctor, "So what if he takes his time to do things? He's all right".

I started to recover from my overwhelming feeling of responsibility for my children. One afternoon six months after my first admission to hospital, I sat in my car in the middle of the park, crying uncontrollably with relief. No one had to be that responsible for another person, could not call him back if he wished to die, could not take away a chosen illness. I saw myself as a young mother trying to manage asthma, a miserable disease. If the child is coughing, perhaps if she gets up she can make him more comfortable. If he is not coughing and sleeps extra long perhaps he is dead. That frightening notion accompanied me every time I walked into his bedroom. And asthma never stops, only takes a holiday if the child is even more ill with something else. Unbroken sleep for mothers of asthmatic children does not exist. I started to see that in fact I had done quite a good job. I had put Sam first, and had tried to hold myself intact at the same time by working, taking a breather from the intensity of looking after the children. As I began to relax, and consider myself more kindly, my emotions started to realign with my beliefs about myself. The panic started to abate, and the depression clouds sometimes floated away.

My religion was discussed too. James' and my families had been Catholic since time immemorial. I tried to love God and obey the strictures of the church, but found that neither my personal stamina nor the bank balance were equal to the task of bearing a child every year even if breast-feeding should give me some respite. Nature was uncooperative. I felt betrayed by life, why didn't it work like the blueprints had shown? The impractical Sibyl at her marriage had planned to work until first child arrived, then to leave work, and care for the other children, six in all. Even the mathematics were bad. Aged 21 at marriage, say 45 at menopause gives 24 child-bearing years, 24 children! I had thrown myself into life at the deep-end, forcing myself to sink or swim through the ambiguity of it all. I had to swim away from the church's pronouncements on sex and marriage. None of the church's teachings on sexuality related to my tentative experience of life. I did the research, and understood precisely how the church had come to its conclusions. Read Saint Augustine, Saint Thomas Aquinas and the Natural Law. What inappropriate models for modern day life. The first, a libertine converted to a life of writing and philosophy, expounding the war against the evils of sexuality, which he had previously enjoyed to the full. Saint Thomas never shared Augustine's foibles, but contributed a weight of intellectual argument upon which the Catholic Church still stands. I understood the strengths and weaknesses of the Church's arguments, and saw also why I did not regard myself as bound by these laws. Laws come from the outside, are imposed by one upon another. Where was the heart, the experience, the truth of life? An intellectual approach could overlie and support the truth of my experience, but never be a substitute for it.

Social realities had to be faced, how do you receive Holy Communion when you are taking the pill? In amongst the strongly-believing friends of your mother-in-law? I knew I was morally in the right, but for many years felt twisted, feeling the eyes upon me in church, and I did nothing to release the emotions of the situation. And resisted marriage guidance when suggested by one of the old guard.

"It helps difficult marriages, and makes good marriages better" was the inducement.

"Leave me alone!" screamed my insides as my throat choked over a polite refusal.

I knew I was honest to myself in the sight of God, but felt excluded due to the persisting split in my emotions. Put up the barricades against my mother-in-law and her insinuating presence (James and I were living in the house built by James' parents). A good woman, but an old-fashioned believer, who took it for granted that her ways were shared 100% by me and James. 25% was maybe nearer the truth. I guiltily cast out my mother-in-law's doctrines.

I needed spirit, not knowing how to make contact, or in fact if spirit existed. I tried various solutions. At one time giving up my beliefs day by day as an experiment, I unearthed the very depths of loneliness. At last, having demolished one by one my beliefs in priests, the pope, the church, the spiritual community, Jesus, and finally God and the after-life, I felt so abandoned that I took back those beliefs which felt good, coming back finally to the teachings of Jesus Christ where I found beauty and support. Eventually for many reasons I had lost all respect for the man-made laws of the church. I stopped going to Mass, edged away from the old friends and made new ones, and fought for a new life.

But at this time in the hospital, I was in the middle of my breakup with the church, there was much probing into my feelings about obligations and duties. About beliefs and logic. About perceptions and family expectations. The whole scene was open for discussion, dissection, put under the microscope. The emotional accommodation of my new understandings took a long time to become reality. During this time I succumbed occasionally to swallowing Valium, to ease me through the worst passages. I continued to visit my doctor, at first weekly, then fortnightly and finally monthly. He stood behind me, his strength and knowledge of the dark waters I was trying to cross supporting me as I made my way alone.

I saw a creek, with the huge trunks of red-gums growing on the banks. The course of the stream had been diverted however, by a self-made wall, taller than I was, of old fallen trees, limbs, twigs, a snarl of crossed limbs making an impenetrable barrier. The water was dammed up behind this mass of debris. But by removing the key log from the dam, the water would burst through and flow normally again. With my tears the huge logs of red-gum shifted, the structure lurched uncertainly, and with a crash released, the flood tearing furiously through the dam walls, sweeping the logs aside, flowing strongly before finally coming to rest in a peaceful green meadow. There were many such dams in the landscape of my emotions, and one by one they fell, and still fall, as sweetness and understanding flood my being. The whole episode of the panic and depression lasted on and off for five years till I had mastered the changes it brought with it.

ꟹ PART 3 ꟸ

THE HOUSE OF DAVID

My body is rounded with experience but empty and longing for love. I dream, and my dreams are a remembering. I whisper, and the wind takes my breath to new ears. Old ears becoming new, remembering long ago, remembering Sirian days. Sirius smiles, and our hearts open, fresh hearts, creating anew from our past.

SUN AND LIFE, Frida Kahlo's magnificent painting, depicts her frustrations and disappointments portrayed amongst a deeply sexual background of flesh-coloured magnolia flowers. In the blood-red sun a tear traces its path through the agony of childlessness. The half-opened magnolia flowers richly moist, housing the erupting phallus, and in climax, the weeping foetus, her own inability to bear a child.

For David and me this picture held the germ of passion in the exploding tumescence of the magnolia blooms, precariously opened to permit viewing by the passing eye of public gaze. Blue and green ribbons carried the ripples of radiance to a waiting world, heavy in its longing for love. A world, eager in its expectation of happiness.

A shared snap-shot, an old post-card recalls the memories, transformed by the experience of years. David stands watching, his eyes piercing me with the intensity of life, just as his presence did when we were together. Moments of gold.

The first time we met was on the telephone. David rang me to ask me to come for a job interview. I was painting the hall, the children were away for the holidays, all was peaceful. He asked if he had interrupted me, and I said I was painting. He took that to mean creative work

"So you paint too do you?"

"Only houses" I replied.

I was then 27 years old, one year out of the severe bout of panic and depression, and with a determination that by finding interesting work and new friends that the depression could be held at bay. We lived in my father-in-law's self-built timber house in a bushland outer suburb, opposite the railway line. I did casual teaching work in the various universities in the city, but although I wished to pursue higher education, at that time I had no clear direction towards my life's work. I had found my priorities during the last year, my children and family coming out first, with my mental health through satisfying work intertwined. The Catholic inheritance had begun to be laid aside, along with a host of misconceptions about how to live my life, leaving me open to the strength of new ideas.

I went to my interview a few days later. The university was brand new, a collection of clean-faced, dust-coloured brick buildings on a campus more builders' rubble than the landscape it would become. I threaded my way between obstacles down the brick-strewn path towards the buildings, searching for the name, 'The Hugo Austin Building' where I was to discuss the new job. I thirsted for the chance to prove myself in the scientific world. Every day spent at home with the children I perceived as a day wasted when I viewed my ultimate goal. Development was everything to me, one degree not enough, there had to be more, more stretching, more love, more work, more interest (not more children) in my life. I scanned the newspapers for jobs which could catch my imagination and extend my repertoire.

I mounted the steps and walked into the office. A man came forward and shook hands with me, smiling he introduced himself and said

"You're Sibyl? I'm glad you could make it. Come and we'll sit over here. Can I get you a cup of coffee?"

"Yes thank you" I answered, and sat down on a straight-backed office chair. I watched David preparing the coffee. He was about ten years older than I was, medium height and build, red-gold hair, and blue eyes. He held himself with assurance as he put spoons of coffee into the mugs. His back was straight, his bearing confident. He seemed familiar to me, but from where I did not know. I recognized him in his shirtsleeves and brown trousers, and responded to his easy manner. I looked around the room. It was the top floor of one of the new buildings emerging on the campus, but not completed on the inside. Everything was new, but not in order, furniture bundled in from the suppliers in full use already, but no tried and true routine superimposed as yet. Sheaves of paper lay in organized disorder, wall charts half rolled up, everything slightly out of place in this vast barn of a building.

David came back with the coffee, and he and I looked at each other and smiled. Life had suddenly taken a leap forward, so subtly, so sweetly, that we hardly noticed.

He began to explain to me about the course they were running. They had only taught the new Environmental Science course for two years, and were in cramped, temporary accommodation. His desk was in the middle of a large room, crowded with other desks, and paper work in various stages of completion. Various staff members were coming and going, occupied with writing lectures and assembling demonstration material for practical classes. Our discussion ranged easily over all the courses in which I had previously taught. We found that we had many acquaintances in common, in the science world of the various universities in the city at that time, and enjoyed discussing this theory, or that new way of running a class. I had studied both animal and plant physiology and our experiences dovetailed. I agreed to help out in his classes due to start the next week. My lasting impressions of this meeting were of contentment, a filmy recognition of life's change of bounty. What a friendly smile he had.

So I arrived at work the next week, a few hours early, as David had promised to show me the procedures which I would be teaching the students. Life at the university was indeed fun. David had to instruct me in some of the slides to be examined under the microscope, and I found it easy and was quite successful. I had always enjoyed teaching, and still have firm friends made during my tutoring years. David and I grew quite friendly, and I found his easy manner so attractive that I sometimes wondered where events were leading.

In those days of deep depression I often had very good days followed by very bad ones. Sometimes the panic would be so gripping that I was afraid to go near stairs for fear that I would lose control and would throw myself over the rail. On those days I could not use knives, and roads were a terror. It felt as if life was glimpsed through a grey cloud. Through this I continued to work, continued to care for the family and the students, and only rarely found someone in whom I could confide. Fantasies of love kept me alive. The tension must have shown on my face, as in the midst of this turmoil one day David put his arm around me and asked what was wrong, could he help in any way? My reaction was surprising, and determined. In spite of my longing for a friendly shoulder to lean on, I heard a voice in my head say, 'Not now, I will wait until I can come to you in happiness.' I smiled and said something inconsequential.

In the short-term events led me to continue working in various scientific disciplines. After two years whilst sitting out the miserable Christmas holidays, regretting the necessity of the 4-month vacation from teaching and contact with my colleagues, I sat in my favourite occupation, scanning the job sections in the newspaper. I suddenly saw my own job advertised, albeit in a more permanent form than I had held it. My immediate reaction was that I wished they had told me personally about it, what if I had missed the advertisement?

True to the formality of the advertisement, I put in a formal application, and soon found myself working half-time, and enrolled for a Masters degree also half-time. I would have gladly worked with David as a supervisor, but he believed in sharing resources, so I had the choice between the animal and the plant stream, working with people who needed a student to help with their research. David said

"You didn't need to apply formally, you could have just rung up."

Thus began a more structured approach to my research career which I had been wanting since I had graduated. Many times I had met the young colleagues of my husband, and heard their laboratory jargon, and had longingly remembered the years of my own involvement in science. It reached out to me, the botany I had learnt roaming through the mountains with James, the picturesque precision of biochemistry, the visions of plant cells as factories, containing power houses and construction sites, demolition crews and sewers. How much fun could be had exploring physiology, the how and why of nature. My teaching work was side by side, complementing the research. I was in my element and thoroughly enjoyed the work. From this time I began to consider science as my art form.

David was second in command in the faculty. After the first year I did not work with him at all, but we met in the corridor and chatted occasionally and gradually I began to forget the attraction I had felt at first. In the interest stirred up by my growing professional life, I learned to cope with my not so interesting marriage, my husband who was more wedded to late-night work and sport on the weekends than to me, and children who always had something extra for me to attend to. One year David and his family went overseas on sabbatical leave, but it made little difference to me. I was reasonably content. My depression was manageable. Everything was quiet. My life was ordered with a touch of boredom added.

Every Christmas my children took their entire holidays with their paternal grandparents interstate. I would pack them off with tags pinned on their shirts, in the care of an air hostess. Sometimes gruesome stories would be relayed, for example, how they had used the oxygen mask in the aeroplane for Sam when he had an asthma attack. This long break helped me to recover my self confidence by giving me some space, and peaceful time alone.

During these summer breaks I found that I made a picture of my ideal woman. I was the valiant woman from the Book of Proverbs, plus the modern career type.

'Who shall find a valiant woman? Far and from the uttermost coasts is the price of her. The heart of her husband trusteth in her, and he shall have no need of spoils. She will render him good, and not evil, all the days of her life. She hath sought wool and flax, and hath wrought by the counsel of her hands. She is like the merchant's ship, she bringeth her bread from afar. She hath risen in the night, and given a prey to her household, and victuals to her maidens. She hath considered a field and bought it: with the fruit of her hand she hath planted a vineyard. She hath girded her loins with strength, and hath strengthened her arm. She hath tasted and seen that her traffic is good: her lamp shall not be put out in the night. She hath put out her hand to strong things, and her fingers have taken hold of the spindle. She hath opened her hand to the needy, and stretched out her hands to the poor. She shall not fear for her house in the cold of snow: for all her domestics are clothed with double garments. She hath made for herself clothing of tapestry; fine linen and purple is her covering. Her husband is honourable in the gates, when he sitteth among the senators of the land. She made fine linen and sold it, and delivered a girdle to the Chanaanite. Strength and beauty are her clothing, and she shall laugh in the latter day. She hath opened her mouth to wisdom, and the law of clemency is on her tongue. She hath looked well to the paths of her house, and hath not eaten her bread idle. Her

children rose up, and called her blessed: her husband, and he praised her. Many daughters have gathered together riches: thou hast surpassed them all … Give her of the fruit of her hands: and let her works praise her in the gates.'

Her attributes I had whilst I held her picture, but I could never hold them over winter. Then the picture would fade as depression and cold came in. Next summer the valiant woman would be back again, stronger and more beautiful than ever. She helped me through the five years climbing out of the depression, to becoming a more assured person, often appearing, encouraging me onwards. Shades of my mother's trust in the Will of God accompanied the valiant woman, a trust in following in the zest of life to the full.

On David's birthday he held a luncheon at his own expense for all the post graduate students in the faculty in gratitude for their meagerly-paid labour. Many of his colleagues were amazed, firm believers that there was no such thing as a free lunch. He had become Dean of the faculty in the absence of the professor, becoming the first non-professorial dean in the university. David and I set sail that day with our feathers to the mast, airborne. David was a real party man, who could include everyone with his cheery smile, even a non-party-going person like me. His energy burst through its boundaries. He sat at a long table in the staff club, calling out to this one and that one, sometimes to me, gently teasing, moving around, making sure everyone had drinks, all at his expense. I was so nervous of myself, my usual unfortunate state, that I came, ate my lunch and promptly departed, to go back to the security of my work. His exuberance overflowed that day, and touched me strangely as I pronounced my 'Thank you', and then later when he himself returned, a little tipsy and bubbly. One of his bubbles bored a hole through my armour. A friend had told me

"He would be the easiest person to have an affair with".

Yes I could see that all right, I who didn't have affairs, thirsting for love on the one hand and bound by restrictions on the other.

David was concerned to give everyone fair conditions in the faculty. He cared about the students, and went out of his way to make sure everyone had money, appropriate jobs, and took pleasure from their place in the department. He himself enjoyed life, security of tenure, new cars, outings to the theatre, even a bet on the horses, and tried to ensure that everyone else had the same opportunities as he had. For the two years that he was dean he spent very little time on his own projects, and much effort on ensuring a strong faculty. He came to me one day to discuss my position. It was a busy day, I was running around with test tubes, seeing to my latest experiment, running between laboratory and cold-room. David asked me about my expectations in my job, did I enjoy the work, emphasized that the department needed my teaching services, saying there was room for my talents and that I would be welcome to stay on. He suggested an appointment which could give me a secure position, as my position was casual, and could be terminated at any time. I was pleased to be thought a valuable member of the department, but was not deeply involved in the idea of security or tenure at that time. After all, I was married to James, the greatest security of tenure in existence. David continued his discussions with the professor and the vice chancellor, and eventually a new position was created for me, a full time position, which gave me three years tenure at a time, and could become permanent in due course.

I kept irregular tea-room hours, as classes and experiments kept me busy. David did likewise, so we did not meet often. But chance plays no part in events when two people are coming together. I met David alone in the tea-room late one afternoon, both clad in our white laboratory coats, and we found ourselves enjoying each other's conversation, as another hole bored its way through my armour. He listened to me, was genuinely interested in my views on life, and my family's progress. This man made me feel myself, allowed the first rays of light to penetrate my rigid belief system and find a real person underneath it all. I was bound in the old bone corsets of religion, tied to the rack of family duty, stretched unbearably through panic and depression, but ready to give birth to an emerging self. The tinder was set.

Even at this early stage of our acquaintance, David and I had started to understand each other. As I think back over those times, so much has fused together, so much I know about him, and yet it is all coloured by my eyes and later events, that I hardly remember how I came to know about it. When I read the magazine from his last year at school, I see a young man with an intense ability, both in sport and academically. An extraordinary vitality streams out from his eyes, as he sits in the centre both of cricket and tennis teams. Knowing him only much later as an enthusiast, and someone who had a boisterous sense of fun and laughter, I can imagine him fooling with the boys, writing (always kindly) parodies of himself and situations. He wore smart, well-cut clothes, a touch conservative. He liked order about him. His approach to administration was 'Do it immediately'. His loyalty to both colleagues and principles in the academic life that we shared was unshakable. And yet he was from another generation, a different lifetime. His conservatism in family life at once saved me many upsets and stopped me in my tracks.

*

Class followed class, week followed week, and the months passed. After work a group of staff sometimes met for a glass of wine, there was always some occasion to celebrate, even if it was only the survival of another class or meeting. David had invited in a few friends and we all sat in my office, chatting about the day. This was a comfort zone. We relaxed and told stories, looking past the cream office walls, past the bright posters I had put up as a cheery signal, and out into the green parkland that stretched beyond the building. Swapping stories of this student's failure, that person's A-grade performance, how to give incentive or how to design more comfortable ways of examining the strugglers, who were often so beset by exam jitters that they failed to do their best.

David and I had offices next door to each other, in the middle of a busy corridor. These 60's style buildings were of the brick and concrete utilitarian appearance, strictly rectangular, a cream-coloured bare-walled central corridor running roughly east-west, with a floor-length window at each end, the offices and individual laboratories on the north side, and the utility rooms and a big class laboratory on the south side. North facing windows in each office, looking out towards the next building and the trees towards the car-park. David and I met every day, but work was exacting for both of us, so we were restricted in our contact.

It was 11/11/75, a momentous day in Australian politics. It was a dusty evening, warm without the bite of summer. As a deposed Gough Whitlam walked with Australia past Scylla and Charibdis, through the gates of uncertainty, David and I followed, on our way to the adventure of paradise.

I had found David, working late in his office. As head of the faculty, he had to administer to the whole staff, prepare special addresses to the students, go to endless meetings with the Vice Chancellor, library committees, deans' meetings, and as well he gave his normal lectures and practical classes. When I came upon him, he was a pale shade of beige, his hands trembling slightly. As I knocked on his open door he startled and upset a cup of coffee over the papers on his desk.

"Damn and blast!"

I silently handed him the blackboard duster, and he soaked up the creeping coffee in the grey cloth.

"I'm sorry, can I help you?" he looked distracted.

"I saw you working late, and I came to say hello. Are you all right, you seem a bit disorientated?"

"I'd just finished. This dean's job needs a 24 hour a day shift sometimes. But it's done for another day. And I've finished reading George's thesis. That's what was drowned in the coffee, but it's only a draft, it doesn't matter."

He looked up at me, standing in the doorway. I had stayed back late to take measurements for an experiment.

"Have you eaten yet? Don't you go home for tea?" I asked.

"My wife and children have gone down to the beach house for a few days, but I didn't have the time to leave this." He looked resignedly at his desk piled with papers. "No I haven't eaten, and I'm famished. I'll go down to the pub soon and get a meal."

On an impulse I said

"Look, I'm going home in a few minutes, and I haven't eaten yet myself. Would you like to come out and put your feet up, have a glass of wine, and I'll get something for both of us?"

"Oh, I couldn't disturb your family, they'll be resting."

"Actually, they are sleeping over at a friend's place, and my husband is away at a conference. I would enjoy some company myself."

"All right then, it would certainly be more relaxing than eating alone in the pub." He stacked his papers in order, put on his jacket and we walked out of the building.

I had not known him very well, but I had unexpectedly found my heart opening to this conscientious man, with his smiling face and hair which curled out above his ears. I was curious as to what sort of a man he was, how did he relate within his family, how did his relatives treat him? What did he think of marriage, religion and politics? So I was not entirely innocent in my invitation, but I can certainly say that nothing more than conversation entered my mind. Not in those days.

I prepared a simple meal of pasta with herbs and cheese, poured two glasses of wine, cut some crusty bread, and we sat and dined together. In some people, no amount of manners or elegant clothes can hide the unformed parts of a personality. His hair which lay in all directions, the bushy eyebrows which formed hairy verandas over the eyes gave a clue to a spirit which although not allowed full reign, was ready to burst with surprises. But it was not only these physical traits which made me think he was a gem. There was an air which he communicated subtly to me, of goodness. I had never detected in him vengefulness, jealousy, or the least bit of power seeking, which one often saw in large measure within the university. This man seemed to come directly from the heart, no calculation in his approach. But covering this goodness were traces of neglect. His exterior was all there, the shoes well polished, the tie carefully knotted, but something was unfinished within him. There was a part which craved knowledge, and not the type which one learns by reading. To put it simply, he was inexperienced in the deeper passages of life, no strong love had laid its hand on him, no personal devastation had greeted him. He was of course wholly unconscious of this vacuum. In fact he'd have laughed at anyone who suggested such a thing. But he was by far the most interesting man I had met in many years. Intelligent, experienced in his scientific work, known in the scientific community in our city. But totally uncommunicative about himself. Of his family life I knew the bare statistics. Married, two sons. He seemed to have separated his home life completely away from his work life. There were never invitations to parties at his place, although this was an accepted part of the lives of many of the other staff. He came to work, toiled away selflessly every day, then disappeared again into his black hole, to recreate himself again the next day.

I smiled at him over the dinner table, our eyes meeting as if to acknowledge some connivance in this unsought pleasure of a private meal together. I refilled his glass with wine.

"Do you know, I've always wanted to get to know you better" he said, "I don't know how this happened, but it feels as if I have been let out of purgatory for a night."

"What is purgatory? The job or the family?"

"Perhaps both, in a way. The job is demanding just now. It is double the workload I had before I was dean, and there is very little help that I can get with it. And of course, not being a professor myself makes every confrontation with the Vice Chancellor or the other deans more difficult too. But if I had more support at home it would perhaps be easier."

"I don't receive much support at home either. I have had to create my own avenues of escape, and coming to work is the chief one. But tell me about your family? I have never heard you speak of them."

"My wife keeps a perfect house, she works hard at it, keeping everything in order. She cooks the food and looks after the boys, keeps their muddy shoes out of the living room, you know the kind of thing."

He glanced around my kitchen, and I was aware of an untidy array of children's toys, rubber boots in the corner, and a basket full of clothes in the hallway, awaiting folding and putting away. I grinned at the contrast.

"Is that what you want?" I asked.

"Well, yes, I suppose so. What else can you want? But there were other things in the beginning. I supposed that our house would be open to my friends, but that was too much work for my wife, every time I had people home it sparked a disagreement so I had to stop inviting them. I began to feel trapped there. She didn't often want to go out either. Then I decided to buy subscriptions to things that my wife liked to do, concerts, ballet, opera, so that the tickets were already paid for, and not to go would have wasted money. So we do those things. But we don't often go to the movies or shows. I'd have liked to have done that."

David spoke as if life was over, that there were no more choices to be made, that the last word had irretrievably been said, and not by him. I said

"If you want to go to the movies and your wife doesn't, why don't you go and let her stay at home with the boys? James and I do that sort of thing."

"It wouldn't be possible. We either go together or not at all."

"Why?" I asked as I cleared away the dishes and opened another bottle of wine.

"She doesn't like to go out alone, and you don't think she would let me go out alone do you?"

"Are you so untrustworthy?" I asked, grinning at the thought of this unsophisticated man eating dinner alone with me in my house. He caught my drift, and shook his head.

"Oh no, I'm pure as the driven snow. In fact I've never had the opportunity to be anything else."

"And if you did have the opportunity?"

"I'm not at all sure that I would take it."

We got up and moved our drinks to the lounge room, where I had lit the fire. We nestled down in the comfortable old leather arm chairs, and continued our conversation. The lamp behind us gave a dull glow to the deep red curtains.

"Why did you get married at all, David?" I asked.

"I needed to at the time, I needed a sexual outlet, I thought we would make a go of it. She is attractive and neat, I like that. We had similar families, it should have worked out. But even before we married, we were disagreeing about quite major things. She actually broke off our engagement at one time, and gave me back the ring. Instead of receiving it gracefully, I threatened to throw it in the sea. She looked at the ring, and you know, she abhors waste, so she said,

"No give it back to me, I'll marry you after all."

I wondered about the sexual outlet, if that need had been unmet, like his need for company, but felt we were as yet circling around each other, not yet ready for the deepest conversations. But he brought up the subject himself.

"So we married, I got drunk on my wedding day, and I've always regretted that. We got started all wrong. I blame myself for being so inept on her first time. And we never discuss intimate things."

I wondered if there was anything to salvaged here? He was too quick to take the blame. And how did it go on year after year with no apparent resolution, or at least discussion? He went on

"I suppose all marriages become boring after the initial fervour is gone. And we had so little fervour."

I thought of James and I, whatever else, we had always been good in bed together, had discussed our sexuality, had learned from each other, and grown together through it. Our problems stemmed more from James' inability to give me and the children the priority we needed. Here was a very different marriage. I saw David's life as a grey curtain behind which, unbeknownst to him, raged uncontrolled fires. The contrary one in me would have loved to drive a sword through the curtain, and glimpse the passion.

"But if we can search a little deeper, what is marriage all about? For anyone?" I asked.

"First for sex, then care of the children, companionship" he answered, spouting the social norms. "What else could it be?"

"Lots of people these days have sex whether they are married or not. And everyone doesn't choose to have children. That leaves companionship. Which is also available without marriage, witness this evening. Granted your answer would have been true when you married, it isn't true now. If you could choose again why would you marry now?"

"I don't know. I'm inexperienced here. But I imagin e sometimes making love to someone who really enjoyed making love to me, someone who showed that she cared. I must be a bit unsatisfied, because when I go to the ballet I always watch the breasts and the crotch of dancers, I am fascinated, as if there is more I wish to experience. But there again, I'm back to sex, and you don't consider that a reason to marry."

"Not necessarily. But I have seen people who are married, who are really devoted to each other, they seem to have something above the usual just rubbing along together sort of marriage. Although they too have been through hard times, somehow they have been loyal to each other, they have discussed their difficulties, tried to accommodate each other's needs. Their love grows instead of waning. I can imagine that that type of marriage would be worth having."

"How do you know it will be like that before you get married? It probably happens only by chance,"

"I don't know. Perhaps it takes a certain flexibility. Perhaps you can be in love, consider whether you would like to give that commitment to the other person. Let's take you and I as an example. We have been married for some time now. We know what it is like, the up sides and the down sides. Suppose our respective spouses were to die, and we were left with our present knowledge. No children, we'd better kill them off too. And no grief, just for the sake of tidiness. What I would do is this. If I fell in love with a person who loved me in return, I would consider, do I love this person enough to make a commitment of marriage to? Do I believe that we, the man too, can work through the difficulties together? Discuss life's situations. Give and take. Do I want to do that? If I really wanted to do that, then I would marry. If I wanted less than that, I would simply have an affair, make love, and see what happened. It could always change, get better or worse. But of course I'm talking hypothetically here. James and I are Catholics, and there is no sex outside marriage, and no divorce, even if we wanted to. So that's my answer, what's yours?"

"Much the same I suppose. You know, my wife and I have had some terrible arguments, we actually came close to divorce and then she unexpectedly became pregnant. Even now it feels like we are putting up with it for the children, and that when they are grown up we will separate."

"James and I have had a time of awful fights too, it was as if I had to assert myself, almost at times I would argue that black was white. But it was some process of gaining self confidence that I was going through. I was half aware of it while I was going through it, but not completely. One day I had been so brutal, that James was crying, he was almost destroyed by my terrible brawling. From that day my aggression stopped. I saw that I was inflicting unnecessary pain, that there was nothing more to be gained. However, I was never as conscious of it as it may seem from the way I am describing it. It was more a mood that passed. These days we are much more peaceful, more dull. Sometimes I think there must be more to life, but I don't know where to look."

I looked over to where David was sitting. He was staring at me, through me, as if he had suddenly seen more than he was looking at. The light was dim, the room warm. He spoke at last

"You and me both then. I am convinced that there is more that I need to experience, but I don't know what I am looking for either."

The fire had burned low, and only the glowing coals remained. I got up and stood behind him.

"I will give you a rub on your neck and should ers, just to relax you, then we had better turn in. I've got a big day tomorrow. Will you be all right to drive home after all that wine?"

"Surely!"

I got him to take off his jacket, and started to massage the muscles across his shoulders and in his neck, taking my strong fingers down his arms and hands. Then I massaged his head, finishing with gentle strokes across his forehead, and smoothed his cheeks. Massage can be strange, it can lead people in certain directions, in the direction of a greater will, so that unusual things can happen, things that the individuals concerned had not consciously suspected. Of course I knew this, but believe me, I had not intended the final result. What happened was that when David had tried to stand up he was dizzy, whether from the wine or the massage or both. He couldn't walk. He lurched, almost falling against the dresser and I grabbed him steadying him. It was clear he wouldn't be able to drive home after all, he would have to stay. I was just able to guide him to the bathroom, and then I steered him towards my bed, he took off his trousers and shirt, and fell into a deep sleep from which he didn't awaken until morning. I slept beside him, all night half-conscious that something strange was afoot.

When he awoke I had alr eady been up and showered, and had gone to the kitchen in my bathrobe and got some breakfast on the way. He was gauche finding himself in my bed. His ginger hair was standing on end, whiskers on his face. He stretched and yawned, rubbing his face.

"Do you know, I feel better than I have in years. What have you done to me?"

"I have done nothing. It is you who have taken the rest that you needed."

David lay looking up at the ceiling, only half awake still. Not ready yet to face the day. He stumbled into the bathroom, and I heard the splashing of water. I was standing in front of my wardrobe deciding what to wear when he came up behind he, took my breasts in his hands, underneath my robe, and pulled me back onto him. I felt his penis hard against me, and the certain firmness of his shoulders and chest. He pushed my robe to the ground, and gently turned me towards him. As I made no move away from him, he kissed me, with such hunger that I had never felt. I acquiesced, silent. He carried me to the bed, we lay together and swiftly he entered me, and was spent within seconds. I lay under him, in the bliss of discovery.

He rolled off me, laughing. Laughing in joy like a young boy. I was laughing too, saying nothing. We dozed briefly, flesh against flesh, breath mingling with breath. I awoke and rolled over on top of him, feeling the firmness of his body, my cheek against his hairy chest. Arching my back, luxuriating in sensuality. I started to kiss him, this time taking my turn to make love to him. I offered my breasts to his mouth, quivering with anticipation. I cradled his head to my chest, stroked his hair, kissed him as he entered me again, and gasped as he pulsed his joy into my receptive body. Deep blue lights flashed in my head. We became silent for a time, resting in each other. As we opened our eyes, looking into each other's gaze, we affirmed what had happened.

"David" I murmured.

"Sibyl" he replied.

In love as in springtime. Flowers coil out from the heart of nature and suddenly the earth erupts with the colours of blossoms, perfect shy faces. The pink-budded trees burst with leaves. Everything that has been written in silence over the winter months is suddenly on view, flooding the senses, highlighting every thought, every mood, every word. Every person, every being takes part in this revival. Longing, meeting, exultance, quietness, waiting, cycled around and around in a sea of tenderness. I dreamed, awake, letting the water of my emotions wash over me.

Love is an ocean, but I play about on the shore, darting in cautiously, and then retreating to dry land. Sometimes I set sail. Music now evokes those feelings of surrender to the beloved, when I float in my dinghy, adrift on the ocean, open to the universe, all in sunshine gold, body tingling with suspense, accepting yet fearful, giving and longing all in one. Tenderness is born, the lover is present in the heart. The body stretches to greet him. Waves of bliss gently rock the boat, swaying in life's breezes, over the deep, blue water. No one is near, but all are embraced. The spirit is open, love flows in. The body lies trembling in its caress. The tide of feeling swells and subsides, accepting light and darkness, the passage of time and loneliness, sure of safe haven, nothing can disturb this voyage. I hear the voice and the tears well up, flowing at the triumph of love even in death. The knowledge that it is so overwhelms me. There are no perils for my little boat, it travels on surely, experiencing rapturous joy and loss. I gasp at the exultance of beauty, giving, receiving, changing. Seasons moving on, spring, summer, and now autumn.

*

This was the beginning of falling in love. Or was it only the conscious beginning? It was clear that love had been lying dormant for a long time, for if it had not been present at all, it could not have burst forth with such fury. It brooked no obstacle, allowed no pause, as it swept through our lives, changing everything it touched, every face, every object every situation transformed in its glee. I was happy for the first time in years. I could love freely, no holds barred.

On the other hand, falling suddenly in love when both people are married to other partners has very little to recommend it. I would never choose to repeat the experience. Is it indeed a choice? It felt not to be. But perhaps the choice had been made before, in the sublime depths of spirit, of which I was almost unconscious. It is the ultimate in light and shade, white and black, exultation and guilt. Daily my mood swung between the two extremes of joy and despair. Everything was on the surface, not that the emotions were superficial, the roots were into my soul. But it was as if my soul was suddenly visible, or accessible to me. The soul knows about love, passion, directness. It has no program that respects social norms. It sails into ecstasy, all banners flying, and watches us scrabbling around within our social confines, trying to pick up the pieces of respectability, loyalty to partners and children, secrecy, embarrassment and the like.

After our joy-filled morning, David and I drove in to work, separately of course. The aura of delight followed me. I went to my office, removed from the banality of the students and my classes. But of course life had to continue, notes had to be written, classes prepared. With my soul shining through, I was blissfully happy in everything I did that day. I sometimes glimpsed David going about his chores, but made no move towards him. He smiled in my direction once, but was racing out to a meeting, so that was our only contact. At the end of the day I went home as usual. The children were home again from their friend's place, and were telling me about how they had climbed up the big tree, had gathered fruit, had thrown pips at their friend's Dad until he pretended to be a leopard and came stalking them. Their souls too were on the surface, I could see that now through my new eyes. Joy was in their faces as they told me about their friend's new kittens,

"Could we have a kitten Mum? She said she has to give them away. Please Mum!"

"Yes, why not." I wondered why joy was not on everybody's face.

But the next day I fell to wondering how David was faring, the thought even crossed my mind that perhaps he didn't feel as I did, and I felt joy recede from me, just ever so slightly. I drove silently to work, and looked at the big brick building towering there. It felt as if it was my other home. I spent half my life there. It was a desolate sort of place, had little welcoming spirit. But it wasn't exactly unfriendly either. I climbed the stairs, feeling just slightly heavy. I walked to my office, unlocked the door and saw on my desk a bunch of red roses, David's signature on the card. I knocked on his door. No answer, of course he would be giving his lecture. My spirits revived as I sat drinking in the velvet red petals, the fragrance equal to none other. So David was probably feeling as I did, the beginning of the syndrome 'Where is she, what is she feeling, is she thinking of me?'

When he arrived back he was all coy smiles.

"Will you have lunch with me today? Did you like the flowers? All right we'll meet at 1 o'clock."

Sitting out on the lawn at lunch he said

"Well my princess, how are you faring?"

I felt awkward. My thoughts had been everywhere. Fortunately James was not due to return till the coming evening, so I hadn't had to think about him. I had considered my children, and David's wife and children. I was inclined to shrug off our meeting as not important in other people's worlds. So I said

"Well to tell you the truth, I feel a little strange. I haven't done anything like that ever before."

"No, you intimated that. And of course it's new to me too. How does it feel today though? Do you want to forget about it or do you want to go on with it?"

"Isn't it a matter of where we are allowed to go? We both have family obligations. I can't stop being married, religion you know. I can't stop loving my children. What do you think?"

"All I can think about is loving you, wanting to make love to you."

"I think about that too" I said, my eyes lowered, as if the noonday sun would be embarrassed by such an admission. "I wonder if it will be possible to go backwards, to forget it ever happened. This morning I was beginning to wonder if you wanted to see me again, and I can't tell you the relief I felt when I saw your roses. They opened me to happiness again. I think I would shrivel up and die without the joy that I had yesterday." I lifted my eyes and looked at him. He was munching sandwiches, nodding his head

"That is why I sent you the flowers, I wanted to keep you in my life, I couldn't bear for you to disappear."

I stroked his hand, surreptitiously glancing around to see that we were unobserved.

"Then I suppose that that is our answer. We will have to see what life brings us in this new love."

A tremble went through my body, and tears formed in my eyes as a shaft of sunlight flashed through the leafy canopy above. A sort of prescience of future joy and pain in the battle between the soul and the rules of society. David saw, and grinned,

"Come on, we're not dead yet. We can work together you know, we will be close at work."

"Yes, I am happy, really happy to have found you. I don't know what came over me."

We gathered our things together and returned to work.

*

James arrived home that evening, bursting with gossip about his colleagues, and with sexuality. I shrugged. I enjoyed making love to him, but now I could see that we lacked the passion I had experienced with David. Whilst not exactly looking at the ceiling and thinking of England, I was not my usual enthusiastic self.

"Are you a bit tired?" asked James

"Yes, it's been a busy week".

He turned over and went to sleep, but I lay awake musing for some time. Where was my life to lead me now?

Before Christmas I was in my sitting room and glanced up at a picture on the wall. It was of a pale child with big sad eyes. It caught my eye, she was suddenly dark, the whole picture now a picture of death. I was afraid, not understanding this communication from another world. I kept my eye on the picture in the days that came. The darkness faded a little, but did not completely vanish. After ten days James came in holding the newspaper with a stricken look on his face.

"Sam's godfather has been killed, with his whole family. A horrendous car accident!" He sat on the bed, shaken, as we joined together contemplating the shift of life into death. The two families had been close, we ate at each others' houses, and shared projects. I remembered the darkened picture, remembered its title Paula, the same name as my friend. So that was it. I shivered, unused to such messages. And yet, this was a prophecy, the first, received by Sibyl.

"I saw something, maybe a premonition. Do you remember I told you about the picture?"

"No I don't remember, what was it?" answered James.

I repeated the story. James could see I was trembling, and he put his arm around me.

"I'm devastated by their deaths" he said. "Perhaps it was some kind of premonition, I don't know about those things. But it doesn't alter the dreadful sadness."

*

Christmas passed, and that year we took a beach house at Lakes Entrance. I went with the family on holiday for two weeks. It was hard to be away, and I phoned David from the beach, to hear that my paper had been accepted but required some extra work. I took the opportunity to return alone to town to do this experiment, and treat myself to a whole day with David. He came to the house, hungry for love. We came together again, our bodies and souls merging into one. We lay in each other's arms talking sweet-talk, revisiting heaven. The heights of bliss are always balanced by the despair of their withdrawal. Best to accept it quickly and keep going.

I travelled back to the beach with the children. The fun of being with them became curiously flat and just a chore. I would waken next to James, couldn't enjoy making love, so the day started badly. Then the children would begin to quarrel, and I had a hard time making peace, doing the housework and getting the children down to the beach. My friend Leah was in a neighbouring house with her husband and children, we had planned the holiday together so we could catch up on our old friendship. We would go out to pick blackberries, talking inconsequentially, as I did not dare to confide my secret. Lacking the free flow of trust, our conversations lost their spontaneity. I felt dull in their company, closed off. But Leah was persistent, determined to keep our friendship.

"What's the matter Sibyl? You're on another planet!"

"Nothing, I'm all right" trying to draw down my shutters.

"Are you having an affair?" I jumped as a wave of relief coursed through my body. I made a grimace of helplessness

"Yes actually. How did you guess?"

"I recognized the symptoms, I did it myself a couple of years ago."

"It happened recently, seemed to come out of the blue. On the one hand I am blissfully happy, on the other hand unbearably guilty."

"Tell me about him?" her eyes smiled gently at me.

I told her, and as I told the colours around me shone more brightly, the taste of the blackberries was sharper, the sounds of the birds sweeter. Joy flowed in my veins again, as I revisited my love, looking over the miles that separated us, into his eyes once more. I conjured up his essence, and Leah and I shared the bliss of the moment. I paused, then after a few moments Leah asked me

"He's married?"

"Oh yes, he has a family to support."

"Do you know them?"

"No. But tell me what happened to you? I didn't know you had been through it too."

"He worked with me at that time, we fell in love, we talked, took each other to visit the places we knew and loved. Everything was the same, but lightened. We made love, trying to hide from our families."

"Do you see him still?"

"He was transferred overseas, so although we never actually broke up, it is in limbo. He is not a good letter writer. I'm sad, but really it is the easiest way for me. I know he loves me, but he's married, we can't break up the families."

"No, there is no question of that. But we work together too, and there is no prospect of either of us moving away."

"Then it will continue, unless one of you takes a step back."

"I feel that I want to meet his family. You know, James was in love with someone a couple of years ago. I knew her and when I found out I wasn't even jealous, I invited her home. I wanted her to be included in our family. But she never came. I suppose James and I have been together so long now that I don't feel threatened by other women. But I know if David had another woman after me I would be fierce."

"Most women are fierce about their husbands, and the other woman in my case was possessive about his money and his time. I never wanted to meet her , I wanted to keep things quite separate. But he used to say that their love affair had faded, you know how it does when you have kids and a mortgage. You haven't time to do lovely things together, and if your aims are not the same from the beginning, as they rarely are, marriage winds down into duty and occasional sex. The sparkle has dulled."

"That is how David speaks of his marriage. And perhaps how mine is. James and I had so much counselling when I was having the breakdown, but it never recaptured our sparkle either."

I walked on, picked another spray of blackberries, and threw away an unripe one.

"So how do you feel about David's family?" asked Leah.

"Another obstacle to our happiness. And somehow, to prevent them being an obstacle, I want to meet them, to include them in my happiness."

"I think this is all right at a higher level, but it won't work on the physical level. Be careful Sibyl, you tend to jump into situations which blow up in your face, assuming that things which work for you will work for everyone else. Don't be too trusting. You will be hurt!"

I paused. I had been considering inviting David's family home, but I allowed Leah's warning to sink in. Perhaps I was confusing the levels of consciousness again. Trying to bring the space where all is love and freedom down to the physical world where different expectations cause chaos. I stood back from my plans as a lightness spread through me. This felt better, I could allow David's family their own space, their expectations of his protection, his income and attention. I need not try so hard to include them, simply to know that we are all included was enough. I could leave them in their dignity, silently.

"Thanks, Leah, that has brought some peace into the situation. Lord knows where it will all end."

"I'm sure He does. And don't forget, no one owns anyone else. Love is a free commodity. It can always be given and received. But keep your expectations out of it if you can."

"That's the hard bit. But I try."

*

James went out deep in the surf. I was sitting on the beach watching the children. This was a job I had done since I was ten, making sure the little ones were safe from the undertow. James was quite far out. Sam too was a bit far out for my comfort. I walked down to the water's edge and called to him to come closer to the shore. I looked out to James. He was swimming strongly, but not making much distance. Well, he was a big boy, he could look after himself. I returned to my watching post and my dreams. I looked up again, James was swimming in closer now, Sam was sitting nearby making a sand castle beside his sisters. James came and sat beside me. He was clearly shaken

"I almost couldn't get back, the undertow was so strong". He sat panting, I put my arm around him, feeling alarmed, and presently he relaxed. I found myself wondering if I would have been glad or sorry if he had been sucked out to his death. Such thoughts! I was aghast. Was the solution so difficult that I had to resort to death as the arbiter? Horrified at myself. He was a good man, but I had had enough of marriage. I didn't wish him harm, but then Catholics couldn't get divorced. My emotions circled gloomily, giving rise again to that sense of dislocation, this time at the behest of my own feelings against the morals of society.

So now my family relationships were being eroded. How could I find the will to enjoy the passion of David's love and at the same time care for my children with the energy that they required? Fortunately, David's affection overflowed to my children, and joined to mine it became possible to love the children together, and to continue that part of my life. It wasn't perfect, but usually it worked out well for the rest of my family.

Back in town, sometimes the calls on my time were too great. It was as if David and I were starving in the midst of plenty. Our time together was limited. We yearned to be able to do the simplest things together. We had our work in common, but no hours to play. When I had been giving everything, time at work to the job, and time at home to family my personal resources began to be used up. There was little left of me but an automaton obeying the wishes of my two employers.

On Easter Saturday we created a crack in our schedule. David arrived early to take me to a country race meeting. James and the elder two children had gone to the country for Easter and my younger daughter had gone to spend the night with her grandparents. I dressed in a long graceful turquoise and white summer dress, straight from Carnaby Street. I had become an elegant woman, fair hair, blue eyes and a mischievous smile. My handsome escort carried me off that day. His boyish humour beamed over the races, the people, the horses. The lawns and gardens were sculpted into delicate beds, the bookmakers' stands behind the grandstand, and the horse boxes lined up in an enclosure over on the right. David showed me how to place a bet, and we ran up to the rails to watch the first race. Good old Paddy Fox, chosen for my Paddy, won for me. We collected our winnings and went to the bar for a beer. We played the game of being a couple, walking around arm in arm, unafraid of detection. Our spirits rose, we laughed, celebrating our triumph. David started to thaw away from his duty-filled life. His protective spirit flowed around me, his joy was in taking care of me. This was all I had ever dreamed of, that someone would care enough to encircle me with love and peace of mind. It was safe to caress, to be passionate, to discuss. He wanted to teach me things that he knew, placing new ambitions before my eyes.

He told about his parents, his life before he married.

"I was the second son of a country teacher, I have an elder brother Tom, two years older than me. My sister Elsa is two years younger. I liked to make friends with everyone, and the dogs and cats and my horse. We lived in the country, always in the teacher's house beside the school. I tried to help Dad. One day a tree blew down next to the house and I overheard Dad say 'I must burn that tree which came down', so I set out to dispose of it myself. But I forgot to drag it away from the house first, and the timber wall of the house caught fire, and the fire brigade had to be called."

"What did you do?" I asked

"I ran away and hid, I was only about four years old at the time."

I smiled at the vision of the scared four-year-old, wondering if it was safe to come out and face the music.

"Were your parents cross?"

"More exasperated. I used to get into a good few scrapes."

We seemed to be forging links between us. The old reminiscences shimmered, joining us together in unlikely places. We had been sitting in the stand, waiting for the next race. But this time our horse had finished in the middle of the field, so we wandered down to the bookmakers at the rear of the stand and considered our next bet. Then we went to the refreshment tent, and sat drinking tea.

He started to tell me about his mother who lived currently in a special accommodation home. He recalled a day in her life that had etched itself on his fourteen-year-old memory.

"It was just after the war. Everyone was poor, trying to put their lives back together" he said, "Country children, particularly us because Dad was a teacher, were courteous and kind, we looked out for each other and for Mum and Dad, we had a very strong code of family unity. You know, Mum had married Dad on the rebound, he told us when we were older. So they were never that close. As we grew towards our teenage years, Mum became depressed. She was a physically robust woman, quite healthy except for her depression." He was staring into his memories.

"That day, outside our house Mum was pacing around the garden, she seemed to have a lion's energy inside her. Sometimes she stopped and broke off the dead roses and threw them on the ground. Elsa and I were on guard, she had to be watched because we never knew what she would do. We were sitting on the front step reading. It was such a hot day, the streets were dusty and baked hard, you know those small towns, and the grass between the cracks in the pavement was all brown. Everyone was tired of the summer, even the houses, they seemed to lean, there were ragged pieces of iron needing a nail, palings missing from fences, the walls were old white or peeling cream, and everything covered with red-brown dust."

He seemed to be absorbed in another world as he described this scene to me. He went on

"Our house was no better than any of the others. The gum trees made hardly any shade and there was a hot clammy north wind, gusting, stirring up dry leaves and papers. So there we were, Elsa and I sitting watching Mum snapping rose heads in the garden. Then she started to pace again, we could see she was muttering something to herself, her lips were moving. We were reading, and got engrossed in our books, just glancing up from time to time.

She must have walked past us to the back door. I looked over to where she had been, but she wasn't there. I asked Elsa

"Did you see Mum go in? We'd better check on her." I ran inside, and found the kitchen door locked and called to Elsa to find Tom, then I ran around the house and jumped up and looked in the window. I saw Mum lying on the floor with her head in the oven. I ran around and turned off the gas. You know I was shocked, I became really angry with her, she was supposed to take care of us, but she tried to leave us. There is something I can't forgive in people not taking responsibility, and it started from that day.

Tom came and threw his shoulder against the locked door, and we pulled Mum away from the oven. She was groggy but she wasn't dead. I've always been sorry that we saved her life, because she had to go into hospital after that. The pills didn't work, and neither did the electroconvulsive therapy. Eventually they operated on her brain, and she became like a robot. And she's still alive, she's gone through it for forty years."

He shuddered.

"How did life go on? Who cooked for you and did the housework?"

"Dad did most of it, and sometimes we had a housekeeper. Our father was a strong man and we absolutely relied on him. But the worst part was the times that Mum was at home. I became scared that she would do something to Elsa. She slept down the other end of the house near Mum's room. I used to get her to come and sleep near me and Tom, so that we were all together. It felt safer.

Eventually Mum was permanently in hospital, so we moved to town, and we used to visit her on Sundays, take her a nice roast dinner, or some cake, she didn't get that in hospital. Then we went to boarding school, completed our education. We never talked about Mum, we kept silent about our family".

"Do you know what made her depressed?"

"She was manic-depressive. I can remember overhearing her and Dad arguing, she used to go out on spending sprees, and he couldn't afford it. I heard her crying once

'I needed that dress, I can't live here, why can't you understand me, there is always money for food.' When she became agitated she would take out the week's grocery allowance, and come home in her new clothes. So then we didn't have enough money for food. Dad would get angry. As a result she started to take things without paying. Then the police would bring her home. It must have been awful for Dad. She was a trained musician and had been used to performing but the people got tired of her moods and her bossiness, and didn't want to ask her to sing. She was no longer invited to play the piano at the church gatherings. I think she was rebelling against her confinement in a country town."

"I've been depressed myself," I answered. "I can imagine how she might have felt. That she deserved better than anything she could achieve in a country town. A bit snobbish maybe, but possible. You children couldn't heal her empty heart no matter how much you loved her. I can imagine her thinking 'This dress now, if I bought it I might feel a bit better.' The craving for relief can be so great that she might forget the purpose of her money. She had to go on, but there was nowhere to go, no one to confide in, I can imagine her proud spirit, refusing well-meant queries as to her health, excluding anyone, anything which could touch her core. An argument with your Dad would serve only to deaden her reactions. She would be screaming to express herself, and through choosing unacceptable forms, theft, she would be crushed further. The self won't be forgotten, it lurks underneath a deep depression. She must have felt her life to be unbearable."

"Yes, I can see that. These days I can see better how it must have been for her. But at the time we were kids, we were told to watch her, Dad had to give time to his students. Our consciousness had changed gear. Our usual childish selfishness had become 'We must help Dad, we must take care of Mum so there is no more trouble.' The family closed ranks about Mum, we tried to protect her. We accepted the situation, it was the only sensible thing we could do to help out. But we didn't think much about what she would have been feeling. In those days you didn't."

"Do you see her now?"

"Yes, I visit quite often. You know, I've noticed that she has recovered a lot of her spirit. I see her bossing the other old ladies around, the ones in the home with her. It seems that the lobotomy has reversed itself to some degree."

"You can't keep a good woman down" I answered.

I told David about myself. How I had escaped the mental hospital, and avoided the sentence of mind-deadening drugs, shock therapy or lobotomy. Partially because I had been born into a different era. It seemed that I had been shepherded through my depression, had found suitable places, a university hospital trying new techniques, and good people to guide me. Not only that, but the times when I had been forced to take decisions about my health, for example coming off the antidepressant pills, I had been able to do it. I had used my depression to learn about myself and become more assured. I was not only grateful for my safe passage through these times, but for the whole mind-expanding experience.

The last race had been run and the evening was becoming chilly. David and I got up to go home where we kissed and said goodbye for a few days. I sat for a while thinking of David's mother. Now I had a clear picture of David's loyalty to duty, learnt from his mother's inability to perform her own duties. This was part of the memory of childhood which had made him the man he was. It was in the very fabric of his nature. I was warned, let no one attempt to disturb David's fidelity to his commitments.

When spirit is acting, everything acts for spirit. There are no accidents, no coincidences. The energy which flows from spirit is the same over the entire world. People meet by its design, events shape themselves to paint the whole picture, nothing is missed. Everyone has their place in this.

I remembered the passion with which I had watched David in those first days we were together. In a group of people he would be talking much more than I would, and I would sit watching his animated face, his ginger hair, receding slightly at the temples, his arms, his square hands, how his clothes sat on his body, engrossed in the experience of loving him. He had once commented that I watched him. I hadn't known what to say, just conceding that I enjoyed it. And I continued to do it. I found myself now gazing at him in the same way, enjoying the shape of his nose and lips, the curve of his forehead, the hair grown long over his ears. Tying the knot. One afternoon as we sat alone discussing a class, he came towards me and knelt down, laying his head in my lap. I held him for a long time, stroking his head and shoulders, not speaking, looking at his hair, now greying slightly, feeling his breathing relax, contemplating our lives.

"Ah, the peace of being with you" he said.

I brought so many conflicts to my relationship with David that it should not have surprised me that another cycle superimposed itself over the cycle of loving. This one dealt with fear and loss. I was in ecstasy one day, and in terror of losing it all the next day. I was still a Catholic, and bound to many of the morals of the times. Thou shalt not commit adultery , thou shalt not steal another woman's husband. Honour thy Father and thy Mother. I was less afraid of dishonouring my own husband, as he and I had been open with each other about various unimportant flirtations in the past; all the same it took its place in the list of sins I was committing.

It was summertime, and classes had finished for the year. It was the time for getting back to research, writing my thesis, to be submitted within a few months. I wandered around the corridors, trying to collect my thoughts back to science. I went and chased up references in the library, bought a sandwich for lunch and went to the tearoom to drink a cup of coffee with whoever was about. One of the students came in quoting an article from one of the medical journals. He started to relate chapter and verse on the penile injuries suffered through the use of a vacuum cleaner with a fan blade built into the nozzle. His audience caught each other's eyes, feeling the sudden pain, dissolving in gusts of anguished laughter. Imagining pieces of male genitalia being neatly sliced. Pleasure with a vengeance! I wondered about men's sexuality, craving, craving release. Was it different from my own? At least I did not gratify myself with a vacuum cleaner! My sexuality had the love dimension. I had only to see David, smile a little, and there I would go again. I was haunted by him, longed for his touch, pined for him on the weekends, and happily accepted his frequent suggestions that we should work back late and go out for a cuddle. One day we went to a lecture in the city and afterwards we drove down to the beach and walked along the esplanade, holding hands, window shopping, David buying gifts for me. Sex becomes urgent for those newly in love. We found our opportunities. We became inventive, secretive. I hated the secrecy. I suddenly understood the cry of all those taken in adultery,

"It felt right, we loved each other". Was it right? Was it wrong? Where was truth?

I would get up in the morning and shower whilst playing loud Abba songs on the radiogram, and allowing their moods to sink into my soul. James and the children had already left for work and school. As I looked out at all the quiet houses in my street I would wonder if they also housed women in such a turmoil of chaos as lived within me. Thinking that perhaps they had achieved a marriage and family life that worked well, had reached 'valiant woman' status. I drove off to work, musing on life's direction. I would walk into the stark brick building, greeting its cold walls and dusty passageways and go upstairs to my office. David would be driving to work too, I supposed. I would sit, ears tuned for his footfall in the corridor. Then I would hear him walk past my office, hear the key in his door, and as I sat at my desk, trying to continue working, he would knock on my door. I would quickly scan his face for signs of acceptance or rejection. We would greet each other, he would come over and kiss me, as my body started to tingle. I would get up and give him a quick hug. We took up our duties, abstracted, but at the same time still achieving well. I was working up a new series of practical classes for David's plant physiology subject. One day, feeling terror-stricken at the thought of men's infidelity I burst into his office, and begged him, commanded him never to deny his involvement with me.

"Don't you ever pretend this hasn't happened", I stormed, not understanding from whence that spark arose.

He was taken aback,

"Of course not" he answered, "It's all right, I'm here for you".

Sometimes I felt utter confusion, guilt towards our families, the workplace, the students, my colleagues. I was so desperately anxious to keep my love a secret, that the most uncomfortable thing I could imagine was that one man in particular amongst my colleagues should guess it. Of course David's and my behaviour together was so obvious that few people missed it. Love and togetherness is communicated in a subtle language that those who are in tune can always divine. The wife of the professor saw it when David and I visited the professor in hospital, and thankfully kept silent. Gradually news spread as the energy between us floated around and involved others. Many were silent , so many men in a man's world, their minds were on other things. They were often emotionally blind.

These were the 1970's. Women may or may not go to work. They may have read Germaine Greer on feminism. They would rarely have a career. If they had studied at University, they would usually have given up their jobs when the children arrived. They might have a part-time job to bring in some extra money. They would very likely use the contraceptive pill. And they would usually remain faithful to their husbands. Would be more likely to cling to a husband for the emotional and financial security he brought the family, rather than to throw him out in punishment for a wandering eye. I wondered if I was unusual in my desire for a full-time career, children and family life, plus a lover. I never worried about money, always had just enough. I felt that the wives would probably think I was extreme. My cup was running over, spilling my flamboyance into life's stream.

I had already had to confront my religion on the contraception issue, now I would challenge the sanctity of marriage. Perhaps it hinged on God, "What God hath joined together let no man put asunder". But how did I know if God had joined me to James or was it just I who had done it? I remembered the words I had heard at my wedding ceremony, that marriage would last for 'some other time'. I was no longer in love with James, but we functioned quite well together. We had three children to care for. At least I had worked out how to keep things going. Maybe time was running out for the marriage. Perhaps the reality of my passion for David which felt so right in me, was at some new level of awareness, some different voice or intention of God.

Our excursions continued. One day David drove me to the botanical gardens. We walked past the lake where people were feeding the swans, through the grove of fringed palms, the garden of oak trees until we came to a secluded nook where the sun's rays through the dense foliage made bright spots on the grass. We sat close together on the seat, David took my hand and trembling with tenderness asked me to marry him. I gasped in astonishment. I smiled into his eyes, treasuring this moment of love and grief,

"We have to come through these things so that we cause as little problem to our families as possible" I answered. I wondered ever after if our lives would have been different if I had answered simply 'Yes'.

I regretted my answer. In the beginning I really believed I could experience the passion without involving the families. It didn't work.

But still, we continued our work. My promotion, thankfully in place before we had come together, meant that I had extra duties, extra classes to prepare and teach. I did a good job and was seen as a reliable, creative member of staff. More responsibilities followed, committees, meetings. I completed my Masters degree, my paper was published. I had the assistance of the professor in this, but behind it all David's expertise helped me to keep everything running.

James and I continued our journey apart. He always had a life I knew nothing about, his work life, and I left him to it. He had finished his degree, and by now had a lecturing position in a College. I ran the house and the children on my own, and he usually didn't come home even for tea, still having various sporting activities and after-hours work. I had been so used to this that I expected very little of him. We went on occasional holidays together, and if a disaster struck he was there. We had had a fighting marriage and now it was serene, but unchallenging. The children were cared for by a baby-sitter who came in after school and cooked tea for them. This was an area that could house a few difficulties.

James came home early one day complaining of a pain in the stomach, he couldn't eat and was in really griping agony. I took him to the doctor, and eventually he was admitted to hospital for a few days. The virus took its course and left, and so did the latest baby-sitter, pregnant and terrified of hepatitis. James was at home then to look after the children, and took over the appointment of a new baby-sitter. He reported to me the results of his interviews from day to day, and soon a new lady rolled up for duty. The martinet Mrs Collis arrived, who cooked the children food they didn't like. Esther took to hiding lumps of meat in the sugar bowl, or sausages in the pocket of her school tunic which often ended up very clean after a trip through the washing machine. I was amused, sympathizing with the children, but unwilling to look for another baby-sitter as they were a scarce commodity.

From this time onwards James came home more often and took much more interest in the running of the house. I paid little attention to him, being only too glad that he was helping out at last, and I was free to attend to my considerable duties at work. I saw what he did and thought

"Sorry, it's too late now to do this together, I'm not interested any more."

Suddenly my marriage began to fail. James started to insist that I pay more attention to him. I couldn't do it, and avoided the issue. As I had started to recover from the depression, we had been in a 'married couples group' at the hospital, for people who had difficulties in their marriage. Every belief system through which we had operated was examined, and often torn up and thrown away. James and I both entertained a few flirtations here and there, nothing serious, but weakening the marriage bond, stretching it so thin that the snapping became inevitable. Over the years our relationship changed, I went from being totally naïve, to questioning everything, loudly and aggressively. This in turn gave way to a person who was fairly silent, but who would not be pushed anywhere she did not wish to go. A person who was bored with marriage whose only rewards were the three beautiful children. Emotional support, love, affection were sorrowfully absent. A mosaic piece waiting to be found.

We decided to move to a bigger house, two blocks away. James came home more often trying to make the marriage work. He confronted me.

"Do you love me?"

"Yes of course" irritated.

"Do you really want to move house?"

"Yes" I felt my world shrivelling.

"I feel desperate, I think you want a divorce"

"No, we can't get divorced"

"But do you want to?"

"No of course not."

I lied, what could I say? Perhaps it was not yet time to speak out. I didn't understand why I could not simply speak the truth. And yet everything in society, religion, upbringing was against me. I remembered a girl at school whose mother had divorced and remarried. The mother had become an outcast, her daughter sharing in the taint. An indigestible mess filled my consciousness. The confrontations continued. At last I said

"Look if you aren't content why don't you find someone else, it's all right with me."

James and I did an enormous cleanout of the house (including his parents' belongings left behind years before) and moved out. I later recognized the importance of cleaning out from the spiritual, through the mental and emotional to the physical level, every time I did it. It always marked the end of an era. If one considered what was being cleaned out in the physical sense, one could find a glimpse of the spiritual dimension. This time it was the parents' baggage, Catholicism at its strictest interpretation, and James' and my involvement in it which was left on the tip.

My mother came to visit us in our new house, and wished us a happy life there. The sinking feeling of that moment stayed with me. I knew that happiness here would be impossible. Catholics do not split up, no divorce is permissible, they just go on and on in desperate marriages until they die. Or they defy the Church's teaching, the upbringing of their families, and divorce in shame. James was still asking for more attention, I still couldn't give it. Hard times.

Times got worse. David's marriage was also strained. David had tuned his life into a polite *ostinato*. But his wife suddenly wanted to know why he was distant. She too wanted more attention. Wanted the impossible, a love relationship recreated magically. Perhaps she too had been trampled and thought her authority over her husband would bring satisfaction. David told me that his wife wanted to discuss their marriage, she had rung him at work to tell him that she was unhappy with the way things were, and he had promised to talk it over that evening. David had told me a long time ago that they had considered ending the marriage previously, and now it may happen. I still felt I was bound to James for life, I saw no escape for myself.

David's family contretemps brought havoc. David came to work with a face the colour of suet, no smile, stiff and removed. 'Hell hath no fury'.

"What's the matter?" I asked when I could get near to him. He seemed to be withdrawn into himself, not anxious to speak to me.

"I had to tell my wife about us" he said, "She got hysterical. I had to promise that I would never speak to you again to get her to calm down."

"Well we don't often talk whilst we are making love!" I said mischievously, but David's face told me otherwise.

"I have to obey her, I have to break with you." His face looked old, lined. No trace of life in his eyes. Despair entered us. In turn, the life drained out of me. There was nothing I could do. I went to my office and sat at my desk. I fiddled with the papers. Went downstairs to check the mail. Taught my class, my mind half there, half dead. Went to the toilet and looked at my drawn face in the mirror. Couldn't recognize who it could be, how I could have come to be in such a state.

*

Unloved, my spark is extinguished by the cruel winds of society, blown out by the refusal of anyone to offer hope of love's survival. My wretchedness leaves me writhing in a muddy pit of snails, who advance on my shackled figure, to crawl over my face, block the portals of my breath, gradually smother me with their thick slimy bodies. I am dying in filth.

My sorrow follows crescendos and diminuendos of misery, unabated. I retreat to the bottom of the garden to sob away its raw peaks with the trees and possums my only witness. Then I return to the kitchen to continue cooking dinner for the few minutes that I can bear before I am forced to retreat once more. There is no hope, we had tasted the sweetness of love and now he has withdrawn, leaving despair. I think that he can go on, continue his life as it was, enjoy new friends, while I sit here alone grieving. So now I become angry, my rage against him seethes until I see again his pale face, not only the colour of putty, but its texture, moulded by external forces into its flat contours of blankness. Then I grieve for his loss. When the doors are closed there is no way to open them. No person, no circumstance save reunion with the beloved.

*

All talk of David's marriage breaking up dissolved in his wife's knowledge that David was in love with me. The strings that bound David were long and tangled. I understood some of them. David had never recovered from the day when he had pulled his mother out of the gas oven, as she lay trying to die. He regretted it still when he appreciated the misery in which she spent the rest of her life, in a home for the mentally ill, the lobotomy ensuring her passivity and compliance. So threats by his wife to kill herself were taken seriously. Another string was pulled by his sons, now in their teenage years, and requiring a father's affection to guide them into adulthood, not to mention the high expenses involved in paying for a public school education. Above all, he wished only to please people. His wife held all the trump cards in this play. The marriage lines, the boys and the home. She was an expert in manoeuvring her filing cabinet of duties into David's escape route.

I continued to work, but the spark went out of me. I went about the department like an automaton, without inspiration. The classes ran, uninterestingly. Nobody noticed.

David still spoke to me, sometimes even held me, in desperation. Sometimes we came really close again , sometimes he was far away. One day he told me his wife had rung the professor to ask that I be removed from the staff. The fear bit deep. I went into the professor, starting to cry as I walked through the door. He said nothing, only hugged me. Then he said there was nothing that would be done about my appointment, it was safe. I thanked him and left.

A few days later the other professor who was now the dean in David's stead called me in, and gave me a lecture on my behaviour. He too had been approached with a request for my removal from the staff. I stood and wondered at his rudeness and insensitivity. I knew that he had been divorced and had remarried, surely he must remember the trauma of these events. I wondered if he would give David the same lecture, or was it reserved for the junior female staff member. He went on and on, until I started to cry. Later his secretary confided in me that he had thought I was brazen because I did not immediately burst into tears. This saga went on some days, each day more excruciating than the previous one. I was aware of the double standard silently preached, but said nothing. No use in such a male faculty. They couldn't see it. They huddled together, the tweed jacket brigade, talking about the lovers with their mental minds, condemning as a nuisance that which they had no way of understanding, the concepts of love and loss. They couldn't do anything against my appointment, I knew , just make my life more unbearable than it was already. Suddenly I wasn't the golden girl any more, was criticized when previously I would have been helped over difficulties. The butt of lewd comments. Excluded from invitations within the school now because David had seniority, and the two families could not be invited out together. Old enemies crawled out of the woodwork and waved their self-righteous banners. It happened in the blink of an eye.

At home I was a robot. I cooked by rote, tucked the children up in their beds with prayers for all in need. I had no interest in anything. One day James brought home some friends for a drink. I summoned my energy and tried to listen to their conversation. Suddenly I was spellbound, my namesake Sibyl returned briefly with a gift. The woman started to tell me about an experience she had had when she had undergone an operation, and had needed resuscitation. She had flown out of her body, floating above the person on the bed, had seen the doctors working frantically to revive her as she turned to leave. Then she had felt the most overpowering sensation of love, more than anything she had known here on earth, and longed to go into it. A woman in a blue dress stood before her, filled with compassion and said

"It isn't your time yet, you must go back." Then the doctors relaxed, they had succeeded. With the utmost regret the woman turned back to her body, and later awoke in the recovery ward.

I found a tiny straw to grasp in this story. The woman had been moved by her experience. It seemed as if everything has not been said here on earth, perhaps there is a greater love that we have not yet experienced. This straw of involvement with the love in the afterlife grew over the years to a raft, then eventually an ocean liner, propelling me safely through the lonely times.

After three weeks of robotic life James asked me what was the matter, I hesitated, wanting to hold my silence. Fortunately he insisted. With explosions of grief I told him everything, my love for David, the debacle of the previous three weeks, my despair. And he in his turn told me of the woman whom he loved. I was grateful that he always let me off the hook of guilt, anything I had done he had always done better.

The next morning driving to work I knew that my marriage was over. Even if I had no future with David, I wanted the love I had found with him, and perhaps I could find it with someone else. It was not with James, so I must leave. So clear, just finish it. Catholicism was suddenly irrelevant, the power of my insight brushed it away. I bounced into work, knocked on David's door.

"I wanted to tell you, I am going to leave James. Our marriage is over. He has someone he is in love with."

David seemed troubled in his own thoughts.

"Don't be too hasty, Sibyl, it is most unlikely that I shall ever be free to be with you" he said. "Don't throw away your marriage so lightly, you and James have worked a long time together, you have the beautiful children."

"Even if you can't be with me I must find love again. Even if it meant leaving you too and finding love with someone else. I know it exists now, and I can't live without it."

"I don't want you to leave me" David said, his eyes lowered, not meeting mine. I sought them out.

"I am not leaving you, I'm leaving James."

I was riding a wave of relief that day, and trusted my own future. David's lack of freedom did not trouble me, I coasted along, the first respite since the news had broken.

James did not agree with me, he wanted to go to counselling, to patch up our marriage. I remembered the married couples group during my depression. It had never helped much. It had gone on for years, and it had always bored me. I felt revolted by the thought of doing it again. James had a friend who was a counsellor, she added fuel to James' fire by recounting the dangers the children faced through the divorce of their parents. I still refused. He pleaded. I dug in my toes. *Impasse*. I suggested we lived close by each other to help take care of the children. It never happened. Eventually I won the argument, if not the war, and James left angrily to go and live with his lover. I was left alone with the children.

Now it was my turn to be terrified of living alone. I had been so afraid of monsters under my bed that I always took a big step when I got up in the night, to avoid their grasping fingers. Now there was no one to run to, I was big mama. The children were at their most docile ages, the pre teens, and helped me through those bad days. James was testy, but came sometimes to take the children out. I was disappointed that he could not be more in their lives. Gradually, slowly I crawled out of the pit.

David was with me as I conquered my fear of the outside world. He held me in the palm of his hand, so that I could take the steps to form my personality. He encircled me, secured me against outside attack. In all the thirteen years I was with him, I experienced no panic. I was whole, a feeling being, tempered by my adherence to duty, but expanding. With him I expressed all my feelings, the love, the pain, the exultancy, the sadness. I was fully alive.

One day as I crossed the campus with a friend I overheard screaming as someone underwent primal therapy. I said

"Do you think that I would benefit from such therapy?"

"No, this is for people who are out of touch with their emotions. You are definitely in touch."

The woman who had five years ago been in panic due to the suppression of her emotions had come full circle. My fears changed direction. In panic they had been involved with who I was, the innermost fabric of my being. Now they were to do with my relationship with the world. I still felt dread and anxiety, but it had become manageable, because now it was not myself which was at risk, but my position in society. By breaking all the rules, taking a lover and a career, leaving my husband and my religion I had set myself up as an outsider. I had to learn to take that role. To make it a part of me. In the face of my background and family this was a large undertaking. I had to take all the pieces of my smashed mirror which I wished to keep, the happy parts of my childhood and adolescence, my career and my spirituality, my love and my sorrow and put them together in a new form, rerolling the sheet of glass to become the mirror of heaven. And without his love I would have been unable.

His personality was already fragmented. He was a locomotive, running on the twin rails of duty and love. Without love he could not function, and likewise, without the discharge of his duty to his family he would fall apart. His ultimate wish was to divide himself in two physically, and live peacefully with both his women. And because he came from another generation, it was likely that he would not be able to achieve more than this.

David and I would be together and happy one day and in despair the next. We evolved a fantasy that 'one day' we would be together permanently. It kept us going. Our love was not diminished, and sometimes flowered again. One day he announced that he and his wife would be taking a trip to another state to consider a job there. I felt as if I had been kicked again. Our personal customs arose, we decided to have a cup of coffee together at 10.30 every morning, and think of each other. David began his habit of sending me a card when he was travelling, and this buoyed up my spirits. It was all a matter of balance.

At the end of the fortnight I was working alone in one of the cold rooms, dark and damp, preparing a brew for an experiment. Suddenly David appeared on the other side of my workbench, as if from nowhere,

"Hello, my princess" he said,

"You're back!" I breathed, radiating relief and happiness.

"I had enough of New South Wales," he said, "I'll be staying here and working with you." He grabbed my hand, and I clung to him, expressing everything I felt through the touch of our fingers. The question of David and I working together was always of utmost importance to me, it seemed that my world pivoted upon us collaborating in a research team. It seemed vital to my being, it was this which brought me joy, and it was to this that David and I always returned when life became difficult.

David coped with his life like an automaton, hounded by the darkness that sought to molest him. He had two lives, one with his family and one at work with me, and never the twain could meet. He drove to work in his old white Mini, past the gates of duty, to lift the shackles and enter the landscape of desire, happiness and fulfilment. In the evenings he returned to family duty . The gates we passed through in order to be together had time limits, we were day-trippers who yearned for a weekly pass.

I didn't understand his situation at first. Later I wondered how he survived something which to me would have been impossible. I couldn't enter his door, or experience his situation. David knew how to placate me, but couldn't reach any further into the ambiguity of his situation. He was from another generation and his patterns were too ingrained to change easily. His desire was to please everyone. He wanted to cut himself in two physically, and this is what he did mentally.

Every Monday morning I would drive to work, chugging along in my baby blue car, looking forward to seeing David again after the weekend of domestic duties with the children. That drive became a panic. I chewed the dashboard in my fear that he wouldn't be there, shook and trembled lest he had been in trouble again, dreading that if he was there he would have his grey face, his withdrawn manner. I wondered what effects this constant fear would have on my body. Being a physiologist I could well wonder about the long-term effects of raised adrenalin levels, never documented because lives are too long.

Some months after we had come together, David and I were sitting on the grass by a lake. It was early evening, I was ostensibly working late, and David was to attend a graduation ceremony in his official capacity as dean of the faculty. It was autumn, yellow leaves floated on the surface of the water, weaving patterns around sticks and tree roots near the bank. We sometimes took our lunch here, to grasp at a half hour of semi-privacy from work. Now we had brought our evening meal, thinking to steal an extra hour.

We ate our meal, admired the view and breathed the air. Then David screwed up the papers that had wrapped our chicken pieces, and stood up. He cleaned up our picnic tea and prepared to go. I caught at his coat sleeve, thinking to detain him. Sometimes the work ethic was strong, but I with my wiles I could cut through it.

"Sit down a bit, there's plenty of time." He was reluctant.

"I have a few things to do before the ceremony, but 5 minutes."

He lay down next to me on the rug, and I cuddled into his chest, my favourite place. We drifted off, feeling the love swirl through our bodies, as the breeze caressed us. It was deep twilight, the last rays of the sun faded, as we lay alone by the water, softly splashing the shore. We dosed, happily oblivious of time.

David jumped up with a start.

"What am I doing, I'm late. Quick get in the car!" I blinked, thought 'Oh shit, now I've done it', and bundled myself into the old Mini and slammed the door. This was my fault, fair and square. We raced to the office where he grabbed his academic gown and fled to the hall, where I heard later he just made it to the end of the procession of dignitaries. His speech barely prepared, he limped through his presentation of degrees, fumbling for words.

David was so able in a man's world, but out of his depth in the female world of feelings, loyalties, jealousy and rage, love and submission. I fought for David's freedom by every method I could find, by love, by Being There, and even bordering on nagging. Love leads one to the truth of the situation, whilst nagging forms a wall of isolation. David treated my lapses from the ideal with grace.

"Ifyoureallylovedmeyouwould ...." was answered with

"I know it seems like that, but really it isn't." I would then stop in mid flight. A part of me recognized the truth in his words, realized the permanence of love and appreciated the irrelevance of the present tangled situation. I made a decision realizing all the difficulties which faced me. I looked squarely at my life as it was, and weighed it against how life would be without David in it. This was the decision of power, was I in or was I out. For the moment I was in. I weighed it up every time life got rough. 'In' lasted a long time.

*

And we decide, consciously or unconsciously, all the moves. My aim was consciousness. My aim was love. My fear was that that which was promised would not be delivered. But how can that be? My spirit, I, had made the promise to myself. I would honour the promise.

Love is the creator, which I saw in every blade of grass, every drop of water in the ocean, all held together in the bond of love. More a force than something sentimental, a force of will. It was this that I contacted when I fell in love, this force which binds the earth, her people, the forests, the seas, animals, rocks, into a glorious whole. Once I had contacted it, I could not walk away from it. I wanted to keep the contact, to always feel 'in love'. I started to develop techniques which helped this to happen, the most important was, is, 'Being There'. Ask nothing, say nothing, stand in my centre, self sufficient, radiate love and be there. It has huge attractive value.

*

Mia meanwhile was growing lanky and independent. At the age of fourteen I caught her in a lie. I confronted the tall girl

"I saw you up in the paddock with those other children, why did you say you weren't there?"

Mia looked at me and said firmly

"I'm not going to do anything you say".

I was taken aback by Mia's directness. I surveyed the situation. Mia was bigger than me, competent in everything she attempted. Headstrong and determined. I could do nothing to make her obey. The power shifted, Mia was ready. I gave in gracefully.

"All right, but I want you always to let me know where you are."

Mia could not speak to me after that, for a long time. I watched her grow into her new role. I worried that something dreadful would happen. What was the worst scenario? Rape, death, or quadriplegia? The situation simply had to be accepted. I learned the hardest lesson of motherhood, to see everything and do nothing. To be the keeper of the energy of the family, remaining silent. Supporting the children's growth through my presence and intention, holding myself ready for them. Another way of 'Being There'. Sometimes I would point out something to Mia, who was galloping into life like an untamed filly. It was not always listened to, but I was obliged to speak. After two years we had found a new relationship. Mia loved shopping and liked to go with me to the supermarket to help choose the weekly food. And from that beginning we became friends.

Sam was growing up, coughing his way through life, losing his shoes and his books, being somewhat of a scatterbrain.

Esther often awoke with nightmares, and would come into my room crying with dread. I took her into bed with me, and then couldn't sleep myself, as Esther was so restless, kicking and tossing. Eventually I made a bed on the floor next to my own bed for these times. When we moved house again some months later, I put Esther's bed in my own room and for years we slept together.

*

I stood on the walkway between the university buildings, looking out towards the library. It was early evening and I was working back. All the senior staff members had gone to a dinner given by the new professor. I gazed out over the grey winter landscape, contemplating my situation. I was not invited, in spite of the fact that the professor had been a guest in my home. It was not even thought that David and I could take our own decisions over how or when we should meet socially. As David had not been called to account for his behaviour, so now he could be received in polite society, whilst the woman, Eve's daughter, should be blamed. In the back of my mind there stirred the feeling that I was in the right. I was learning patience. I was standing alone, firm. Even if it felt terrible, it was the way through.

So I kept walking through the minefield of relationships within the department. Gradually I began to feel stronger and more at home in my new world. About this time the oppression I had felt amongst the other members of staff began to lift. Some of them gave me what little support they could, would say

"How are things these days, I'm sorry to hear you and James have broken up" leaving me free to say how much or how little I wished. With some of the women staff I had a closer association, they chatted at length. Others kept their distance through disapproval I guessed. As I continued my work, and performed well, the staff acknowledged the changes which had occurred, and it seemed to me, they filed the previous year away in their memory banks and got on with their business. I began to take my position in the department once more.

Now the work that David and I loved started in earnest. Some students had done an experiment, and confused their results. I sorted through their calculations, presented the amended results to David who found a story describing a new idea about the regulation of mineral metabolism in plants. This formed the basis of our collaboration. David became my mentor and supervised my PhD. He had other students, other projects, some of which I was involved in.

In his book 'The Tucson Zoo', Lewis Thomas speaks of the habits of scientists who try to find out firstly the details of a process, then secondly the details of the details, and so on, until in the end the plant or animal on which one is experimenting is not seen any more.

David taught me the opposite approach. We were interested in the details as they gave light to the growth of the plant community as a whole. We gauged the effects of minerals, light and water on hormone levels, and production in the whole plant, then the whole community. Some people would say,

"This is too difficult for me" whilst others would comment

"Your work is easy, the analyses are simple, you don't use any expensive machinery to get results."

But the plant is the most intricate of machines, and runs perfectly until its death. Its signals, dials and meters are indirect, and require meticulous interpretation, much preknowledge, and often extra delicately balanced experiments to probe gently into another aspect of the situation. It was like joining science to poetry, without losing any of the accuracy of the science, nor the ecstasy of the poetry.

David was interested in the philosophy of science, read Karl Popper, discussed the implications of the hypothesis that a scientific theory can only be disproved, and the most inventive one can be is to design experiments to test if it is consistent with a certain theory. Scientists are always open to challenge by someone more inventive. David read widely in science and in other disciplines. He had an accurate view both of science and human behaviour. He understood how things worked in the university. In the faculty there was a chemistry lecturer who was always pushing for modifications in his chemistry course. Year in year out he would press for this or that change. Eventually, there came a new professor who having his own agenda, swept away the entire chemistry unit and replaced it with biochemistry, justifying the action with 'Well the chemistry course has always been unsatisfactory, look at all the complaints.' David said it had been inevitable that this would happen. Many times he would observe to me, 'So-and-so is trying to achieve *this*, but it will backfire, and *that* will happen eventually'. Time and time again I saw the truth of his predictions revealed, often after a number of years.

In science it was the same. David read science prolifically, and explained scientific concepts using diagrams to people without any previous background in science, opening new doors of understanding for them. For me it was quite difficult as a student to both take advice and learn from him, as well as striking out on my own and making my individual contribution to science. My first efforts came after several experiments. When I finally collected all the results on the page, I was surprised and delighted to see patterns there, previously unsuspected. I worked on these patterns, exploring their significance for another five years.

I travelled the world, visiting laboratories doing similar or related work in many countries. I flew out of Australia on cloud nine, rapturously enjoying every moment of the voyage. David stood in spirit behind me, assuring my progress, as I zig-zagged across oceans and continents. And then home again, self confidence growing, my ability to present our research increasing. More experiments, testing the response of the plant to this mineral, that perturbation, a new fertilizer, why not measure this hormone. David attracted grants to employ helpers, and the group grew stronger.

*

David had sons, much loved. It was always my wish to give him a daughter. Not a conscious purpose in any way, but a wish which floated in and out of my mind. I never analysed the why of it. Perhaps I felt that he would enjoy the affection which men often feel for their daughters. It was not that I wished to bring up another child, as with my full time work and the family that would have been impossible. At first I was impressed with how well he liked my children, wondered if my younger daughter could be a surrogate daughter for him. Then I was brought up with a start of realization that Esther loved her own father, was not eligible for transfer. However, the wish persisted for many years, in the background of life's activities. The life of the spirit world began to enter my life. Every step I took away from the clutches of organized religion enhanced my appreciation of my inner voice, who never led me astray, who was there at my lightest wish.

But we still had upheavals from time to time.

David was gradually withdrawing from me, he went home early after work every day, curtailed our contact. He was still there, in my life, but I felt his commitment had failed me. I shrugged my shoulders and continued my life.

From the days of my first university degree I had friends who had visited me from time to time, often with an invitation to intimacy. I had always refused, but now seemed to be the time for a tentative 'Yes'. I found this activity quite interesting, but it did not reach my soul. Towards the end of the year I met someone who tapped on my innermost door. This was better, perhaps I should forget about David, just find someone else, forget the hassles, the jealousy, the expulsion from university life, have a fling. The person I had met lived interstate, and as usual there was a planned work project holding us together. I agreed to take my techniques interstate, and work in my new friend's laboratory.

The outcome was different. For a start, David noticed. My usual ardour deserted me, not difficult for him to guess that something was up. I kept no secrets from him, readily confessing my flirtation. His response was to say he would leave his family and live with me, come interstate with me, help with the project, remain a part of my life. David had tentatively handed over the reins and began to glide towards me.

Now I was invited to be unfaithful, to continue my liaison with the new man, deceiving David. I started to think in this way, but my insides howled, 'No, never again'. My relief at leaving my husband had forever put a stop to that situation. I said no to continuing the new affair, returning to where my soul was content, risking the cancellation of our work. Thankfully it didn't come to that and the project went ahead.

Now that David was about to leave his family, we began to discuss how we would go about the separation and when we would leave on our interstate journey. We obtained the necessary permissions from work. I had organized my children to stay with their grandparents, which they did every year. In a flurry of activity, we made preparations for David to leave home. I prayed that all would go smoothly, knowing in my heart that it wouldn't. My own possessiveness came into play and I required enormous strength to behave with decorum. Eventually after many painful happenings, very much 'Being There' on my part, we set off on our journey, to another land.

In this land I was accepted without family references, respected for my work, and achieved much. I had a fairly busy assignment, and we performed eight experiments in a few weeks, with the cooperation of our colleagues, and our own technician who had travelled with us.

We enjoyed anonymity, and some peace. David's contact with his family caused me such acute distress, afraid that he would return to them, that I wanted to beg him not to ring them. At the same time, respect for David's feelings pulled me back, and I accepted the pain of the situation. Leah once told me that when two people separate from their families to come together, that the pain is so great that it eats into their relationship, usually causing it to break also. The pair often turned to new partners following the split, and this had a better chance of survival. I wished it were not so, and tried all I knew to save our closeness.

I found David a quiet companion. He had let his duty go, and with it went the engaging part of his nature. He read, corrected papers, wrote articles, and in the evenings we watched television together. Our lovemaking was desultory. If he had spoken to his wife on the telephone his face became grim, he turned away from me, his head down, his shoulders hunched. He had tried to thwart his generous nature, and it wasn't having any. His strength was in his upbringing, his adherence to duty, his care for those dependent upon him. It was the most lovable thing in his nature. In its absence his character began to disintegrate, his charm grew thin, his smile weary. Not that he was ever mean to me, or less than polite, he simply lost his sparkle. I had felt clear when my marriage had broken up, light and unhampered. Not guilty for a moment. For David it was not the same at all.

The consequences to me were obvious. Either he would grow out of this sadness, which I could see would take perhaps many years, or he would go back to his family. This moment which I had so longed for, David's freedom from his family was a bitter blow to me. I could not see that David made any progress through his guilt. I was not happy with this sombre man, and did not know what to do.

*

I didn't do anything. We completed our project and returned home. David to his family and I to mine. In the brilliant March sunshine I was standing on a ladder, cleaning out the guttering, knowing that I would cope with the grief, knowing that I had presumably lost David forever, and calmly determined to get on with life alone. I was relieved that David was back with his family, the tension of his absence from them was resolved. It felt right for this half-hour at least. But in any case, it wasn't so.

Now that David's train was back on the rails of duty, it stabilized. His jovial self re-emerged, and fell happily into the life he had known before. He still needed me in his personal life, and we became closer than we had been before he had left home. Somewhere, somehow our lives had straightened out. I was much happier than I had been both before and during the episode. I knew now that although he would never leave his wife, neither would he leave me. As we still worked together we took up our professional lives where we had left off.

For my part I moved house, this time to an old house in an inner suburb, a workman's cottage. The house was beautiful, many rooms, peaceful, with a huge almond tree covering the entire backyard and blossoming throughout every August. Echoes of a gentle past. I sought refuge in the high walls and lofty ceilings. This was my house, my chapel, my sanctuary and my retreat.

*

In the course of all this, one month my period was late. I sighed and thought this was really the end, how could I cope with anything more. I still had my wish, to give David a daughter, but we were in the midst of such upheavals just then, I did not want any more problems. I never discussed my wish with him, because I knew it wouldn't work like that. I would never purposely become pregnant, but if a mistake was made, then I would accept it.

My sister Alice could not have children. We had discussed her attempts to conceive by the IVF program, which had been unsuccessful every time. A voice in my head used to say 'I could give you a baby.'

I had had my babies easily, I could as well have one for my sister. I never discussed this voice with anyone, but it spoke to me for some years.

My sister and I understood each other in spite of the six years and the distance which separated us. We met seldom, and had never been close, but the tie of the family gave us a perspective on each other which made up for the distance. She had been a successful nurse, working sometimes with school children. She was an outdoor woman, good with horses and sports requiring balance. We suffered many similar pains from our upbringing, but at different times, so that we often were unable to support each other in the ways I would have liked. When I had left James she had helped me over a rough stretch, simply by inviting me to her place for a weekend. We called each other sometimes and had long conversations, and I was happy to find that we were similar in our outlook on life.

But now that I suspected I may be pregnant I called Alice and heard how the latest IVF attempt had failed. I was exhilarated. I said to Alice

"I may be pregnant, would you like to bring up the baby?" She was surprised, pleased

"I'll talk it over with my husband and call you back".

Meanwhile I flew interstate to a conference, arriving without breakfast at the airport. Neatly dressed, paper prepared for presentation, I started to miscarry, hypoglycaemic, nauseous, trying not to throw up on the plane. No baby. When Alice rang back to say yes she and her husband would adopt the baby, it was long gone. I was disappointed and promised that if it happened again I'd contact her.

*

At the end of that year I was so wrung out that I went to a counselor, and asked if I could talk out the pain of the year. Just talk it out, no advice sought. Over all the hopes and tears, over the biting anxiety, over the broken promises, the move, the money strains, the children's traumas, and on top of it all the usual work, the usual family caring, I had survived. As I finished my recital the counselor said,

"I think you ought to…." But I had made my bed and preferred to lie in it.

David and I often considered moving to another job, either as a way of splitting up and putting some distance between us, or of being free from the eyes which were always on us at work. On one occasion, after a rough stretch, we both applied for jobs, and both were successful. The outcome would have been that we were again working together, but travelling a lot further to work. It seemed to be ordained that we should work together. We stayed where we were.

David was always concerned that I had a secure job, and often advised me that my tenure at the university was not to be relied upon, being very much at the whim of those who were in charge at the time when my three year contract came up for renewal. He watched the newspapers for jobs and heard through his acquaintances what was around. He would urge me to apply here and there. Once I was shortlisted for a prestigious job as editor to a scientific journal. I was interested, not overwhelmingly, but would have accepted the job if it were offered. David gave me a lift to the interview, I dressed in my best sparkling clothes, black tight pants and a smart flame coloured jacket. The interview proceeded well, I was encouraged. But David said later,

"Well you didn't want that job, did you?"

"What do you mean?" I asked.

"Those sexy clothes will never get you that sort of job!"

I looked at myself, and wondered what I had been thinking about. He was right, I didn't get the job.

*

It was about this time that Paddy died. She died young. We had kept our contact and our delight in each other, but she rarely travelled from her home in the country. I saw her rarely, we phoned each other for birthdays. She encouraged me, had no hard words to say about my marriage breakup, and was enthusiastic about my relationship with David. The year before when she turned sixty, we celebrated at her daughter's. I showed her pictures of him.

"He looks nice, very nice!" she told me. So warm, so easy to communicate with. No hang-ups, just love and acceptance. She knew the road I had taken.

"We will come and see you again!"

"You will have to make it soon!" she warned us. But before we had returned she had died. Unable to attend her funeral, I went to Mass to mourn her, but it was the wrong thing to do. I should have gone to the forest, to the beach or the countryside. At Mass I was treated to a sermon on the holiness of marriage, and no matter how I twisted about in my seat, I couldn't escape, I was bruised once more.

☙ PART 4 ❧

CONCEIVING THE CHILD

Sirius dreams and I catch the lilt of song in my body. The tune is meat and drink to me, I rock in bliss. I am the goddess of love, blessing my creation. A new star is shining, dancing, preparing its own lightning path.

A YEAR HAD PASSED and again my period was late. A shiver of anticipation lanced my spine. But no need to think about it yet. Go to work as usual, teach the classes, correct the reports, talk to colleagues as if nothing was out of the ordinary. Just at an angle, not in my direct view, stood a glimmer of light, nothing definite. I didn't tell David at first either, keeping my precious hope enclosed in my body. Perhaps, perhaps. The holidays were coming up soon, I was to travel to New Zealand to attend a conference, and present a paper. I forgot about my body in the responsibility of the moment. Preparing the poster, organizing the children, climbing on board the flight to Christchurch. Looking down over the white snowfields of Mt Cook, I remembered again. No sign yet, there still could be something. It felt more stable somehow, more present. The glimmer of light trembled slightly, but did not move into view.

On my way to the university I looked out at the springtime gardens, early, too cold for flowers. A still wintery sun lit up my journey. I had arrived earlier than the other participants. I unpacked my clothes in the college room and went downstairs to look for a cup of tea. Wandered around the deserted corridors and dining rooms feeling bored. Walked out into the garden, but the trees were unfamiliar, and still in their winter dormancy. The bushes pruned bare. I found my way to the office, and asked the staff when the other participants would be arriving.

"Mostly this evening, some tomorrow" was the reply.

"Could I find a cup of tea?" A woman standing at the copier looked over and said

"Would you like to come home with me? I'm going home now and need a cup".

She was the supervisor of the women's college where I would stay. As we sat in her bright sitting room, knick knacks everywhere, next door to the college, and chatted about university life, I felt strange, a little out of place. I enjoyed conversation, but again became filled with the idea of pregnancy. I was wary of giving away too much. What would the woman think if I came out and spoke openly of my love for a man married to another woman? And how I wished to bear him a daughter? How we were so happy working together? I felt dislocated again, in my conversation. The worldly me, who was able to make people feel at home, welcomed into my space, listened to. And the other me, trembling with anticipation, with the reality of my life, which sometimes burst out through my eyes, my breath, but rarely through my throat. I felt constrained, as if the two parts in me were at war, and could not coexist without bringing chaos to my protected world. All the time drinking my tea, eating a cake, smiling, listening, talking.

The conference proceeded, I performed adequately, remembering little, except moments of 'It still hasn't come, I must be, I'm now three weeks late.'

Walking up the bare concrete stairs, looking out the window to the pale sunlight, 'I'll get it checked when I go home.'

Hope and dread together. Nothing so public as pregnancy. All the people at work, all my family to be faced. 'Now I've really done it!' loomed inside me.

The glimmering light spoke of nurturing, weaving its cocoon of safety, glowing silkworm, tiny bud. Making its home inside me, interlacing its capillaries to drink my blood. Baby vampire. Adored child. I was swept into joy.

The aeroplane touched down, I was home again. First stop the Women's Clinic, take the test. Certainty stood out on the plate.

"Yes, it is positive, you are pregnant".

The nurse looked into my eyes. The light stepped forward, no longer a faint glimmer but a flesh and blood person. This time it had registered. I was aghast, horrified, delighted, the feelings chased themselves across my face, I was overcome, the hugeness of it terrified me. I knew what to do, and yet I knew nothing.

"Are you all right about this?" asked the nurse, "You're not married are you?"

"It's all right, and no," I gave a tight smile.

"Will you have the baby?"

"Oh yes" this time a real smile, filling the universe.

I drove to work. It had been a week since I had talked to David. I knocked on his door. He recognized my footsteps, my knock,

"Come in."

I was nervous for the first time with David. I had considered what he would feel, my working beside him, flamboyantly fertile, he could almost die of embarrassment. To say nothing of his fear of his wife. I walked into his office, closed the door. He got up and gave me a welcome-home hug, and a warm kiss.

"I've got something to tell you" I said.

"Oh?"

"I'm pregnant." Pause.

"You're sure?"

"I had a test."

"Mmm. I suppose you're not going to do anything about it?"

"No."

He sat down and looked at me, combed his fingers through his hair.

"Do you feel all right?"

"Yes".

I sat down opposite him. We looked at each other. Accepted each other. Digested the situation in silence. My being was split in two again. The first was now an unwed mother, in common with many, receiving pensions, downtrodden, brave victims of religion and society. In the second, my determination to have this child, a gift to David, a gift to my sister, a gift to the world. My strength lay in my knowledge of correctness , right was being done according to my soul. No other choice was possible. David seemed torn by the same lights. He knew his child would come to earth. He welcomed her, from his strength and love. But his personality quaked. His wife, his sons should not know, he could not cope with that. He wondered if I could bear to part with the child, when the time would come. But he did not doubt it. Whatever else I was, impulsive and soft, I was also determined. He wanted to run away. His insides churned like buttermilk. He looked across at me. Light of his life. The meaning in his existence, if he was honest. Without me his life was as dry as the stubble after the wheat was harvested. He would support me, to his last particle of courage. Just praying that it could all happen anonymously. No talk, no publicity. My child, for my sister, as far as the world could see. He would not acknowledge his involvement at work, amongst our colleagues. Only with me, and the closest friends. He blessed his second job, glad he would be spending a lot of time away from the university in the next months. He took my hand, stroked my fingers, let his affection enter me, flowing down to his child. I clasped his hand strongly, thanking him for his presence. Understanding his silence. Grateful he was still in the room. Another job to be done, bearing a child together. An incantation of tenderness. We surrendered to a new level of commitment. In the bare office, the walls covered with books, the passion of creation passed between us, as we accepted the path.

Motherhood opened me to new satisfactions. I welcomed the growing child, stroked my belly, talked to her, encouraged her into the world. Sat sewing, creating baby garments. Sat for hours just in my happiness, souls entwined with each other, the three of us. Work was harder to do now, it was barely possible to concentrate. But I scraped through nonetheless. I took to spending time in the library near where David had his second job. Then we could meet for lunch, I could work on my thesis, and take some time walking in the gardens, watching the men playing bollé. The baby grew.

Alice was pleased with our plans, offered financial support for my confinement. We talked, planned the birth. We were both happy. I agreed that the baby should be adopted. I knew about the pain, but couldn't look at it, it wasn't the time yet. I needed this time, so short, to be a complete mother. I gave the child everything I had. Remembered my older children, their gestations, became closer to them as they were interested and eager during my pregnancy. As we sat in the old lounge room, Mia playing with our old tabby cat Tiger, Sam and Esther looking on, we shared talks about babies. Mia enjoyed the differentness of our family, and found my pregnancy made us even more unusual.

David watched me, saw my waistline spread, lifting higher every month. Felt the joy of the baby's first fluttering movements. Filled himself with my calm and contentment. Tried not to worry, and engrossed himself in his work. Wondered how he had become involved in this bizarre situation. So conventional, he had been, was still. Silent, hardworking, it did not suffice, his soul had burst through to love, he had not been able to leave me before this, now could never leave. Sealed in blood now by the child. Life was a mystery to him, a rational man. It should be so easy, how did it become so entangled? He went to work every day thinking his thoughts, but being bound in his rationality he could not come to any answer. He loved his sons, and me, even to his wife he had a dutiful affection, coupled with apprehension. Love did not fit into rationality, so where did it fit? He was too constricted by his ignorance of spirit to come to any conclusion , he remained outside spirit's understanding, while participating in its joy. Work took over, spreading its claims over the lack of life understanding, a void which remained to the end of David's life on earth.

"Beth, my daughter, joy of my heart, song of love."

I caressed my baby and sang in my exultation. The baby lay peaceful, stars in her blue blue eyes, a furry fuzz of fine gold hair on her head, tiny fingers clasping mine. The room seemed filled with angels, singing in the golden light. I lay back tired from the birth, holding Beth to my breast. I watched her every movement, the quivering breath, feeling the softness of her hair against my cheek, the silk of her skin. Perfect child, a daughter for David. Our love now incarnated.

Beth was born into the world very early one Sunday morning. David could not be contacted until Monday morning, family obligations. I could not sleep all that Sunday, but lay weeping tears of tiredness, relief and gratitude. Outside the sun shone and the trees waved their greeting to the new soul. Through the windows streamed the healing heaven's blue. The red-roofed suburbs in their luxuriant green gardens stretched away over the hilly suburbs. Serenity and calm filled the room. Beth slept deeply, the sleep of the newborn, welcomed to the world of matter. Slept beside her mother, under her tender gaze. I longed to share these moments with David, my only sadness was in waiting a day for him.

That night I slept from early till late, healed my body in bliss, and awoke refreshed on Monday morning.

David and I rang each other at the same moment. A few seconds confusion as the call was transferred.

"You have a daughter" I laughed.

David felt the impact, breathed it in, his fatherhood.

"Come and meet her" I begged.

He arrived within the hour, bearing gifts, flowers, a card, still treasured.

He brought his essence, love to the core of his soul. His delight at the newborn, saw her sleepy face, her rounded arms and legs, the tiny fingers and toes complete with pearly nails. Felt her grasp, heard her cry, watched her suckle.

"The youngest baby I have ever held" he told me.

Tenderness flooded his being for Beth and me, transmitted in his kisses, and received in ecstasy.

Delight once experienced is permanent. In the earthly life however, it is overlaid by ever newer experiences, and becomes hidden from view.

Her sisters and brother took her into their hearts, held her and welcomed her. Although they accepted that Beth was to be brought up by Alice, she was always their sister too. Little Esther asked me if I would have another baby just for us. In my heart I so wanted to keep the child, but my decision, for whatever reason, was from my soul. It was a necessary path for me to follow, and I never questioned that. What grief was to come I would deal with. The interrupted motherhood, and for my children their sibling relationships would be solved delightfully, much later.

I was on the train, travelling away from my baby. The pain had entered my heart as the train lurched onwards into the darkness, away from Beth in her new home with Alice. I remembered above all the pain. I was bleeding from everywhere. I couldn't sleep, I had taken some pills, but they had just made my head fuzzy. Alice had tried to help me, but in the end the task was hopeless and she turned to the mechanics of driving me to the station and dropping me off to catch the train.

I had left Beth in her basket at Alice's home. As I looked down at my sleeping child, so contented, wrapped in her blanket, her fists curled against her face, I again felt the despair of love denied. I choked on my goodbye as the sword fell between us. She had been the pinnacle of my commitment to David. I wondered how could I be so stupid as to think this would not give me grief?

It felt like the ultimate violation, an amputation of the heart. I wanted to tear out the pain of loss and bereavement. The astral umbilical cord, normally disintegrating over seven years had been cut roughly and too soon, giving forth displacement in its premature separation. It felt that everything was lost, irrevocable. No tears would come, or just starting on their path, were stifled in my wretchedness.

The train pulled in to a station, doors banged, people hurried by, oblivious that inside the carriage a part of me was dying. Tormented by a million spears, self administered. Then we were on our way again as the train pulled out of the station, and I fell into a fitful doze, rolling from side to side in black despair.

Home again, I could just function, I could walk to the kitchen, could make a cup of tea. Last time I sat here, Beth was with me, curled up in my belly, playing contentedly, safe from the world. A world away. I craved to see her father, to feel his arms around me comforting me. The telephone rang, it was David. He would meet me at lunch time. I went to lie down, trying to sleep as I had been so restless on the train.

At lunch time I drove out to meet David, I saw his car parked in the street under a tree and ran over to it. I threw myself into his arms, the tears spurting from my eyes, my whole body shaking, sobbing. He stroked me, murmuring tender words, smoothing back my dishevelled hair. He was there for me, in this my greatest hour of need.

My breasts were engorged, no baby to suckle. I had tried to wean Beth gradually, but at such a young age it had not worked out. My milk was pushing out, looking for her lips, and aching.

I began to call Alice, begging her for news of Beth. David saw more than I did, saw that I was making impossible demands.

"Leave her alone," he counselled, "Alice has enough to deal with, a new baby, everything unfamiliar, let her learn her way, I know you aren't trying to interfere, but she is vulnerable, give her space." He was right of course. I tried to relax.

I saw an advertisement for a meeting of women who had given up their babies for adoption. Here I thought I would meet some people to talk to, to share the pain. But here the pain was not fresh, it had set solid during years of mishandling. Some of these women had never seen their babies, they had been taken away immediately after birth. An outrage. They often had tried for years to make contact with an adopting family. Sometimes it had worked out well, sometimes it hadn't worked at all. Their grief was still as strong as it had been twenty years ago. If I learnt anything from this encounter it was to keep crying my pain out, express it. Two years of normal grieving they said, the experts. Two years to soothe the rawness of the grief, but the wound would never heal.

David was nearly drowned in my tears. At first I wept daily, but after a week or so I became calmer and returned to work. My body gave up trying to make milk, accepted the vacuum and returned to normal functioning. After that I wept when something happened to stir up the pain. Premenstrual tension was a good time for an explosion of grief.

Returning to work was impersonal. Very few people mentioned my baby, one or two asked how I felt now, and my sorry face answered them with intellectualized impressions. My family likewise, had no ability to deal with grief, no words were said, no feelings ever shared. I felt an outcast. I wanted to visit Alice and Beth. David understood the situation better than I did.

"Let her be" he told me again, "she is insecure with you ringing. Perhaps she thinks you will take Beth away from her."

I understood this, but as my resolve to go through with my plan for Beth had never wavered, I was slow to realize that perhaps

Alice thought I intended to take Beth back. On my part, this decision was in order that there should be no lack of clarity in Beth's life, but clear borders between the responsibility of a normal mother, taken by Alice, and the responsibility of the love bond, the biological bond, which I myself would always honour. No amount of pain caused me to waver in my decision.

After two years of grieving, my tears dried up and I could talk about Beth happily enough. I stopped talking about having another baby. I received pictures from Alice, and we met occasionally, sharing the baby's growth between the two families. But my wound lay dormant, tender to the touch. My father with his accurate sensor occasionally touched the wound. My comment,

"Today is Beth's birthday" was attacked with

"She's Alice's child now, you've given her up so leave it alone!"

My mother once said that I had an ability to do hard things, and that I would not make old bones. And another time commented that it was obvious where Beth had come from, so there was no need to seek more acknowledgment than her looks.

The years passed. I was busy in my work and saw little of Beth. We lived far apart, visited seldom. One Christmas we met at the house of a relative. After the feast, the tiny Beth came up to me and tugged at my dress. I looked down and stroked the smooth hair.

"Sibyl, did I come out of your tummy?" asked Beth.

A wave of recognition flowed through me. These moments of truth sidled up to me unexpectedly then flashed in front of me. I looked down and smiled,

"Yes you did, and I was really happy about that".

I was always glad to see Beth but knowing of her existence was enough. I did not need or seek contact. When we did meet it was sweet. Sometimes David would take us out to lunch, even sweeter to see the father and daughter together.

I had always felt under an obligation to Alice, remembered that when Alice was a baby, my father, concerned with a sick wife, had said,

"Sibyl, take the baby round the block in the pram".

Mother Sibyl, not more than seven years old pushed the heavy pram up the hill, down the long side of the block, down the short side, then up the other long side and up again to the garden gate. I reached home relieved. As I entered the house my father called out

"Take her round six more times!"

Ughh, tough. I took on the mantle of obligation, too heavy for my young body, too great for my few years. Pushed and pushed. A couple passed us by as I toiled my way up the hill.

"Gee there's a baby in it!" said the woman. My unspoken response was

"Why else would I be doing this, it is no fun for me!"

When Alice was eighteen months old it was found that she had to have an operation and spend a long convalescence, immobile. This was hard for Alice, who was an active child. It was hard on the mother, who grieved for her baby's discomfort, spending hours of time rubbing the tender points on the fretful body. It was hard on the other children , the mother had less time for them. Alice was not easy to approach, and I at eight years old, felt myself rebuffed more than once, even felt guilty that I had made the child cry again. Alice made a clean recovery, and had become a fine sportswoman. We had had fairly separate upbringings. I left school when Alice began. Had married when Alice was still in school. I wondered why I had given Beth to Alice. It had been something I had felt strongly about. Was I trying to appease Alice still for a long ago childish rejection? Some truth in that. But not the whole truth. It would have been difficult for me to have continued to support my other children financially as well as to give a new baby the time she needed. I had absolute faith in Alice as a mother, and have never been disappointed.

Shared motherhood required silence of me, years of silence. Being there, as I had been with my older children. No words can be spoken to a rebellious teenager. Their mother must be there, supporting, loving, guiding only by her presence and her readiness to talk when the rare moment comes. An active time for a mother. Actively being there. Saying little. With Beth I observed, said nothing. Saw her infrequently. Waited for Beth to speak to me. Responded when asked. Sensitive, more sensitive now than I had been with the others, almost raw.

As I sat writing about these times my agony was reopened, and I went back to the beginning, to my first parting from Beth. I tried to look into my soul. I became a multitude of frantic butterflies, enclosed in a metal container, beating their wings in a frenzy, fluttering into each other and into the container itself. And every surface of the metal was molten, scorching their tiny feet and wings, so that they dared not rest.

Eventually a space appeared that was cooler, the butterflies swarmed to it. It was in the shape of the word GUILT. It is all my fault, I deserve this pain for daring to love a man I have no right to love. And there was more, I remembered my thought,

"If I am feeling so wounded, then Beth must be feeling the same. What a terrible start in life to give a child, it is all my fault thinking I could give away my baby without pain, that everything would just work out. A miserable mistake, to be borne throughout our long lives."

At last the butterflies had ceased their swarming, and stood resting in the guilt, absorbing the feeling of it, the hideous black despair, which was at least preferable to the molten frenzy. I let my mind wander over those long ago events, and at every point came to a new wave of realization. That Beth was not necessarily affected the same way as I had been. That love prevailed over us all, no matter what had happened. The mass of dark energy began to give way to the cooler blue-green hues of understanding. I wondered how I had carried this poison within my system for sixteen years, unsuspecting of its presence. It had showed its face in my kidney imbalance without giving any clue as to its origin. Now it was starting to release into my body for elimination, it would bring the familiar symptoms of headache and nausea. This time it was the worst it had ever been, the migraine unremitting, the nausea becoming vomiting, which continued even on my empty stomach. I became dehydrated and for a day I could not even keep water down.

I judged myself harshly as usual. I wanted to forgive myself, to treat myself to kindness and sweetness as David had done for me years ago. I took the wig and gown off the judge and marched him out of my chambers. I opened my roof and let heaven's healing blue flood my space, my rooms, furniture, clothes. The sun through the picture windows played over the surfaces of my desk, the green leaves of the tall trees casting dancing shadows on my face as I sat in the multihued light. So interesting to contemplate light, so mathematically correct, so close to God. The waves of gentleness wafted down in a fragrant perfume, the bird's song melded in with the soft light, as my body accepted my recognition of freedom.

Balance, so elusive. Worldly happiness, evanescent. I go to the source. Take love from the creator first, allow it to trickle down through the way stations in the spiritual world, through the realms of astral imagination, to us here in earthly forgetfulness. I remember each step, so that I am not tricked into shortcircuiting the process.

I was not strong enough in those days, and indeed still falter over that one. The child within is so needy of love. She clutches at my jacket, screaming at me to pay her attention. Reminded, I turn to her and stretch out my arms, as she throws herself at me, quivering with desperation and denial. Fill me, fill me! She cries. Don't leave me without love! I look at her history. Be strong, don't give in. Stop crying, stand up straight! When all she wants is a gentle hand to stroke her shoulders, to take away the pain of emptiness. She is content with very little, but cannot be content without that little. So I remember her, caressing the little one, holding her to my breast and letting her be there, to heal in peace.

I saw Beth as a swan, its graceful white neck arching forward over a patchwork of fields below, rivers, lakes, dark blurs of northern forest. Its wings each mother, beating in unison, perfect balance maintained. I on the right and Alice far away from me on the left, united in the rhythm and grace of shared motherhood. The purposeful swan was flying strongly, finding its own direction, supported by the mother wings. I had given up Beth in faith and love. I must hold this recognition. At this thought, I saw two hands come up, one from each wing, clasping each other over the back of the swan. Reassured, I looked again inside. I knew that I always did my best for everyone, absolute loyalty and honour in the family my code. I recognized many instances where I had been tempted to the contrary and had held firm. At that thought, two people emerged from the wings of the swan, turned to each other and embraced, two souls in a unison of purpose. The swan flew on unnoticing, determined and balanced towards its destiny.

Leah was home from abroad, we met in the botanical gardens by the lake for lunch. Spring sunshine streamed down, a gentle breeze tickled the leaves high above us. Across on the next rise, roosting bats swayed in unison.

We hugged. I had not seen her during my pregnancy. Since her divorce she had been working in Italy, and we had kept in touch with infrequent letters. Her eyes searched my face, sussing me out. I in turn saw a new radiance about her which intrigued me.

"You're sprung! Tell me about it," I said. She grinned, acknowledging my truth.

"It's special. I've met a new man. Different this time. We are loving each other and at the same time giving each other room to be ourselves. Not in each other's pockets as I've always done previously. So far it is working like a dream."

"You aren't living together then?"

"No, we meet every few days…." We chatted on munching a Greek salad between words. I considered David and I, we met daily. I wondered about a new level of freedom, to know love so strongly it was not necessary to meet so often. It reminded me of the relationship that was developing between Beth and myself. In spite of all the anxiety and sadness surrounding her and my sister when I had given her up, the thing that had carried me through those dark days was a deep knowing that this was the way ahead, everything was in supreme order, guided to its perfection by unseen hands.

The waitress brought our lemon tarts and coffee. We settled back to enjoy each other's revelations. Leah was saying

"You know, before we were together, I used to meet him sometimes at work. He called in occasionally from another branch and had to liaise with me. After several of these meetings I would go home and when I was resting, a feeling of deep love for him would come over me. All I would do was to be in the feeling. There was no urgency to contact him, or any of the usual jumpy things I do when I start to fall in love. It was so serene. Then the feeling would fade, and I would be back in everyday life, totally content with that. It took some months before we acknowledged this to each other and began meeting outside work. Now it is simply the joy of knowing his love. If I never saw him again it wouldn't matter. Love is, and it is eternally!"

I took a deep breath as I realized how closely this mirrored Beth and me. Leah was taken by my joy and pain as I started to spill out my story to her. The parallels in our understanding of love drew us closer than we had ever been.

"But there's one thing that puzzles me, why I felt so absolutely drawn to give my child to Alice. It would not have been impossible for me to have kept her. Difficult yes, but nothing is impossible."

Leah's eyes moved to my left, staring into the distance, I relaxed and waited for the conversation to resume. Eventually Leah spoke.

"I'm picking up a scenario, in England, maybe Bath, Jane Austen's times. You had a sister then too, called Hannah, but your roles were reversed. Hannah was the older, more serious sister, as you are now, and you were younger, pretty and a great favourite with the boys." I grinned, remembering how I felt almost staid beside Alice's vivacious personality.

"Hannah kept the books for your father and helped out in the house." I gulped again; this was so often my role.

"As Hannah was the elder sister, it was anticipated in that society that she would marry first. There had been an expectation that she would marry the eldest son of a neighbouring family, the parents had had this wish since the children were born, although there was no formal engagement. But all that went out the window when the lad fell in love with you. Society's rules were flouted when you and he married, and had a contented life together. Hannah was left out in the cold, with the household tasks and the books. Imagine how she must have felt, her secure future undermined by the innocent love of the happy couple. So now, to make amends for this is a high priority for you. And one further twist to this story, the lad whom you married in those times was the being who came to you as Beth. So you have done the one thing which has totally erased this karma for you. You have given your precious child to a sister in need of a child. You have done it in love, with grace, and you have borne the consequences for yourself."

I was astounded. What a neat signing off. I had not imagined that anything like this could be true – had up till now had no experience of 'past life' stories. But what grabbed my attention was the intricacy of the detail, and how it felt 'YES'. The gaps in my understanding had been filled, and as Leah had said, the slate was clean.

꧁ PART 5 ꧂

PACK ICE

Sirius flickers, and the ice freezes over. Good intentions, honest toil are lost in an instant. No movement forward is possible, the direction is now faulty. Go back, go back. My new way is undiscovered as I struggle to see without light, and stumble in the darkness.

I HAVE BEEN A PERSON who does not respect rules for their own sake. I've been ready to rewrite my own rule book as I have seen the old codes cease to serve my situation. It seems to me necessary that life is so, and that we are ready to change not only our behaviour, but our personal rules whenever the situation demands. But suddenly at work I found myself in the way of someone else's beliefs. This was much more difficult, to find my own codes breached by someone in authority. Which way should I jump? I could not follow my own conscience and that of authority, and I had to acknowledge the legitimacy of the authority. The events which unfolded gave me the opportunity to observe myself as I experienced the pain of these changes.

Our Environmental Science Department had been set up by our first professor with David as second in command. Not only was the school good academically, but there was a loyalty which flowed to everyone, coming through the professor down to the last student. People took a pride in being able to give assistance to the students, and to each other, and it showed.

The founding professor had resigned, and a new man had been appointed. This had happened a couple of years before Beth had been born, but time had passed and now it was two years after her birth. The new professor was interested in research into agricultural chemicals, thus endearing him to the Vice Chancellor and explaining his selection. But this was an Environmental Science faculty. The ecologists amongst us were orientated towards balance in nature, and would have done many things before introducing such chemicals into the fragile ecology of Australian nature. However, no pleas or suggestions from the staff were listened to, and Professor Bullgate was appointed. The staff, receiving mixed messages from their leaders and each other did not know where to place their loyalties.

The Environmental Science course had been set up with great care and attention, had been assembled piece by piece, by trial and error over many years. Suddenly the course was up for grabs, and little thought was being given to the suitability of the changes. I had difficulty finding room to teach my classes as Professor Bullgate's staff had moved equipment and personnel into the teaching laboratory. When I asked for time and space I found that I was on shaky ground. The staff did not support my views and accused me of being paranoid. I became apprehensive for the first time that the renewal of my contract, due in a year or so, may not be approved.

Then I met the president of the Staff Association. In the course of conversation I found that she would support my request for a tenured position when the next renewal was due. It seemed that I had amassed a number of goody points, a list of publications, length of service and the holding of office in a professional society being amongst them. So I wrote my *curriculum vitae* once more and went to see the dean. I requested that I be given tenure, and when he looked dubious, I mentioned that the staff association were backing me, and added for good measure that there were no female members of staff. Equal Opportunity was an issue in those days of the early eighties. My answer came back quite soon. Yes, there would be a tenured position offered, it would have to be advertised but this was a mere formality. The person holding the position was almost certain to be chosen. I ignored the fact that by now I found my position in the department almost untenable with all the friction which surrounded me. The devious Professor Bullgate was apt to plan the removal of staff rather than to give them the support that they needed, and this situation made it impossible to feel secure. The staff member concerned would be the last person to be told. And by now I had been fifteen years in the faculty. I had quite simply been there long enough.

At the same time David was receiving his own cues that time was running out in the department. Two of the final year students had offered to raffle a car to augment one of the Professor's research projects. Most of the staff were delighted at the generosity of the students, but David saw further and was horrified at the position in which the students had placed themselves. He explained to me

"They are having difficulty in selling enough tickets. Their final year is really busy, and now they will have to divert their time to selling tickets to break even with the price of the car. If they don't do well at the end of the year, they could ask for special consideration on the basis of their involvement with the raffle. And this brings them close to a situation of bribery, as the money is to be donated to the school. In any case, departmental funds are the business of the University, or the granting bodies, not the students."

Some of the staff thought that David was insensitive to the undoubted good intentions of the students. Others told me that he was bitter and twisted. Relationships within the department soured, cliques formed and gossiped poison.

It was time to leave the department, but first life had a treat in store for David and me. David was again due to take his sabbatical leave, and I too could take a sabbatical at a reduced rate. The previous year I had visited a colleague in Switzerland, and had asked about the possibility of a joint project. My colleague Janina had been enthusiastic, and had applied to a Swiss granting body for money to finance my stay.

Mia and Sam had left school and they would stay on in the house and it was only for me to arrange support for Esther.

Before I left Australia, I went to one last departmental meeting. I sat amongst my colleagues and heard them discussing work for the coming term. It was a fine winter's day, they had gathered in the professor's room, and for that day the sourness was absent. We drank a glass of wine together as they fumbled through their papers, and completed the agenda. Finally Professor Bullgate asked the group about the advertisement for my position, how should it be worded, and the meeting approved a formula which was satisfactory to me. The group smiled their farewells to me and as my eyes sought each familiar face the voice in my head said 'Which one of you will betray me?'

I had arranged to buy a small Renault in France, and we set off on a month of travels to various laboratories and talk-giving before we were to take up our positions and begin our projects. Here we were, on our holiday of a lifetime, we could stay in hotels together, eat out, drive to exotic cities. We were blissfully happy. However, there were sometimes restrictions to our freedom.

In Prague David attended a conference, and as a part of it we were to go to the opera. David was in a tight-lipped mood of wife-terrors. He sat with his colleagues, anxious that I shouldn't meet them in case they took stories home to Australia. I climbed to the very top of the opera house to my seat alone, feeling excluded and angry. The opera 'The Bartered Bride' was beautiful, but I could barely enjoy it. Perhaps I felt I was a bartered bride. I stomped downstairs during the intermission and walked up to David, who reluctantly introduced me to another man from the conference. I hated myself but could not see how to change either the situation or myself. David reserved, I gritting my teeth. Here we were in the middle of Europe, on the other side of the Iron Curtain and we might have been in the next room to his wife. Would he ever relax? As ever these situations took their own course, fading out gradually, I later apologizing for my temper, David saying no its my fault, then the gladdening of lovemaking and everything was back to normal. We rocked our way through Europe, happier than we had ever been or would be together on earth.

We explored Paris and Berlin, drank the cappuccino of Bolzano in the luscious outdoor market, and drove into Padua. David said

"There is a chapel here, I saw it in 'The Ascent of Man' on television, the walls are painted by Giotto."

We walked into another world. Giotto, the Arena Chapel. I had learned about Giotto in school. The first painter to use perspective was all I remembered. Certainly that was there. But it was Mary's life which shone down from the walls, her birth and life with her parents. Mary, the role model for all young girls, had changed her significance for me. Now I saw her as another woman, who had suffered every type of anguish, experienced every type of love. Her parents, Joachim and Anna had dreams and angelic visitations also. I looked at the stylized faces and wondered what they thought of their dreams and visions. In the bible it seemed to be taken for granted that people were given messages in dreams, but now it was out of favour. To talk about a dream these days was to invite ridicule, unless your name was Carl Jung. However, I was open to trying to interpret the world that they portrayed. In biblical days they were important enough to be recorded, often bringing warnings and being acted upon. The annunciation of Jesus' birth, the visitation of Mary to her sister Elizabeth, the flight into Egypt to escape Herod's wrath, were all mediated by visions or dreams, now thought to be in the realm of the impossible. I had heard my own interior voice several times. The first conscious time I had heard it was when I was twenty, driving down the street on my way home to my parents' house. I was excited by my reading at that time, I had been given CS Lewis' books, and had plunged into his world. I was fascinated by his logical way of putting experiences together. I revelled in his account of the Christian life, more down to earth, or perhaps easily lived than the more traditional approach of my church. As I drew near our gateway suddenly I heard a voice in my head asking me a question,

"Do you want the spiritual life or the material life?" My answer rushed in, no hesitation

"Oh, the spiritual life." I saw the infinity of what I had decided upon, there was no doubt in my mind. Then it had seemed that my spiritual life had vanished, for I had married, had children, divorced, lived with David. But when I thought that way, I immediately knew deep inside that life is long, the spirit infinite, all will happen in time.

I said to David, "Do you ever wonder about the spiritual life?"

He looked a little perplexed,

"Not often, but sometimes. For example when Beth was born I found myself wondering where such beauty and joy had come from, why I didn't experience it more often. But I can see that you do, I sometimes think you should go back to your religion."

"Spirituality is without the rules and regulations of religions" I replied. We walked on to the next picture, the nativity of Jesus.

Now looking at Mary's devoted face as she looked down adoringly at her infant I entered into a reverie of Mary's reactions to all this. She was a young girl, she had the same womanly feelings as other women. The passion for a child I could understand. The truth of the dream world? How strongly it impacted at times. I still remembered in minute detail the times when spirit had contacted me. As if chipped into the rock of my being. Unerasable. And not only that, but almost iridescent in its content. Fluttering in from a colourful world and just as suddenly vanishing again. Another consciousness, so difficult to grasp from the earth plane. I did not know how to enter it at will. Was this the 'spiritual life' that I had asked for? And Mary, how had she come to receive such honours? The gospel said she prayed a lot. I found prayer in some ways distasteful. In the church people were always miserable sinners, whinging for forgiveness. Too bad, I thought, for the self confidence required to function. At school we had gone to meditation every morning, sitting in the Lady chapel and looking up at the young Mary in her pink dress, sitting so serenely in her own meditation. This made more sense to me, a sort of reverie where one thought led to another, gently passing through the mind with an overmantle of harmony with all that is. One of the schoolgirls had said to the nun

"But my mother doesn't meditate, she wouldn't have time." The nun answered

"Meditation becomes a way of life, once you learn to go into that space you don't have to sit down and *do* it, it happens of itself."

This made sense to me also, this was how I felt when I walked through the streets near my home, looking at the gardens. I would sniff the roses as they brushed past my cheeks, smile at the gracious trees spreading their shade for me, and laugh at the voracious insects, so intent on eating, eating, eating, as if the last great famine was just around the corner. The colours intensified, the reds and blues seared my being, yellows sparked my optimism, orange brought vibrancy, and the deep greens spread peace through my soul. This felt to be a much more effective meditation than sitting in a chair reading words from a book. That had a place too, at certain times, but to me did not compare with the joy of gardens. Perhaps Mary too had had her own special way of meditating. But why were they all so serious? Did they ever laugh in the bible? Too bad for them if they didn't! I caught David's eye with a mischievous twinkle, and gave him a hug.

"Just something to help us lighten up!"

*

We entered the old anatomy theatre in the University of Padua sparking a remembrance of past academia. The forerunners of David's role as an academic and researcher seemed to be assembled here.

Astral eyebrows were raised, heads turned at the entrance of these travellers from the antipodes. The lecturer perhaps Vesalius, the Belgian anatomist, a professor here in the sixteenth century. The empty spaces were peopled by the scholars of centuries, delving into the function of the organs of the human body. In the times when this anatomy theatre had been built it had been illegal to dissect bodies. Was it out of respect for God's temple or because man may not pry into the handiwork of the Lord? Or because it conflicted with current ecclesiastical beliefs? The theatre was a circular space with galleries up the wall where students could stand and look down to the large oval table in the small circular space in the centre below. The stairs were outside the theatre, and one entered each gallery through a side doorway. The table was constructed with a trapdoor in the top, which could be operated in case of a police raid, and the body and dissecting paraphernalia would disappear into a space under the floor, and there would be left the lecturer sitting at a clean table, speaking to his audience. Police raids in those days threatened death, Vesalius himself had been condemned to death for body snatching and dissection, his sentence commuted to a pilgrimage to Jerusalem during which he had died. Galileo had spent years in prison and house arrest for his scientific belief that the earth was not the centre of the universe. I had read Bertolt Brecht's play, 'The Life of Galileo' and had seen how deftly Brecht had portrayed the ecclesiastical authorities. They were so filled with their false belief systems that they refused to observe the planets through Galileo's telescope, and could not use their logic to understand his claims. Michelangelo had made deals with the body collectors to let him have corpses for dissection, unbeknownst to the authorities. The ultimate authority in those days was the pope. How things had changed. And yet the core was the same. The sad comedy of the efforts of authorities to preserve the *status quo* was unaltered. And people still sought academic truth, it pushed through them like a charging rhinoceros, disregarding social conventions and precepts. They congregated in the places of learning, many of them. Often the younger ones were more dedicated to the pursuit of academic excellence, being free from the pressing social obligations of spouse, mortgage payments and children. Older academics were often hampered by their seeking for tenured positions in the university, or excessive writing for grant applications. It got in the way of an individual quest for knowledge. And yet David was able to continue his research, he read widely, almost every evening spending time with his papers and books. He would often intuitively know the direction that research would take, fascinating me with his predictions which I would see fulfilled in the years which followed. I was more technical in my approach to my science, and would spend hours calculating, collating and expressing data in various forms until I perceived a pattern in the numbers. I liked to talk to David about his reading, but loathed to have to do it myself. A session in the library for me usually meant sleep or distraction. But together we made a good team, with our dovetailing interests and skills.

Here in the ancient anatomy theatre I felt in my place amongst the scientific community assembled there. Everyone has their own niche, be it reading, experiment, calculation, or pondering. Or their specific combination of talents to develop. I felt the tradition of academic excellence which pervaded the old woodwork, dark railing supported by carved balustrade which made up each gallery. I could feel the enthusiasm of the audience, the erudition of the lecturers. Copernicus had studied medicine here, Gabriele Falloppio had described the fallopian tubes between ovaries and uterus, his student Girolamo Fabrici had become professor and had taught William Harvey, who in turn had discovered the circulation of the blood. And how many other well-known names? We soaked in their presences.

*

Suddenly the car turned for Switzerland, the travels were over for now and the projects must begin. My friend Janina had found me an apartment in a house with an old couple, because she thought I would enjoy living with a family. But the old families of Geneva had a rigid code of morality which didn't include approval for David and my love affair. I stayed at this house for a month before David spent a night there, and then returned the next day to find a note on my bed accusing me of prostitution, and giving me a week's notice. An impassioned scene in the old-fashioned sitting room with the owner of the house followed, his wife avoiding the conflict skulked in her bedroom. I defended myself in abominable French, shouting my outrage at being judged by someone so meaningless to me. The old man stepped backwards into the safety of his traditions, ducked my wrath. I marched upstairs to David, enraged.

"He says I have to leave next week"

"Why don't you leave now, this isn't a suitable place for you, and never has been?"

How was it that David kept his perspective and saw the whole picture so often whilst I was attacked by trivia? Together we packed up all of my belongings into the car, thrust the key under the door, and drove to Berne, arriving after midnight.

As I continued to flout the conventions of society, society continued to rise up and slap me in the face. There was no escape , I was out of step with a large number of people. It remained for me to seek the company of those with whom I could find a resonance, to move away from the others, and leave it at that.

I travelled to and from Geneva daily in the train, a two-hour journey. My colleague looked at me in surprise as I entered on Monday morning.

"Your landlady phoned me, said you had left, she complained about the smell of your cooking. I wondered where you had gone."

"To Berne with David. I didn't know what else to do ."

"Is there any hope I could smooth things out?"

"No, I felt uncomfortable there."

"Then we'll advertise for another place, where will you stay in the meantime?

"In Berne"

"It's too far to travel each day"

"It will have to do for now".

So began the most productive of my time in Switzerland, Janina and worked together, expanded our science and published papers.

Two weeks after I had moved to Berne, an answer to our advertisement for an apartment was received, and I moved into a one bedroom flat close to the railway station and the telephones. This was much better, it was still within walking distance to the university, and near the centre of the city. I spent much time on the phone, talking to the children or to David. I developed my weekly program, spending long weekends with David in Berne where I calculated out my results for the week, wrote my reports and read the literature, and my week in Geneva where I performed my experiments. On the weekend proper, David and I walked the streets of Berne. A quaint city, old fountains standing in the middle of the streets, painted and glowing in gold, reds and blues. The Chindlifresser was my favourite, a giant shown gathering and eating children, the worst bogeyman for a naughty child. We saw movies, ate fondue at restaurants, bought food to cook at home, and then made love and spent the night together.

Our relationship had become deeply contented. Interference was minimal, no neighbours, no one to pry, freedom to live together.

David sat in the driver's seat of his train, steered straight ahead by the parallel rails. The train represented the core of his being. *His* direction, *his* wishes, *his* likes and dislikes. His ideas of love were restricted and he was not able to incorporate them into the fabric of his professional life. His personal life was one rail of the train track, and his professional life the other. Try as he might, he could never see them coming together, he stared down the long track ahead, peering into the distance, but no resolution came into sight. His personal life with his wife had become so devoid of energy that the train could not have continued its lopsided journey without intervention. The brakes on the 'personal life' side were in danger of seizing up and stopping the train. I had become a part of his personal life, balancing the whole. At the same time I fuelled the train, shovelling the coal of my energy into his boiler and making it possible for him to speed onwards.

If there was one time in his life when he had seen the parallel tracks shimmer and a bridge start to be built between them, it was during the time he spent with me in Switzerland. Love entered his life at that time in a way counter to his old beliefs. His upbringing had said, 'The man goes to work and brings home the money, the wife takes care of the house. Love is at home with the wife and family, it doesn't have anything to do with one's profession'. And this was how his life with his wife had been. I had always refused to take that role, neither with James nor with David. In front of me lay a long straight road of life. David started to understand how love could penetrate life. He saw my successful project taking shape, saw my discipline and dedication to my profession and to him. There was no separation in me. I invited him to join me on my journey. He drifted towards me. Now we were living together, there were no time barriers. Our days stretched out endlessly, inviting experimentation.

We sat together after our evening meal, reading, looked up and caught each other's eyes.

"Shall we go to bed early?"

"And see what happens?"

Echoing the movement of our souls, our bodies moved gracefully together. We learnt to love for hours, poised on the edge of the precipice, careful not to take the final step, but skirting around it, taking another path, prolonging our enjoyment, waiting in rapture. Always a new trail to be explored, new blossoms to be kissed, exotic birdsong to be heard, unknown brilliances to be caressed and honey to be tasted. Our bodies twined like vines, sprouted new tendrils of affection, green leaves of happiness, radiant flowers of bliss. Refreshing dew collected on the delicate buds to be licked clean. Our souls echoed our satisfaction, pouring fresh water onto thirsting soil. The springs of hope gushed into our lives. He kissed me, all over, his lips teasing the opening of crushed petals. I took his fingers in my mouth, fondling their divinity with my tongue, burying my face in his golden hair. Cradled his head on my breasts, rocking him gently. I bent backwards, offering myself to my man. He reached into the depths of me, my body and spirit one. Gave the gift of joy through my shuddering body to the end of my being. Took in return the comfort of my kisses, the caressing arms, the softness of my flesh into his own vibrating body. Then precious rest, contentment, legs everywhere, arms spread wide, delicate words of endearment. *Repose à ma tendresse*.

David began to become lulled and accepting in our relationship. He relaxed and swam in the drunkenness of ecstasy. He almost forgot the thorny cactus invading the garden, creeping under the lush vegetation, until he felt its prickles. He was constantly jerked back to his reality by a phone call from Australia.

I was happy and unhappy. I felt the movement of our souls, and the new harmony of our love. It made any intervention all the more difficult to bear, and as the months of our sabbatical flew by, the time for parting drew close.

My car had been bought on a contract which obliged me to resell it to the same firm where I had bought it. In Paris. We planned another trip. We visited the Art Gallery at Nancy to see the paintings of Georges de la Tour. His paintings enchanted me. Often one, two or three figures, illuminated by a single candle. Their faces had a supreme depth, understated emotion, centred. My favourite was 'The Newborn' a mother held the candle for her daughter and the infant, who lay sleeping in his mother's arms in the middle of the painting. I was reminded of Beth, never far from my heart.

We travelled on to the killing fields of Verdun, reading the information boards by the headlights of the car as by now the sun had set. I felt close to the soldiers who had died in the First World War, I had read of the battles, learned their plight and mourned their passing. I became aware once more of my name, Sibyl, the one who could walk on both sides of the underworld. I had read in the works of Rudolf Steiner of spirit people who sought out the souls of soldiers after they had been killed in battle, and took them through their fear to places of safety in the realms of death. I shivered. And as I stood there a story floated into my head.

I had become a South African soldier, fighting for the allies in the First World War, in the trenches in France. Surrounded by the dead or soon to be dead (of the South Africans, two thirds were killed on one day, on the Somme). I looked down at my hands, holding the rifle instead of my pen, death flowing where there were once stanzas of beauty. Unbearable, that I should shoot to kill an unknown innocent, probably as afraid as I was. It was too much, I refused to do it. They must not make me kill a man. It was my decision, I was forced to take it at that moment. Desertion was impossible, I couldn't take that route. They'd shoot you for that anyway, and besides you would have the waiting, the suspense. Best take it on the chin, do it now. I put down the rifle and stood up. Pieces of metal were flying around as usual, my mates yelled at me to take cover, 'You idiot, lie down, What the hell's he up to?' I thought of home, the grassy plains of the veldt, my mother's gentle sitting room with the lace curtains filtering in the sunlight, my rosy-cheeked sisters, my poetry. I longed for them, for help from somewhere. Help, in the shape of a piece of shrapnel, flew into my eye, knocked me down but didn't kill me. I had failed as a soldier, and now I had even failed at killing myself. Everyone was angry with me, I had caused an incident, I had to be carried to the dressing station by grumbling mates, it would have to be investigated. The sergeant was screaming my guilt at me. At the dressing station the nurses, who didn't know my cowardice, told me how lucky I was, getting metal in the eye and suffering only minor damage. My shame at letting down my mates grew. I looked out at the nurses, in long white uniforms, flat-chested aprons, enamel buckets with cloths, rows of beds with groaning men, or still forms. These were the people I had refused to support. They will never cleanse my shame, it would take a million enamel buckets. Eventually, after all the rumpus I was sent home, a dishonourable discharge. Not good enough to kill people, or not good enough to defend my country? Very, very deep inside I remembered that I had refused to kill innocent men. It was an impossible sentiment, a traitorous thought. Unsolvable ambiguity. Back with my family there was not enough love to heal me. My self confidence was at zero, no feelings, no poetry. My life was over, my spirit broken, and soon I died. Now I had to wait to be reborn into a suitable time when pacifism is honoured, and war is a disgrace. It could take a long time.

This story felt familiar, did I imagine it, was it another past life story or from the collective unconscious that Carl Jung used to speak of? I had no way of knowing.

Later that evening I told David my story of the soldier, and the story of my name. To my surprise he looked at me and replied gravely.

"I have always thought you were attracted to the spiritual, and the life beyond the grave. I think you should take up your interest. Do some research, read up on it. And I can tell you something else about your story of the soldier. On the ABC a few years ago I heard a program where they hypnotized people and found that many of them had memories of past times, and that each memory had its own particular reason for its existence, within the present life of the person. The events did not seem to be random. The people who made the program were researching past lives, but I'm not convinced they found evidence that would persuade me. All the same, there is something in the consciousness which gives rise to these stories."

"I knew when the soldier put down his rifle and stood up that I remembered that feeling. James and I had been arguing, he was trying to stop me from going out, and was almost violent. I couldn't get past him, he barred my way. I suddenly started yelling at him, 'OK hit me, do what you want, I don't care what you do to me!' It was the same as how the soldier felt, a sort of final despair."

"That is what I meant about these memories, or stories, whatever they are, not being random. There is that point of contact within your life. And if you are interested in working with the dying, perhaps one day you will do that too. There is always scope for voluntary work once the children are grown up."

*

We had occasion to look once again upon death during our travels. We took the train across Europe through Belgium to Germany. Near Liège the train stopped and the loud-speaker announced that there had been an accident.

The two occupants of the compartment besides David and I were conversing in such a way as to make me squirm. A young Englishman, the most puffed up and pompous imaginable was lording it over a middle aged French commercial traveller. A short plump man not even understanding fully the insults being thrown in his direction. David sat dozing, and I escaped into the corridor and stared out of the window. The train moved off slowly after ten minutes or so, and passed another train which was stationary. I had always been aware of the fact that train wheels were lethal. Imbued with the spirit of Anna Karenina, I always looked under trains, ghoulishly expecting to see bits of bodies or congealed blood on the undercarriage. And this time I was not disappointed. At the end of the train I saw first the new pig-skin brief case, flung aside. Then a bloody mass of minced thorax, lungs perhaps. It was so bright red. A trail of blood. Then further on, the lower half of a man in a dark suit, severed neatly just above the waist. The train officials stood waiting for the ambulance, one walked along the other train track, no doubt tallying up the bits.

I had always dreaded seeing what I saw now. I had been afraid of dead bodies forever, had seen dead and decaying sheep on Paddy's farm. I had imagined all the horrible things which are described in detective novels to be haunting my nightly passage to the bathroom. And here I was looking at it. What surprised me most was my reaction. Almost no reaction. Was I dislocating my emotions again?

"It's just a piece of meat" I thought, "Why have I been worrying about that for so long?"

I felt I had been liberated from a primal fear, in looking on death and accepting the inevitability of the physical mess, with the knowledge that life, whilst still existing, had moved on. Another step along my road to Sibyl had been taken.

I had put in my application for my reinstatement to my job before I had left Australia. After that I had heard nothing, nothing at all. The months in Geneva flew past, and eventually I received a handwritten, shabby letter from the Professor saying obliquely that I had not been given the appointment in the first instance. I for some reason, thought that this was not the end of the story. At the same time, David received a phone call from one of our supporters, a secretary, who poured out a story of intrigue and machinations in departmental politics that brought the Borgias out of hiding. The direction of policy had changed, and I was the first sacrifice. The chemical herbicide buffs were marching onwards in the Environmental Science Faculty, sweeping away all opposition. David rang me, alarmed. I was almost in denial, not comprehending the seriousness of events.

"But you will have to address this, ring the Staff Association, get some support. This man has gone crazy, he has no respect for you as a member of staff."

I suddenly felt sick, as the prospects of no job, no contact with David, and no money leapt simultaneously onto my horizon. The thought of spending hours toiling in boring employment, working for someone I didn't care for, simply to provide food for the children was unthinkable.

I put the situation into the care of the Staff Association and tried to put it out of my mind. Meanwhile David's wife had joined him in Berne and I was relegated to my position as 'the other woman'. My unexpressed misery gave me a bad cold. I soldiered on, wearily working out my last days. Sniffled my way through the old quarter of Geneva to the university, clinging desperately to the opening that my soul had known. In vain now, for it had finished. Evolution is only upwards, and if it can't continue in its old way it must burst, sometimes painfully, through a new opening. I had six weeks left to complete my project, and fly home to Australia. I wept miserably, flushing out my cold with my tears.

I had one more ambition to fulfil before I left Switzerland, and this was to write up my work in a form ready for publication. I had still more experiments to perform, rounding out the statistics, but I had a strong intention that it would be written up before I departed. The weeks plodded by.

Easter came and went, there was only one Sunday left before I would fly out. Sunday was always my day for writing. I would rise early, eat breakfast and tidy everything off the kitchen table. Then I would lay out my papers, tables and graphs already prepared, take a big block of new paper and write a summary, indicating where the tables and graphs fitted into the text. Then I would write the whole paper, pouring endless cups of tea, sometimes pacing up and down briefly, then sitting down and continuing to the end. I had written several papers in this fashion. It seemed to be the end result of weeks, sometimes months of an inner activity of mulling over the subject material. I would find myself thinking over the intricacies of the work in bed as I dozed off, or when I was walking in the street. It would begin to permeate my being until suddenly a free Sunday would present itself, and the complete story would be written down. This final Sunday in Switzerland was like that. The powers that organized my life gave me the opportunity, and I wrote my experimental story. Another chapter for my thesis was complete.

David rang me sometimes, or I would ring him at work. One glorious day before I left he travelled down to Geneva in the train, and we spent the afternoon reenacting our past exploits in bed.

Then I flew sadly home to Australia, torn in two in the joy of meeting my children and the teeth-gritting experience which awaited me at work.

*

The day before I arrived in Australia my delightful colleagues at the university had removed my appointment from the books. The staff at the meeting before I had left Australia had actually all betrayed me. The professors avoided speaking to me as far as possible. No one admitted responsibility.

"It was just an administrative necessity" I was told. People from the other departments spoke of their surprise at my plight.

"It was all signed and delivered before we knew anything about it. I'm sorry, but no opportunity was given to say anything." Gossip flew around the campus.

"She doesn't really want a career, she only wants to work with David!"

"The students have criticized her classes."

"Her demonstrators don't think she works hard enough."

It was really coming out, old grievances, people wishing to climb into my place, excuses, passing the buck. But it never came out into the open. Someone would poke his head out from behind a screen, make an accusation, then disappear again behind his protection. My ally the secretary talked to me, damning the leaders of the department. Told me even more incriminating evidences about who had sat on which committees, and had been involved in self-seeking skullduggery. I meanwhile was severely jetlagged, not sleeping, and coming to work each day for a fresh onslaught of the horrors. Rachel in the staff association had done her best. She was genuinely amazed and disgusted by the gossip which had reached even the Arts Faculty and her ears. She discussed a few alternatives with me. Eventually Rachel persuaded the Vice Chancellor to appoint an enquiry to look into the debacle.

I was teaching my classes, I had to work out six months, the nominal time of my sabbatical before I was allowed to leave. I needed that time and perhaps more to finish writing my PhD. David wrote to me, wanting to know what was happening. He would be home in a month now, at least I had that to look forward to. I struggled on, all the departments of my life asking for a spirit which I had lost. Deep inside me I saw that there were powers at work which I didn't understand. 'One door closes, another door opens' was a maxim which floated into my head. For the first time I looked at my job, not to the joy of its beginning, but what it had developed into. It wasn't what I wanted any more. I wouldn't mind not doing it. Actually, I would rather be anywhere than in the building with those colleagues. But I had a reasonable income, and it was always completely used up with the three children, the mortgage and the car. What to do about money. Panic? Not this time! If I could fight a good case through the Vice Chancellor's enquiry they might give me some extra money, that was worth fighting for. I started to prepare my case.

David came home, choking with rage at the treachery of the department. He criticized everyone and every decision. Gave his lectures with his temper clamped down. The conditions which had been difficult before we had left for sabbatical had now become untenable. He resolved to leave with me if it came to that.

Brightness came into my life as I strode down the middle of the corridors, clothed in uncharacteristically gorgeous clothes. I held my head high, and scorn flashed from my eyes. I dared people to come out and say publicly what had filtered back to me from across the campus. Some people remained my friends. Some people avoided my gaze. Others were unwittingly implicated. They would be noted and forgiven at a much later date. Some, also the mistreated, were constant allies. It was a scene that demanded to be left behind.

The Vice Chancellor's enquiry worked the opposite way from how I had hoped it would. When I was criticized, I had hoped to be able to present evidence refuting the criticism. Instead the woman heading the enquiry called in students and demonstrators who had worked with me and asked them if they had made any complaints, stirring up a cauldron of innuendo. The whole situation became unbearable to me. People were called in one by one to give their opinions of me, openly discussing the enquiry, sometimes telling me how it had been. I was called too, to explain the case which I had presented in written form. This too was dreadful. I felt judged by these women, who wouldn't put a foot wrong in society, whereas I was apparently caked in sewage up to my knees. I got a migraine after one of these encounters, and David sent me home to bed. My greatest relief was David's continued support which could cut through all anxiety. In his anger, our love could not continue as it had been. Evolution cannot go backwards. The joy that we had known was gone. But we still met at home, still made love and tried to recapture old moments.

The enquiry gave its decision, I must go, no change of decision, no compensation, not even an apology were warranted. The consolation prize was an extra two months employment, as the presentation of the enquiry's findings had been so delayed. I felt dirty and dishonoured. I had hoped to be able to show that I had been badly treated by the university, and now the shame seemed to rest on my shoulders instead.

Looking back as I write about these times, it seems a jumble of mixed goals. David and I had aims relating back to the founding of the department, the training of students, and loyalty to them and to the other staff members. It was inevitable that the old ways must crumble with the development of the school. The new professors came in with their personal agendas, they must command their own loyalty, and the new staff gave it, even most of the old staff. David and I could not. It was clear that a clash of principles was involved between me and the authorities, and the only way out was for me to leave with dignity. But I took with me an understanding of how badly people can feel under these conditions, how careful one must be when the rules are changed, and the amount of compassion that is required to help others through the transition.

*

My work was drawing to a close. The PhD was ready for submission. David had decided to take the rest of his four months sabbatical leave at the University in Adelaide. I would go too, it was close enough to home that I would not have to make new arrangements for the children, and I could take one last holiday with David away from prying eyes. It would give us a chance to cool off after six months of purgatory. I had leave accrued, also long service leave, and my superannuation would be paid out in a lump sum.

David was down the street one day and met an old friend from his schooldays. She worked at another university, where David had many colleagues.

"There's a lectureship advertised in our department, did you know?" she said.

"I thought it would have been filled long ago" he answered, "Is it still open?"

"Yes, it is."

David told me he would ring up and inquire about it. The Professor he knew well, all on the old-boy network. He talked to me again.

"He said I could have the job if I want it. And he has a job which would be suitable for you too, if you're interested. Send in your resumé. Of course we have to go through the formalities, but it sounds promising."

The universe had begun to breathe out good things again. Its object had been achieved, David and I were out of the old jobs which had become so constricted, and into a new field still working together.

*

Adelaide was hot. I had a lot of library work to do, which I disliked. I spent much time sleeping there. But to my credit, I wrote my best paper yet, for a prestigious American journal. As I wrote it, taking pieces from my thesis, including new data, biochemical assays that David had done in Switzerland, I felt it was good. It expressed my experiments as a mathematical model, and tied up the ends with a big bow around the whole idea. It was accepted with no trouble and only minor corrections. My PhD too was passed by all examiners on their first reading. I was pleased. I had taken the view that if the chapters were already published in refereed journals, that there would be no trouble in having the thesis accepted as a whole. And it proved to be the case. Hard work was paying out its dividends finally. In my work life at least.

In my personal life with David, things were not as rosy as they had been in Switzerland. We were battle-scarred and weary, the year had taken away our *joie de vivre* and we were as yet unskilled in dealing with emotional wounds. This meant that we were at a disadvantage with each other, the closeness that we had known in Europe could not return until the wounds were dressed properly, and this took me many years. David would never attempt it.

I had always promised myself that when I had completed the PhD that I would take better care of my body, which I had neglected for so many years. I started to learn Tai Chi.

Eventually David began to believe that there would be no new job, as it was so long since we had heard any word from the Professor. But when David rang, he was assured that there was no problem. He should take up his new position in April. I too should come for an interview, there was another applicant for my position, nothing to worry about though. I travelled to the city and met my employers. I was appointed, to begin in two weeks.

℘ PART 6 ℘

CHANGING

The light has a new beam, rays of colours, spangling and glittering, as Sirius shines again. I have turned to catch his voice, refilling myself in ecstasy. The world is lit from a different source, exposing layers previously only dreamed of. Endless levels of matter, each less dense than the one before. I plunge into this ocean of joy, swimming strongly towards my purpose. Infinity! My hands respond, glowing in their tasks as I begin to build my future.

"HOW'S THE NEW JOB SIBYL?" Leah had rung me.

"It's certainly different. I'm paid by industry now to test a potential medicine for biological safety. It's not at all in line with how I think about health, using too many foreign chemicals in the body. But it keeps me off the streets. And what are you up to?"

"I rang to see you'd like to take part in a course I've enrolled in, to study hypnosis. They say it can be useful for children who stutter, which is why I want to do it, for the children at school. But it is also used for asthma sufferers, and I wondered about you with Sam."

"Hmmm, it sounds like fun. I'm at a bit of a loose end now that I've finished the PhD and moved on."

"How are you and David?"

"We still work together, but our jobs are enti rely different now. He has unfamiliar lectures to prepare, practical classes to run, and he's still applying for grants. I can't help him any more, there isn't time. And although we see each other every day, our private time together is difficult to find. So actually, our situation is not good at all. Sometimes I feel that all our good times are bath water swirling away, and I can't find the plug in time to save us."

I was becoming despondent over my life. The new job gave me lots of money, daily contact with David, and the rest all went against my grain. Having to use animals as test subjects, a test regime that was interesting but didn't touch my soul and the competitive feeling I had picked up amongst the young scientists around me were not helpful to me as a woman approaching her mid forties. I continued

"This course could be a bit of fun, can you let me have the details?"

We rang off, and I went and told David about the hypnosis course.

"I've heard that it can be helpful in stopping smoking too" he said, "and it would be right up your alley. You've always been interested in the quirks of the mind."

So Leah and I turned up at the hypnosis course. The night before, I was agitated, feeling that at all costs no one would take over my mind. I tossed about in the bed and arrived next morning looking like a wilted lettuce, after sleeping only a couple of hours. Leah raised her eyebrows at me. We started our lessons, a week's course, with practical hypnosis included. We learnt procedures to help people stop smoking, to assist with medical procedures, and finally tried to set each other in trance. I worked with Leah. She and I again were polar opposites, me being resistant, and she going easily into a deep trance. I suggested to Leah

"Can I practice the quit s moking procedure with you?"

"Yes" she agreed, "But remember I go easily into deep trance"

I heard but did not heed. We sat in a quiet corner, and I began the relaxation patter, saw Leah relax, and as I continued I saw her give a swallow. This we had been told, shows that the subject is entering a trance state. I started to talk about smoking, as Leah sat before me, eyes closed, far away. And yet when I asked her questions she responded.

"And what does the smoke do for you?" I asked

"It relaxes me," she said calmly, then burst out "And it stops me breathing!" She was screaming, gasping

"Help me, I'm burning!" I tried to salvage the smoking procedure

"Everything is all right, just keep calm Leah, you are here on the chair"

"I'm not Leah!" she was yelling, dreadfully agitated "They're burning me, I'm tied up on a bonfire, I can't get away, they're taunting me, screaming abuse. Help me, help me!"

"You have survived this, you are here with me!"

"I'm going to die, I can't escape. My feet are burning."

Now I was seriously alarmed. Leah was not obeying my directions as we had been taught to give them. She had gone into another world. We had touched on this in our classes, but this was my first hands on experience of it. I was close to panic, but there was no one near to call on. I raised my voice, urgently calling out

"You are back on the chair, 1,2,3,4,5!"

Leah was sobbing, but she opened her eyes. I put my shaking hand on hers, and after the crying spent itself she said,

"That was very real! I was in another life, I wasn't me. I was Sarah, they burnt me as a witch, and I was only trying to help people." She started to cry again,

"I keep feeling the injustice, the fear, the crowds jostling me, tying me up, yelling insults."

"I didn't know what to do, you weren't obeying what I said."

"Well you know I always like my independence" she smiled, "I can still smell burning, are you sure there's nothing burning here?" She got up and walked around, looking in the other rooms. I could smell nothing, and was bemused. I could not enter these worlds, or could I? I remembered the young soldier I had seen as I stood at the memorial at Verdun, and Leah's story of Beth. I had known little of 'past lives' or the mechanisms for getting into them at that time, David had known more than I. I felt I had undergone a baptism of fire, in more ways than one. This was the first of many visits in which I accompanied Leah to the world of the subconscious. But I always stood outside, my feet flat on the ground, holding the physical energy, as Leah spun into worlds beyond my consciousness.

*

Since we had moved universities and jobs, I felt the need to explore and release my negative emotions. This time I worked through the New Age movement, instead of the psychiatrists which I had used during my first major breakdown. I had not experienced panic since David and I had become lovers. I thought it was over. However, feelings had been generated in the previous years, losing my job the way it had happened, David's constant awareness of his division between two women, my children, family, Beth. All was bottled up inside and began to manifest physically. I began to become beset by minor ailments, small things but telling. Headaches, gastrointestinal upsets, liverish, colds and sinusitis, for which I invariably had a prescription of antibiotics. My response to the antibiotics became less every time I took them, and the sinusitis continued unabated. The aches and pains of middle age had started to invade my body.

I had started to become interested in alternative health care, as the medical drugs were not helping me. I tried to involve David but he could not find a spark of interest in anything outside science. He encouraged me, but he just smiled at my enthusiasms, and left me to them.

I started to understand how to clear out the morbid emotions which clogged my system. I admitted my anger and frustration, and shook it out of my body sometimes crying and screaming. I learned to allow self esteem and respect to enter. 'Take responsibility for your feelings' was my style. 'Don't blame other people for my feelings, take them on my own shoulders and express them privately.' It was not necessary to confront others with my anger or disappointment, only if there needed some clarification of one's position. Or a third person could be used in a type of 'debriefing' exercise. Louise Hay helped through her books. She made the link between emotions and illness. A bladder infection could be attributed to feeling 'pissed off'. Back pain could be due to 'needing back-up', wanting to 'back off' or maybe 'get off my back'. She invoked language in her quest for healing, and I found that her method worked. I did courses in massage, reflexology, Chinese medicine, shiatsu and Reiki. I combined them all into my own way of dealing with life and its situations. From my reading about psychoanalysis, it seems that the processes I followed were identical. Marie Cardinal in 'The Words To Say It' describes her analysis with such beauty, and I could see how my life also followed similar troughs and grey clouds before being liberated by a sunburst of insight. The whole process in me has taken many years, and continues, but as some of the techniques are different these days, it now seems possible to move through emotion more quickly. Again I invited David to join me in the emotional cleaning work, as I saw how much dross we had accumulated over our time together, but although he encouraged me, he was unwilling to accompany me on the journey. His train was charging down the tracks, and he did not notice that one side was starting to seize up again.

I began to attend short courses, began to meet new friends on the same path. I contemplated the emotional predispositions of illness. My understanding of life expanded. I had never understood the point of naturopathy. How could potions containing 'nothing' be effective, except as placebos? Suddenly I became aware of the energy which was not physical. So that was how homeopathy worked, and the flower essences, not through chemistry at all, but through the energy of another dimension. It became so simple. The flower essences worked on emotional states, releasing tension, and allowing the body then to heal itself. Although I was still a scientist, I began to see the human as being composed of body mind and spirit, and became fascinated by the possibilities inherent in bringing the physical world consciously together with its intangible parts.

I used my intuition to guide me. It sorted through my dream life, giving special emphasis to certain dreams. It catalogued the information I received from friends and acquaintances. It looked at frequency of language. Frequency of feelings. It marked feelings into type and strength. Measured my responses. Noted my likes and dislikes, helped me to come closer to the seeds of beliefs or emotions, to select the truth in my personality.

Sometimes the understanding of the emotion behind an illness stopped my own aches and pains, sometimes those of people I sought to help. These energies were easy to feel, simply follow the thought which brings relief, as far and as strongly as you can. Much of my armory of the use of herbs and foods to bring balance to my body had come from the inspiration through others, or from my own dreams. Without the antibiotics, which were no longer effective, the sinusitis took nearly a year to beat. But my immune system gradually responded and I eventually became free of illness.

My eye was quickened and my insight strengthened. My eyes, so used to perceiving small details in plants, to cataloguing their characteristics, now changed their outlook. It was patterns of behaviour that caught their focus. So watching a TV program on shellshock, I found myself watching the men, severely disabled as a consequence of their service in Vietnam. Close to suicide, beset by nightmares and terrors, I identified strongly with their panic. I saw them resolve to revisit Vietnam, overcoming their loathing of their experience and their fear of taking the plunge. I perceived the process which they underwent. First they were nervous, greeting new people with tight smiles, but coping. Then one by one they went into deep trauma. I observed the old horrors coming to the surface. For each one the triggers were different, for one the density of the jungle, so that when an incident occurred, it had been terrifyingly close. For another it was the water, the slush of the monsoon. For another the constant proximity of the Vietnamese people, the sound of their voices, the smell of the streets. As the men traversed their anguish they became silent, withdrawn, weeping. With one a volcano of grief erupted as he laid a wreath in a war memorial. The fears that they had borne for thirty years came to the surface, and began to evaporate, leaving only the beauty of individual personality. As they traversed their fear, they emerged in openness and joviality. They met with some of their former enemies, the Viet Cong. They swapped stories, reminiscences of the war. Compared nightmares. Drank, laughed, arms around each other, the Aussies and the Viet Cong, all forgiven, all brought together. And as they left, smiling, said they would never have believed such peace was possible.

Most people have something that they avoid facing, perhaps dreading the process of seeing and healing as being worse than the event itself. With so very many people I have listened, heard their anguish, together we have undergone the process that I have described in the shellshocked men. The steps into the horror, the engulfing experience and the pathway through to peace.

Sometimes I met people whom I could help in another way. A woman told me that she had had a slight shock from an electrical appliance some weeks previously, and that although she had no physical injury, she could still feel the shock in her arm and shoulder. Something in me knew that I could fix this. I had never encountered anything similar before, but I trusted the inner knowing, and offered to help. She assented, and as I placed my hand on her shoulder, and I immediately received the shock in my own arm. As swiftly as it entered me, it vanished, and I was left puzzled, and rubbed my arm. The woman said

"Oh, it's gone, it disappeared as soon as you touched me!"

There was nothing more to be said, the episode was complete. It seemed that I could heal these slight dislocations which occurred from time to time. I wondered if it was related to the emotional dislocations I had so often fixed in myself.

One of my girlfriends who was in hospital having recently given birth. When I visited her two days later, her belly was so swollen that it seemed that she was still pregnant. She was depressed, couldn't pass faeces or even urine with ease. Again something told me that I could help.

"What anaesthetic did you have?" I asked.

"I had an epidural, the injection in to the spine."

I suspected that it could have been this that was affecting her, preventing her recovery. I placed my hand next to her buttocks, not touching her body, and focussing my attention on producing a clear, functioning body, I raised my hand upwards, over the top of her head. This time I felt that the work was done, but I had no physical sensation. My friend reported to me later that she had begun to recover from that moment. Her body let go its waste, her belly resumed a normal size and her depression lifted. This seemed to be another instance some type of non-physical damage, this time due to the use of an anaesthetic. I do not assume that this always happens after the use of this or any other anaesthetic, but it may happen, and I found I could easily reverse it in this case.

Through my friendship with Leah, I had become interested in the life of spirit. Her psychic powers had begun to unfold even more since the hypnosis course. She had had some contact with the world of spirits but now her experience broadened and she taught me as an apprentice. Leah introduced me to this world. Although I was aware of the life of the Sibyl, and her ability to walk on both sides of death, I had not made the leap of integration that was now required. Up till then I had suspected and feared the world of ghosts and spooks. This seemed to be a different world to Sibyl's. But through Leah's tuition I learned to bring both sides of the picture together. The life beyond the physical grew into a timeless, spaceless realm, peopled by spirits involved in their own pursuits. They were outside my senses, but were known and appreciated by a part of me that was growing in its powers of perception. So matter of fact did this world become, that soon I accepted it with the enthusiasm of a new convert. But the most important thing to me was how I learnt through Leah's clairvoyance about the fate of souls after death.

There are many books written about near death experiences, some by those who have been resuscitated after a crisis on the operating table. I had met two people myself who had survived and come back with stories of immense love which had changed their lives. There are stories written by psychics about the experience of souls after death, my favourite being 'Seven Steps to Eternity' by Stephen Turoff which describes the fate of a young soldier killed during the first world war, and how he helped others into the world beyond death. There were my own experiences of being out of my own body in which I had been aware of watching my body from a vantage point outside, always brought about by stress of some kind. And again in my own life was the voice in my head, infrequent but so direct and clear. It often placed choices before me, or pointed out aspects of a situation which I had overlooked, without the slightest coercion for any action on my part.

I read widely, everything I could find about the afterlife. The usual scenario which is described is that after death souls are met by previously deceased relatives or other workers in spirit form, and are taken to their next port of call in the spirit world. They often traverse a dark tunnel, and reaching the light at the end are enveloped in love. This became the theoretical idea from which my life as a Sibyl developed.

Leah showed me that certain souls, often through the circumstances of their deaths, fear or loss of loved ones, remain fixated upon the physical world. They do not see the people who have been sent to guide them over, and follow what they have been doing during their physical lives. I never understood exactly why this should be so, but I have observed the consequences often enough. Leah could see these souls in her inner eye, and converse with them. I could perceive energy changes, changes in mood or pressure differences, but rarely saw or heard in this metaphysical world. Leah and I were together on many occasions when these souls made themselves visible to her. She would ask them what they wanted, and they would often not realize they were dead, making some strange reply. They might say for example

"This is my house, you aren't wanted here!" when that may have been true fifty years ago. Another common story came from mothers who had died leaving small children

"I am looking for my babies!"

Leah's approach, and the one I learnt, was to tell the soul firmly that it had left the physical world, and counsel them to go into the light where they would find people to help them. Then we would surround them with love and light, directing it through our intention and our imagination, and we would feel the change as they entered it. They often reacted in fear or disbelief to the news that they were dead, but were amenable to persuasion, and always went off with the helpers eventually. On one occasion a crowd of such people appeared, and we summoned in greater powers to assist. In war torn countries there have been many psychics who have assisted with the passage of lost souls. The religions pray for them. Halloween, or All Saint's Day are dedicated to the safe journey of souls.

Once when Leah was in my house I called in next door to speak to the woman there, a staunch Anglican, and a lecturer at the University. She answered the door with a look of pain in her face, and confessed that her back was out, was giving her enormous trouble, and that she could barely walk. Back home I said to Leah,

"There's something strange about that house. I've seen three different owners there, and each time something goes badly wrong or they are forced to stay at home, ill. The first people had a premature baby who was spastic, then the second people were always fighting, their marriage eventually broke up, and this lady, she was so fit and healthy, but her back is so bad now that she is incapacitated."

"Do you suspect something is wrong in the house?"

"Yes I do. Do you think you could tune in and see what is happening?" I was hesitant to ask Leah to use her psychic powers, and yet was eager to understand. We sat quietly, and she tuned in to the little house. It had been a dairy a hundred years ago, a single-fronted shop, on a long narrow block where the horses had been stabled. Now it was painted white with iron lace around the porch. Leah spoke finally

"It was a shop, selling little things, buttons, needles and pins, cottons, that kind of thing after or as well as being the dairy. The woman was saving up her money, she hid it from her husband somewhere in the house, she called it her 'Running away money'."

"How difficult lives were" I commented, "But how does this fit in with all the illness?"

"She had the money hidden somewhere, maybe in a wall or under the floor, but then she died before she could use it. She was anxious that nobody should steal it, and so she is still there, and she makes sure that there is someone always in the house, so that they are her guards. This is why people who come to the house get ill."

"That gives her a lot of power over people" I was not comfortable to imagine that the dead could make the living ill to fit in with their perceived needs. Especially if they were dead and had not reconciled themselves to 'You can't take it with you'.

"Is there anything we can do to help her to move on, and allow my friend to get well?" I added.

"I think so, but it will be best if you go in and speak to the woman's spirit from inside the house."

So the next day, I called in on my friend. I never knew in those days, how much to tell another person of the life I lived inside, of my contact with the spirit world through Leah. People could be alarmed, if they were not directly disbelieving. This woman was of the first variety, when I mentioned what had happened, she backed to the other side of the room, saying she was afraid of people who used these contacts, wasn't it trafficking with the devil? I was now committed to this conversation, and however unwillingly I blundered onwards. I tried to point out that I worked through the love of Christ, and as I was trying to allay her fears, I stood in the doorway between the front room where Leah had seen the spirit of the dead woman, and the kitchen where my friend was backed up against the far wall. I resolved to kill two birds with the one stone, to speak to both women at once, my intention being to comfort both, to allow the spirit to leave and my friend to recover from immediate fear and later her back pain. I repeated the story of the dead woman. I mentioned that the money could not be of use to anyone now. Because of inflationary pressures it would now be worthless. This was quite apart from the fact that the spirit woman was dead. I said firmly that she would find someone to help her if she would walk into the light with which she was surrounded. (I projected light towards her in my imagination.) Soon I heard the wooden ceiling of the front room give a great crack, which often happens as a spirit leaves. My friend started to relax her grip on the bench behind her, and took a step towards me. I reassured her and went home. To my relief her back recovered quite quickly. She told me later that she had asked the minister to come and exorcise the house, that the spirit had left now. I reserved my judgement about the efficacy of the minister's prayers, pleased at least that she was still able to speak to me.

I decided to do this work whenever it needed to be done. In this and other events around this time I had a number of psychically gifted friends who worked with me, so my lack of clairvoyance was no disadvantage. In later years I developed my ability to intuit what was going on, and feel the change in mood and to interpret symbols, so that I became able to perform this service alone. To become aware of a soul in trouble, I often picked up on the stories which people told me. If they recounted dreams of a departed loved one, for example, doing something inappropriate, accompanied by feelings of fear, confusion or grief, I would suspect that a soul was searching. Not seeing directly, I used lights and darkness which flashed in my inner vision. When I willed light and consolation to go to the lost one, I could feel the energy of confusion give way to relief and gratitude.

I heard a young woman telling a story.

"My brother died, he was electrocuted with a power tool. He had been close to me, we had shared his despair and his loneliness. His marriage was floundering, he did not know how to come to grips with his problems. Then all of a sudden he died. It was a tragedy, he was young and had life ahead of him. I couldn't get to his funeral, so later I visited his grave. But I came away with a feeling of such dread and despair, such grief that I didn't know what to do with it. I was crying but the sadness and fear stayed with me."

"That sounds nasty" I murmured, "What happened next?"

"Nothing really, the feeling gradually lifted. But recently I dreamed about him, I saw his body, decomposing, but sitting in his wife's house, sticking pieces of bread and Vegemite on her face. But she was paying no attention to him. It was as if he wasn't at peace, and was trying inappropriately to capture her attention."

"I think he may be stuck, perhaps in his grave, that would be enough to leave anyone in despair. But I also think that we can help him." The woman telling the story was not familiar to this way of working, but as I explained my previous encounters, she relaxed, she was open, and agreed to meditate and try to help him to release.

Later as I sat at my table, playing solitaire, the image of the trapped man came strongly to me. I addressed my thoughts to him

"Do you want to do it now?" I had held back slightly, as I had wondered if it was my job to assist him. But no, he was pushing at me, trying to get my attention once more. I opened myself, opening to the inner world which is all light. I flooded him with the whiteness, he came into my heart, sobbing quivering with fear and relief. It seemed that he was begging me to let him stay, fearful that I would withdraw from him.

"Love is always here, you can stay in it forever" I told him, as his dismay gave way.

For some days I felt him around me, basking in love, until the feeling gradually faded. I met his sister later that week and related to her what had happened. She too had gone out walking to send solace to him, but had not noticed anything special. But after I had gone home that night, she had felt him around her, in peace and gratitude that all was well with him at last.

This was typical of the way souls in trouble would make themselves known to me, and also typical of the way I handle such occurrences. I am a scientist. I would like to be able to quantify, to measure, to collate, or at least to see what I am doing. Feelings and emotions are not quantifiable in this way, perhaps will never be. They span different dimensions to the logical world where science has its domain. But we all experience feelings and emotions. In my family they have been swept under the carpet, not given in to and it has taken me my whole life to admit them, to use them consciously. And now I find that feelings are at the centre of life, the language of soul. The power which results from the fusion of the feelings of intuition with logic and emotion, the three parts of the human mind, is immense.

*

Leah and I sat in the Spiritualist church, the psychics up on the stage prepared to channel information to the congregation. The man was pointing at me,

"The woman in the red jacket" he said. I nodded, agreeing to accept the message.

"I can see a neat woman, dark hair tied back" he said, but I looked puzzled. Leah was sitting beside me. She could see who it was.

"It's Paddy" she whispered. I was jolted into immediate attention. I had known Paddy too well to have described her in any terms but love. The man continued

"She reminds you of a conversation you both had when you were very small, about the meanings of your names. She congratulates you on your work. She says it has caused ripples to spread out, which will affect many people!"

I was engulfed in a mad delirium of joy. From beyond the grave Paddy had returned to encourage me. I am a Sibyl! I will always be true to my name!

"She also says she is back on earth to reunite with a lover – she knows you well and even has the same name as before." I wondered for years over this – no one seemed to fit the description.

*

While I was content, embracing this new relationship with spirit, I was growing further and further from David.

David and I sat in a pub waiting for our lunch, watching the black and white clad waitresses passing between the tables, the other patrons quietly chewing and reading newspapers. The light was dim, dark wood-paneled walls contrasting with the bright October sun which glanced in from the leafy beer garden outside. I felt strange. I didn't understand why really. Technically we were still lovers but David's new place of work placed more demands on us than previously. Not so easy to go to David for a kiss and a cuddle when we were surrounded by glass. We were obliged to limit our daily conversation to lunchtimes, but it was too short a time to make a sure contact. Over the last two years David and I had not come closer, rather I felt the barrier against me had become stronger, harder to sweep aside. David was always unable to resolve the ambiguities in his life. He was hiding under a mountain of work, students, grant applications, lectures to be prepared. Eventually my position was terminated when my employers realized they didn't hold the patent on the drug I was testing. I was free to come and go, to pursue other projects. Money was all right. I was drifting.

My meal had arrived, but I sat unable to eat it. I suddenly felt I could do no more, I would be better off on my own, searching out a new life. Exploring the limitless world of spirit.

Even a new man. The David I had fallen in love with was hidden under layers of insulation, I couldn't find him. I started to cry and held David's hand,

" It feels as if our time is up. I think we shall have to part."

He looked puzzled

"Do you dislike me?" he asked, "Do you want to avoid meeting me?"

"No, it is not about liking" I answered, "I shall always love you. But I need to move further. I have tried and tried to bring you with me, but you cannot come. You are so hidden behind your science, and I can't continue in the old way. I need to continue to develop my spiritual life."

"It has changed you, you are less of a scientist now, believing in ghosts instead of chemicals."

I caught a whiff of disapproval.

"I have to think more widely than science, modern medicine is miraculous when dealing with acute problems, but really poor when it comes to dealing with chronic illness. Finding the emotional basis of illness has to be taken into account when treating chronic conditions."

"Hmmm." He looked older and sadder. My heart went out to him.

"Well, we will always love each other," I reached for his hand and he gave me a tight smile.

I mourned the loss of David in my life, but merely skimmed the surface of my feelings.

As we had a daughter the relationship was carved in rock, indisputable and unassailable. I didn't understand this. My physical being and my mind were firmly earthed in matter, I thought it would be possible to put David aside and find another partner. The world of spirit has other ways, different intentions. No one can guess how life will turn out. The tiny twists and quirks of existence from which events develop hurry by almost unnoticed.

David did not fare so well after I withdrew. Now there was little respite from the impossibilities in his life. He threw himself even more energetically into his work, took more students, and allowed his creativity and affection to flow to them. But even this could not heal the canker which came from his refusal to allow himself the full expression of life. First he became ill with a huge gall stone, which he showed to me after its removal. "Gall stones, concretions of anger and frustration" I acknowledged privately, remembering how we had left our jobs.

At first David and I met quite often for lunch, cups of coffee at the University. I asked Alice to keep contact with him for Beth's sake, even if I lost contact myself. I was sad to have broken off our affair. I would walk to the children's playground, and sit swinging and crying for what we had not achieved, the gum trees nodding their agreement. At first I lived in the country, then three years later I moved overseas, and from there I kept a reduced contact with David.

Leaving Australia, I felt as if I must place myself in voluntary exile for another cycle of time. As I flew out of my homeland I also passed away from the 'New Age' ideas which had been, on looking back, the most exciting, freeing, unlimited part of my life. I entered a period of community living. Leah met me in England, and we travelled together, ending up at 'The Findhorn Foundation' in the north of Scotland.

Findhorn had moved away from its origins to a new phase, where people were learning to live in close harmony within a group. A worthy objective, but nevertheless not interesting to me. I was not enthused by community life. I had contemplated it when the children were small and I had needed help. Then I would swoon in gratitude if even a vacuum cleaner salesman had appeared at my door, another adult face to help me through my day. Now I was on my own, and enjoying the challenges of life and development. My spirit had to coax me into this new life, strewing cosmic carrots in front of me, still longing for a man with total commitment. Leah and I had enrolled in an 'Experience Week' program, and we were with 16 others in an intensive week's events. There were 'get to know each other' games, dancing, meditation and tours in nature. Three afternoons we chose to work somewhere within the community, Leah in the kitchen, and I in the garden. There was a group of Swedish people at Findhorn during the same two weeks as Leah and I, three families including small children had travelled together in a Volkswagen bus. One of the men Olof, was in the Experience Week group with Leah and me. He became friendly with me and invited me to visit their sister community in Sweden. I assented, not so much out of any interest in communal living, but because it might be fun to travel a bit further. I had never been to Scandinavia, and had wondered about going there. Leah had said

"I think you will be invited somewhere"

"Yes, and there will be sexual overtones in the invitation" I replied.

I had had no hesitation in deciding to travel further, and it seemed that Olof and I were drawn together. In the dancing, on the way to and from our gatherings, sitting in the great hall, he would invariably be beside me. He was fun to be with, and I enjoyed his attention. I had never enjoyed sexuality if I was not in love, and wondered if this would be a problem. Still, it was not yet , I would worry about that 'tomorrow'.

What impressed me about Findhorn was the honesty of the people there. When one lives in a community, to be successful one practises a code of openness in relating to other people. Gossiping and spreading rumours does not work. For one thing, everyone is aware of it at some level, so one cannot speak undetected about people behind their backs. It is easier to be up front about issues which need clarification. My Scorpio nature preferred to hide. I was happier alone without the conflicts of society. But at Findhorn, I perceived the uprightness of the women who had been there for some time, and although it scared me, I agreed internally that it was a worthwhile trait.

*

I took the carrot, and travelled eventually to the Swedish community. I arrived one evening in early winter, the ground was covered in snow, I was met at the train station by Olof, who drove me through dark pine forests and winding roads to the village where he and the community lived. I was led into the big dining room, not knowing what to expect. The women had left out some food for the travellers, and Olof and I sat alone in the big dark house. It felt as if it watched me, summing me up.

"Tomorrow morning you can get breakfast here in the kitchen" explained Olof, "After that at eight o'clock there is a meeting here in the library."

He took me to a room in one of the old houses owned by the community, and promised to introduce me to their life the next day. I was in a white room, polished wood floor, two single beds, and in the corner a tall stove. The stove was old and unusual to my eyes. It was round in cross section, tiled from floor to ceiling, glistening white, some of the tiles around the top decorated with a lacy design. The room was pleasant, even elegant, but Swedish in its reserve.

Next morning I met the other people at 'Morning Meeting', was welcomed and explained my reasons for coming. Or part of them. Cosmic carrots were private matters!

I had kept in touch with Olof by letter in the weeks before I travelled to Sweden. He wrote well, and my fear of opening myself to him vanished in his friendship. We enjoyed a brief love affair which lasted long enough to induct me into the life of the place, to find my feet, and make friends, thus binding me to a longer stay. But I often had dreams of David in which he would stand at the end of my bed looking aggrieved.

The community had no religion and few rules, but was based on the ideals of the Findhorn group about which much has been written. Basically, one undertook responsibility for oneself, physically, emotionally and spiritually, and worked together as a group. Of course to live within a group was a difficult way to function, one must remember what has been passed in all the many meetings, and must bring all requests and queries to a group meeting for discussion. Usually it functioned well.

It was very much smaller than the community at Findhorn, only about 20 members, and I was glad to be with fewer people. There the people who became my friends were also on their way out of their 'new age' beliefs. They were strongly principled people who were committed to living and working together. They met often and discussed the running of their guesthouse, the garden, the renovations on the old houses, and the selling of articles in the shop. Sometimes they met to discuss spiritual matters, to share insights and iron out difficulties. The guesthouse was booked by course leaders and the community serviced the guests' living arrangements, cooking meals and cleaning and decorating the house with flowers. I cleaned and cooked and later worked in the garden. As many of the meetings were spoken in Swedish, I had a ready excuse to miss them if I wished and at first I took the role of an observer. I grew to appreciate the meditative space of peeling a bucketful of potatoes for the midday meal. I remembered St Therese of Lisieux who had learnt to love the same job. Using the hands in silence was a beautiful contemplation.

Early in my stay I looked up one day to see a dark man standing beside me, teasing me about coming from the bush. He had a mischievous smile, and my eyes lit up as I teased him in return. Georg was from Denmark, and had a sense of fun that was almost Australian. He also had a wife who was dying of cancer. Pathos and humour sat side by side, endearing him to me. Soon his wife returned from a treatment, and I was invited to meet her. The stately Anita looked out from sunken eyes, her face gaunt with the disease. As our eyes met, an arrow of compassion passed between us, and we became firm friends. We sat long and often, trying to find ways of healing which would alleviate Anita's suffering. We walked in the parkland surrounding our houses and shared confidences and tenderness. Once I walked by the lake sobbing at the thought of leaving, then wondered why was I crying, as I was not leaving. I found myself weeping Anita's tears at leaving Georg, the community and life. It was my first experience of expressing someone else's feelings when they were unable to address them themselves. Anita was apprehensive about death and could not look at it, much less discuss it. I found favour in part because I was positive about the powers of healing. Georg and I accompanied Anita to the hospital, many times, held her hands, wiped up her vomit when the cancer prevented her from eating. Anita's life ebbed away. On her final day Georg, I and another girlfriend sat at her bedside. I felt the room to be filled with unseen presences, and I was aware of being used by them. One's physicality confers an advantage which can be given to those in spirit. Anita sometimes knew she was going, and became terrified. There were no reassuring words for one who was so afraid of passing. I had my job to do, holding the energy of transformation, and was not distracted by emotion, that would come later. I observed Anita's breath becoming more and more shallow, eventually just the upper part of her chest was moving. Soon it was only a flutter in her throat, and then nothing at all. She went silently in the last, no struggle no noise. She was surrounded by loving hands. Her earthly friends sat at her bedside for two hours, gently grieving this unusual woman. Anita lay there, so white, so still, her eyes closed. I thought

"Now you have really gone" and ignored a flicker of dissent. Georg drove us home, and as I sat in the car, I thought of Anita lying cold in the hospital. I heard a voice in my head, with Anita's exact intonation in the English words,

"I'm not there, I'm here!" Many people in the village were visited by Anita in the next few days. Her funeral took place after three weeks, and after that she seemed to be at peace. I sat alone in the church on the morning of the funeral listening to a friend practising her violin solo. The coffin was covered with white and red flowers. My tears for Anita flowed with the music, as I sat making my farewell. But by the time of the funeral that afternoon, my tears were spent, and I joined the procession around the coffin honouring my friend.

Anita gave me a reason for staying in the community during her life, and she gave me the experience of attending a death. She showed me the mystery of this transformation, and I remain in awe of the process. The Sibyl in me reawakened, and became grounded in experience.

I made friends, and learnt to live as a part of a group. I did not really belong here, and in spite of enjoying life, I returned almost every year to Australia. I met David in Australia during my brief visits, we had lunch and a talk. Sometimes Alice and Beth had lunch with us. But the relationship with David was waning now, on my side it was almost without spirit. David took refuge with his family, his new students, and his work. He barely wished to be jolted out of his routine even to speak to Beth. His love was now buried beneath a concrete slab of everyday duties, and it would take a cataclysm to uncover it.

My spiritual life was now a sober affair. I had dreams of David occurring infrequently, perhaps once a year. Other prophetic dreams came to me occasionally, often about my health, and there were always fulfilled within a few days. I wondered where the sparkle had gone, and missed it. Inside, in a deep silence I knew that all was well. I watched the new guests who came to courses. They asked the strangest questions, and I recognized myself from several years back. I remembered the explosion of detail and complexity which I had enjoyed. Even at the time I had been surprised. Everything I touched apparently had the capacity to grow to unmanageable proportions, as if the will to create spurred on an ever widening field of endeavour. I looked back further, to my first research project. It had been necessary after a while to stop the broadening of my interests and come back to the original concept, firming up only a small part of my ideas into the publication of my thesis. Perhaps this process of stopping and consolidating was not only a scientific necessity, but also a spiritual one. I felt now as if I was integrating something within, that my gathering had finished temporarily and that the ingredients were synthesizing or grounding themselves in the flatfoot world in which I now lived.

℘ PART 7 ☙

THE CLOTH OF GOLD

Seeing through the layers of existence, I have learned to traverse the portals of life and death. I take his hand and draw him through the veils, until safe on the other side he is set free. He takes with him the woven cloth of his earthly life, his cloth of gold, to be reworked into his future.

DAVID NEVER WROTE to me now and I wondered if he had forgiven me for leaving him, if he still thought about me, or remembered our love. I knew he remembered the pain, it was obvious in his avoidance of contact with me, but what of the joy?

Old friends told me that David was growing tired. He still met people and had lunch with them, walked with them through the university paths, talked of the future. At home the garden claimed his attention. He could no longer maintain the garden in impeccable order, his tiredness coming from deep within. His soul was withdrawing even then, so early. The erosion of his body had begun. He was torn, always trying to keep everyone happy but unable to meet the physical demands required. He pushed himself beyond the boundaries of health.

Nor did David leave me alone. Sometimes in Sweden I dreamed of him, dreams of reality. I would be walking in his house, terrified of discovery by his wife. She would come into the room and not see me standing there. In a later dream I was in David's house again, looking around, and he was irritated, asking me to leave. Again his wife was there and didn't see me. I wondered if David was angry with me leaving him. Or angry with himself for not being able to resolve his ambiguity. I didn't understand that dreams sometimes tell the opposite of their true meaning.

I returned after five years away, and Alice told me that David had had bowel cancer, had been in America when the crisis hit him, and managed to return to Australia for the operation. David wrote to Beth, explaining about his cancer, (genetically aware) and said please not to write again, he could not cope with any more deception. I rang him at work, and he told me he had made an excellent recovery, in spite of fears that the cancer may have spread to his liver. He told me what had happened. One day he noticed he had passed blood. Too busy to go to the doctor, anxious to finish the grant applications he had begun. He was to attend a conference in USA, must finish the paper for that, so no doctor's visit. He managed to finish his work, and arrived at the conference, but presented no paper, for there his cancer presented itself to him, blocking the bowel, and in great pain he was admitted to hospital. They patched him up well enough for him to return home to Australia for the removal of the bowel. The doctors thought it had spread to the liver, but David brushed aside their concerns.

But he wanted to leave our relationship where it was, couldn't cope any more. I looked out from the dark hallway where I sat, through the door, into the leafy street. Saw the sun making patches of light through the lush greenery. Two opposite worlds confronted me. I felt relief for David and for his honesty at last. I felt despair when I thought of many years still to be spent in his straightjacket. I knew suddenly that there would not be so many years, he would not be able to bear his confinement, but would die soon. I had seen people die of cancer, or survive it. A disease about something one feels helpless and hopeless about. The survivors had invariably changed their life completely, drastically. Addressed previously neglected issues, eaten very clean food, taken massive vitamin therapy. And it didn't always work. My own father had retired, and defeated his cancer in leisure. I couldn't envisage David changing his life at all. He wouldn't receive any benefits from retiring, so much was clear. His life with his students was the only porthole through which David could experience the ocean of his soul. David did not believe in my way of healing so I said nothing. And no one knows the decisions of another man's soul. To live or to die are private matters.

It was more bearable for me to think of David dying, death held no fears for me. I as Sibyl had ushered many lost souls across the river of Death, souls who had died with unfinished business here on earth, who had lost their way and who welcomed my light. I often met them in cemeteries, sometimes mothers of young children, terrified of leaving their babies to someone else's care. They could be anywhere, just needing a kindly word and a reassurance to walk forward into the light. The energy of these encounters was unmistakable, tough going at first, explanations, gentle reassurance, and finally the breakthrough of the sun, resolution and peace as the soul moved on. I was unafraid of these meetings, welcoming them as a service I could perform. I made contact with David's spirit and promised support if and when...

I returned overseas, but still dreamed of David. Unfriendly dreams. On my next visit to Australia, a year later I visited a friend who had seen David recently.

"He had a lump on his hand, the doctors told him it was a secondary, he was not ill, looked quite good, he was a bit apprehensive."

I was jumped into awareness that his time was running out. The sun leapt behind a cloud. Here was face to face contact with the other world. Everyday reality altered, the flowers took a step back, the colours faded as David's apprehension swamped me. I felt my limbs were paralyzed, I lost strength from my being. I tried to telephone him at work, unsuccessfully. I talked to Helen, a mutual friend with whom David was corresponding.

"I don't think it is anything, bowel cancer doesn't metastasize in the hands, he was clear not so long ago, he wrote to me," she said. I believed he was on his way out, and said to his soul,

"If you need me I am here", and received no response. Again I returned overseas.

Months later I was on holiday in the Swedish mountains, stretching my body to the utmost, carrying my pack, and hiking long distances. The pure air, clean snowy peaks and valleys carpeted in flowers gave me respite after a hard stretch of work. It was unaccustomed exercise, and in the evenings I collapsed into a deep sleep.

I dreamed of David, his relationship with me and his relationship with his wife. I waited for him to tell me to leave, but this time it didn't come. Then the dream told of his relationship with Helen, and that she would be the messenger. Clear dreams are always short and to the point, no words were wasted here. I related my dream at breakfast, believing that something was happening for David. No confirmation from my earthy friend. I again went into my soul and promised help when appropriate. No answer. We wandered on in the peace of the mountains , I kept David with me, wanting the love to flow to him, aware of nothing.

Back home in the community two weeks after the dream I received an e-mail from Helen, the messenger. *'David died two weeks ago. The lump on his hand which had been there since January, and thought to be nothing important, was diagnosed at Easter time as a secondary cancer. Then soon after he had pain in his back, and they found it had spread to the soft tissue around his spine. He was in hospital for a month having treatment, then went home on a morphine drip, and two days before he died he returned to hospital. You were so right to worry about him at Easter.'*

*

Much later I contacted David's relatives and friends, and from their stories I put together an idea about David's last illness.

Serious illness at home, a morphine drip in his arm, the brain started to sleep. In fact the whole body slept most of the time as it wound down, surrendering to the cancer which was slowly but surely consuming him, creeping into the spinal bones themselves. He had pain in his hands. He was eroding away from the inside.

The dulled light sneaked through gaps in the drawn curtains, his bedroom spotlessly tidy. Concerned students, knowing he was on the way out, wrote letters of thanks for his life, appreciation for his support. These became treasures, to be read and reread. Friends sometimes rang or called in. Eventually the kidneys failed, the toxicity became greater, the cancer was pressing on the nerves, causing massive pain. The stomach had shrunk, occluded by the growth, he ate a teaspoonful at a meal. The intestines started to give up, they too were becoming blocked. It would have to be drip feeding, he would have to go to the hospital.

The hushed bustle of clinical death in hospital.

"I'll just give you some morphine, it'll make you feel better", another drip in the arm, stiff white sheets, catheters here and catheters there, the failed kidneys increasing the toxicity, brain clogged with drugs, pain, fear, lack of human closeness or warmth. Semi-comatose. Murky, dirty. Couldn't grasp at anything, consciousness blobbing up and down in a sea of oblivion. The only resolution his academic training. He stirred occasionally and knew exactly his stage in the dying process. Nothing comforting in this knowledge. The pain came back, the fear of death, the great vacuum. Animals and humans have a sixth sense about when the time is up. Complete disbelief in an afterlife, but the active brain revolts at the idea of nothingness. The fear of the unknown was strong.

"He hasn't got long now" he heard in the next room. The feeling was transmitted to him. His whole life spent apologizing. It would be a private funeral, just his sons. He didn't want any funeral, didn't believe in religion. His brother the priest came to give the last rites.

"I know you don't believe in religion or prayer, but I'm going to give it anyway, do you understand?" David flickered an eye, just aware.

"Enlighten my eyes that I never sleep in death. If I should walk in the midst of the shadow of death I will fear no evils; for Thou art with me O Lord, Thy rod and Thy staff they have comforted me." The cloth of spirituality and eternity was offered to David, and accepted by him, through the muddied consciousness and the mess of drugs. He just managed to remember he had love hidden away in his bottom drawer. The cloth was almost threadbare, had to last a little while yet. Take care not to tear it!

David died alone and was privately cremated.

*

I was shaken to my core by David's death. One I had been so close to had gone over. I had wanted to work with him, to send him healing power to help him make a painless transition to the afterlife, but nothing had happened. Now with the knowledge of his death, my consciousness altered.

"What are you doing over there?" I said. It seemed that suddenly my thoughts could reach him. We were flying, reunited after so long. All I felt was ecstasy, all I knew was joyful acceptance. Every time I thought of David I was aware of his delight and surprise. All day and all night. I awoke many times with the realization of union with David. I tossed in the bed, my face crumpled against my pillow in the space between waking and sleeping, aware of him. He was strong, able and beautiful, and alive again. I was washed in his glory, bathed in his spirit, intoxicated with love. The body dies and the spirit soars.

Life continued, there was work to be done, and gradually David's presence receded from me. But after two weeks he came again in a dream. This time I saw him in his earthly personality, the one who would not consider a spiritual perspective on life, but would listen sometimes to my enthusiasm for healing and the otherworldly. The man who had begun to bore me with his dedication to science. Although his perspective had altered he still held many of his physical attributes. This time he was full of smiles and affection, although still slightly withdrawn from me. This David said

"Well, going over was nothing to write home about, but now that I'm on the other side, it is just the same as it was on earth."

I was astounded. This man who would never admit to any truth in religion now spoke to me in words I understood. He had no problem to reach me. He made none of his usual apologies, and made no mention of his family. He could never countenance my belief in a life after death, and here he was, invading my dreams and telling me about life in the world of spirit. I was so at home with the idea of life after death that I omitted to tease him over his change of opinion on the subject.

Over the weeks David faded away from me again. Another dream intervened. David was with me, but the noise of the passing trucks was so loud that I couldn't hear him. I interpreted this as meaning that the conditions of my life were preventing me from being aware of David's presence.

Over the years I spent in Sweden I developed an inner calm that had been absent before. I looked at the people with whom I spent time. Each one mirrored someone from my past, often my family members with whom I had had some difficulty. Some caused me grief, others happiness, others joy. They were my present family, blessed. When I had seen each one in their special place, I felt released and decided to return to Australia.

I was back in Australia, my sojourn in Sweden over. I was about to meet David's sister Elsa, for the first time. In all his years, David had never confided in Elsa his intimacy with me, or the existence of his daughter. The family was aware that somewhere David had a person he loved, and would have been glad to hear his side of the story, but he in his self-imposed schizoid life remained closed to them. I had contacted them, and now it had come to pass that we were to meet. I parked my car and tried to put some money into the parking meter, but it was jammed and I couldn't push the money in. The time stood at 40 minutes. I decided to take the chance, and left it. I met Elsa and we greeted each other like old friends. I showed her my photos of Beth, thereby expanding the families on both sides. Sharing her birth through David's death. We wept and laughed together.

At last we walked back to our cars. I glanced at the parking meter, wondering if it was still stuck on 40 minutes. Instead it stood on one hour and 50 minutes!

"There was more to that meeting than meets the eye!" I thought.

Suddenly the symbol became clear. I became aware of David again, of the overwhelming memory of our love, but now coming in more strongly and more poignantly than when we had been together on earth. As I drove home I felt waves of bliss streaming through my body. A dream of two years ago had come true, I had married my ex-husband. A part of me wondered why these wonderful experiences of love took place in such unromantic places as driving through the streets of the city, swarming with people and traffic. I tried to drive carefully, to take my inner life as well as my outer life home to a place of peace.

There I lay in a reverie of remembrance. David came to me from his world of spirit to rekindle our love, to express love in ways we had not experienced whilst he walked the earth. Now he was omnipresent, he could help me in my earthly life. I could invoke his presence over the planes of existence. No longer in a body his relationship to me altered. In my being he found solace. I welcomed him with passion, this part of my soul, always sought and suddenly found. We had been separated by our creation into physical selves so that we could see our beauty reflected in one another, could appreciate the fine detail of our nature. Separated by our own choice, to experience who we were, reflected in each other's eyes, felt in each others arms, swimming in each other's embrace.

David had remnants of his physical life that caught at his heels and prevented his further development. I realized that I could help him to heal these parts. Working as a spiritual healer, I used the techniques I had gathered. I allowed his feelings to come into my physical body, and I felt them as if they were my own. Then I expressed them, as he had never been able to do. The dregs of David's suffering I experienced, all the time fully aware that it was his and not my pain. His anguish of double dealing, conflicts of loyalty, love forsaken for duty. His inability to stand up for himself, and his unawareness of the spiritual dimension. I felt every part of his wretchedness, it racked my being, grated over me as I brought it out through my system. I rode my bicycle up to the overpass over the big freeway and screamed out his disgust as it passed through me. I yelled at the passing traffic, whizzing by under my feet. I bellowed it to the grazing cows, to the aeroplanes taking off in the local airfield, to the golden canola growing in the next paddock. I howled it on sunny days and on cloudy days. I shook it out through my own body. My earthly self laughed at the procedure, hoping not to be noticed, discreet still. I was the only one who knew how it had been for him and was therefore the only person who could help him to resolve his life. As suddenly as it had begun, it finished. The whole procedure took three days. Then I felt surrounded by his gratitude that now he was free to move on.

"Lift the veil and trust my words, I'm ready to speak from my heart, Sibyl. The healing is complete."

*

I think of David, Beth and myself now. My gift to David had been accepted in joy, and with a degree of responsibility that the situation demanded. I shall never forget the leap in his voice when I told him he had a daughter. 'Ohh, I feel strange, all hot and cold!' he had said. His soul had spoken. But his life had not permitted more than presents for Christmas and birthdays. After his death, he spoke to me through Leah. 'I awoke, I could see everything all around me, I was fully conscious. I knew I could be anywhere I wanted to be. With Beth. I could help her in ways that had been impossible whilst I was on earth.'

*

How was I so sure that David was with me? What I was sure about was that the feeling I had had when I fell in love with him was with me whenever I called it, and sometimes whether I called it or not. It was stronger than it had been when he lived on earth. It filled me with grace, lightness and strength. If I asked him what he was doing, I would see in my head that he was sitting with a newspaper, reading a journal, looking through papers. Standing at my shoulder, stroking my arm. These things I have no ideas about. They may be literally true, they may be translations into my mind of the answer to my question. It didn't matter to me. I could play with whatever came into my head. What mattered was the love, the energy which fulfilled something inside me, took away that emptiness and craving, and came when I felt the need for it. Like living with a partner, we would come together in ecstasy, then move apart, working separately for a day or so, and then slowly begin to turn to each other again until the tension reached another peak, and he was with me again. A cycle of separation and uniting. Union all the time would not be challenging. I suddenly understood the reason for the great Separation, so that there could occur the great Reunion. Again and again and again. If it becomes routine, change the parameters. Change life. Die, be born, journey far away and travel back together again. Marry the wrong person and then meet the beloved. And if I became tired of this playacting, I could retreat to the reassuring security of the spiritual world. It felt as if I could go out and play in Disneyland to my heart's content, and when Disneyland became too much I could return to my swimming pool and lie back basking in love.

I sat in the sunshine outside my parent's house, trying to do my tax return. The print sat darkly on the page, black and white. But my eyes could not claim a focus. A nest of panic hovered in my chest. Every time I started work on the numbers the panic swirled faster. I was heading for trouble again. I got up and walked inside, made a cup of tea and brought it outside. But the panic was not to be diverted from its goal. My breath started to come in gasps, as my feet jigged and my hands twitched nervously. The figures stared blackly at me, daring me. I was writhing in my chair, not feeling, not speaking, not understanding.

I heard footsteps behind me on the gravel, and turned. Leah was walking towards me.

"Hello Sibyl, I was steered in your direction today and I wondered why. How are you?"

Being back in Australia had meant we could take up our old friendship. We knew each other so well that we wasted no words. I was relieved to see her calming eyes as I replied

"Desperate! I can't work, something is coming up. Can we go somewhere and talk?"

I got up and we walked down to the end of the garden, and stood under the purple jacaranda tree. Leah was a perceptive counsellor. Her insights had often helped me to unravel a situation when I was so close that I could not see its details. She took my hand and feeling her touch my tears started to fall. The panic dissolved as I took the lid off my steaming cauldron. I looked inside and saw my disappointment and anger.

"What is your trouble?"

"I think I am angry with David" I said, surprised at my sudden reaction.

"Is that what it is? Well, you need to cry your tears, accept and express your anger."

"I feel so stupid when I do that"

" Just accept the banality of the situation. Your feelings just have to be assimilated one way or another, into your emotional and physical bodies. Stamp on the ground, or roll up my jacket and put it on the bench here, beat into it."

Leah had assisted many through emotional crises.

As I began to punch and stamp my emotions started to flow, and I began to see more clearly the incidents which had caused me such pain. I began to relive the agony of David's loss as my tears began to drain the abscess of unspent grief. Images of death, betrayal, unfaithfulness, lack of courage sprang up smothering the new flowers in the grass.

Suddenly I knew that after all the years that had passed, all the emotional expression I had spoken of, that I was still unable to acknowledge my grief at David's failure to commit himself to me. Old habits die hard! And for his death, his final defection, I had never shed a tear. It was not surprising that my grief had had to wait to be reawakened, as at the time of David's death he had been reunited with me through his presence in dreams. But now I felt alone again. His physical commitment was forever denied.

As the bitter anguish of our wasted opportunity burst over me, I cried and cried. I sat sobbing the hurt away, flooding the garden with sorrow. My emotions circled through grief, tears, resignation, anger, and more tears. David was gone, he couldn't love me as I wanted him to, he couldn't trust himself to break with his tradition and be there for me. I need love, I depend on love. In love I give my life away. Without a lover I am a shadow, barely functioning. I have been alone for ten years. Why couldn't you love me? Why did you withdraw so far, so far that I couldn't contact you any more? I worked and worked for you. I tried everything I knew to get you to come to me. I couldn't understand why you were so restricted with rules and regulations when I was so free. At last my sadness began to settle and I rested a while, then stood up and looked at Leah, wearing a bleak smile.

"You have been holding on to that for some time" she said. She was standing close, her hand on my waist, watching me, and at the same time taking in the pond at the end of the garden and the metallic blue-green dragon flies which fluttered amongst the water plants.

"Yes, I thought I had cried enough, but it takes time to come to the bottom of things."

The tall trees, lush and verdant in spring enclosed us as we passed under the branches. The trees brought in contentment as I cleared the dross from my spirit. And now that I had cleared a space, I could refill myself with a draught of love. I stretched and breathed in. Ferns grew nearby, in the bright understory sheltering even smaller plants. We sat down on Mother's old-fashioned chairs.

"Everywhere I look I see relationships filled with difficult situations, falling apart when expectations are not met," I said turning to Leah. "I see people who are not willing to listen to each other, who make up their minds and turn away too soon. When they begin to come close to one another they close the shutters, batten down the hatches, take to the life boats. There is too much hurt in there, people escape any way they can. It takes courage to grasp at love, to be prepared to go through the difficulties of living together. But in the world of spirit love is perfect, and immense. I am always searching for it here on earth, but never find it."

"I have been disappointed in the same way as you" said Leah. Her face changed as she remembered her own loss. "But these perfect love relationships don't exist here on earth." She came back to the present, ruefully.

"I don't understand why not" I answered, ready to stamp my foot and assert my rights over the lovelessness of life, "This is my greatest vision."

"You must keep your dream then," she encouraged me, but neither of us understood the way through to this dream. It was as if the goals were out of reach, affixed to vehicles parked half a mile from our sportsground, but you never knew if someone would get in and drive the goals within reach of our play.

"I wonder if I am mistaken in the way I interpret the messages I receive about love. My longing is strong, grows firmer all the time. I am often told to follow my dreams. I always choose the best. The ultimate closeness, the ecstatic relationship. Perhaps something new is happening that I don't understand at all."

"If this type of relationship is to come to earth, it is certain that no one understands it."

"All I can say is that I am willing to be a part of new experiments." Leah smiled.

"There must be something afoot" she answered.

She had guided me once more through the maze of my feelings. She personally had passed through so many difficult situations. I remember her now, at ease with her life, coming through thick and thin, always ready to help others when they came to hard times. Life is made bearable by such beautiful people.

We sat talking, ranging over feelings and experiences. I told her how I had searched and searched for love, never finding it in the physical world. Or finding people whom I loved, but who didn't love me. I had learnt that the worst thing was not being alone, but not loving. If I was in love with someone who did not return my love, I learnt to simply let the love flow. It felt so much better than saying 'He doesn't love me therefore I can't love him'. I described how my love flowed to many, to fantasies, to friends, to the unattainable, to the energy of love and to the memory of David. How I learned to say to myself, 'The best that I can imagine, the tenderest love, the brightest day, exists by virtue of my knowledge of it. It is what my spirit is giving me now.' This was a sure way to end fruitless longing and unhappy days.

Leah knew these paths, she too had travelled them. Then I spoke of the white hot metal that sometimes pulsed in my veins.

"I am always on the other surface of something I am afraid of. A cauldron steaming so fiercely as to be uncontrollable. Sometimes creativity, sometimes anger when I am frustrated."

I described how it glimmered through the cracks in my armour plate. I simmered often, fuelled by the molten emotion which I perceived in tiny flashes. Years of schooling by parents had covered it with layers of guilt and superstition. 'Little girls don't speak like that to their elders and betters!' The anger seemed to be in touch with a power of a different order of magnitude to that normally encountered. Or through my obedience to rules and regulations, I had succumbed to the building of a socially acceptable cage. It took nearly all my energy to keep it under wraps. Underneath there was something raging, it could kill or love with equal ferocity.

"But what is this power? Where does it come from? Of course it brings irritation when things are not going well, when nobody listens. But it seems more than that to me. I feel there is a misunderstanding somewhere," I continued.

"The fiery source is not anger like a naughty child, talking back to her parents, but a glimpse of the creative will," Leah explained. "It is a violent power, but also the origin of all artistry and inventiveness. The wells of love and creativity will always be there, they are part of us, our own being. But there is nothing negative about the fire of will. It is there with love as a resource, burning in eternity. It is pure radiance, the fuel of life." She went on

"We come to earth in our forgetfulness of our true nature. It is the cosmic joke, the divine comedy that we enjoy as life's experiences remind us of who we are. We live to remember not only ourselves and each other, but our relationship to all creation. Our creation. Everything we attempt broadens as our creation proceeds. To stay within our physical limitations we choose to concentrate on a tiny part of the whole, the part which bring us the most fulfilment. If God stays in himself all is well, but He has no experience. All adventures come through God's creating parts of Himself in forgetfulness and encountering our feelings as we gradually remember ourselves as limitless beings."

We heard a cry from above and saw two eagles flying overhead, swooping and climbing together, dividing the sky in the harmony of flight. We looked at each other and acknowledged that all has not been said, there is more to be created here on earth. We have the patterns, we know in our souls where we want to go. The creative will, the white hot passion which I had met at my birth was the fuel. I vowed to use it. To join my will with the greater powers and see love flourish here on earth.

*

I started to think about my life as Sibyl, midwife to the dead, and my contact with the world of spirit. It has brought with it a new dimension to life and such peace that I could not live without. I remembered the contacts I have had with the dead and dying. A relative who had died, leaving young children. I had come across her grave by chance whilst looking for graves of Ned Kelly's gang, and remembered her story. After her death her family had been racked with grief, it had seemed too intense, too shocking to lose a young wife and mother. Now as I left the cemetery something clutched at the back of my neck, and I felt uncomfortable. Talking later that day to Leah, she said

"You have somebody with you who died leaving small children."

"Is that what it is? I visited her grave, and she must have come with me."

I settled myself in a corner, to explain to the relative that time had passed, her children were grown up, married with their own children. I sent love and light to the woman to open to the passage of time, felt her relief, and her hold on my neck was withdrawn as she accepted the possibility of moving onwards.

My daughter Esther is now a nurse, and in the course of her work has witnessed some strange events. She told me the tale about the dying Vietnamese grandmother, arguing furiously with unseen people. Her son had explained to Esther that she was arguing with her dead relatives who had come to collect her, refusing to go with them.

On another occasion she told me about a twenty-eight year old boy who was admitted into the intensive care ward, transferred from the cancer hospital. I found myself involved, seeing her story as she told it.

The young man was ill with advanced leukemia, not long to go now. But he hoped against hope that this wasn't true, that it wouldn't be today, that he'd have a few more years, months? Days then? Minutes? His eyes pleaded for time, whilst he knew it was running out. Fear erupted out of him. I'm too young to die, I haven't lived yet. His life blood was spurting out through an arterial cannula, put in to aid the staff to monitor his life, to watch as it ebbed away. It wouldn't be ebbing away if that artery continued to bleed, it would spurt away as fast as the precious blood. Just as well Esther was aware, was holding the blood in for now, calling for help which was slow in coming. The older nurse sat at the desk, not attending, not allowing her attention to be given to the younger nurse, 'not much more than a student, she should have gone off duty now, what is she doing here still, her shift is over'. The boy had diarrhoea too, said

"I need to be cleaned up." Esther was still standing there holding in his life.

"I can't clean you now" she said, "You'll be all right", knowing she lied.

The nurse from the new shift was coming over, wanting to change the soiled bed linen. The desk nurse looked over, decided to answer the call.

"Why haven't you gone off duty?" she said.

"I'm holding a bleed" was the answer.

Esther snapped angrily at the lack of commitment, the laid-back attitudes around her. She glared at the older nurse. Suddenly things started to be mobilized. The registrar was called, people hastened in with more technology; the rescue was in progress. Taping up, jabbing, tubes in this hole and out that one.

The dying, bleeding, frightened boy brought his fear into my heart as I listened to Esther's story, and I carried it with me during that day, sending him all the love in my being, hoping it could break through the well-meant technology feast in the hospital. Prayed that he would find someone to hold his hand and be with him as he died. I wondered if he was at all receptive to nature, or beauty, or was he too entrenched in his physical youth? He crashed so suddenly into my world, that there must be some way I could help him. I strode deeper and deeper into his fear, allowing it to take hold of me. The only way to deal with events is to go through them. They cannot be avoided or brushed aside. I take them in to the full, my spirit is always strong enough to deal with anything that comes. Suddenly I saw David standing on the other side of a bridge from me. As I looked at him, the anguished bundle of the boy's life moved towards David, who took it from me to take care of from the other side. The boy became free like a dolphin, swimming for eternity, embedded in healing, peace and freedom. This was Sibyl's work.

For David himself, how had it been? He had left his family in death, and would miss them, and maybe have no way of contacting them. He had died under the influence of morphine, which causes the sleep of not only the physical bodies. He would have been numb when he died, not able to see the world of spirit, his family funeral, or even the gathering which his colleagues had organized in his memory. He had been dead for three weeks before I had received the news of his death. Then suddenly, as I called to him over the layers of existence, he was awakened by my tap on his shoulder. Perhaps he remembered our time together, and the cloth of eternal life that his brother had spoken of at his deathbed, for he had answered in bliss.

In my dream I saw an aeroplane flying over the ocean. A woman fell out of the plane and was lost in the deep blue-green water. The aeroplane flew on but soon crashed on a distant mountain, on rocks that resembled chocolate cake. The metal of the plane broke up and reformed into six tiny dolphins, embedded in the rock. I was the woman falling from the plane and becoming lost in the emotion of living. David the aeroplane, losing his life eventually, before its time. Crashing too fully into matter, believing so strongly in the physical world.

I was singing in a performance of Verdi's Requiem. This was the epitome of Verdi's dramatic power, stirring one to the foundation of one's being. All fear, all dread conjured up in the massive drumbeats of the *Dies Irae.* Explosions of vibrating harmonies, soaring sopranos and growling basses. As I practiced, tapping my foot to the rhythms, finding my entrances, I felt David's presence. If I should sing it for him it would give a new meaning to the music. My voice would lead me into a new state of affinity. An idea started to be born, to give David, the man who liked people, a towering send-off. Many of his friends and colleagues whom I had met had said sadly,

"He was dead and buried before we knew he was ill."

About 1% of his life had been present at his funeral , so much morphine puts even the non-physical bodies to sleep. Only his nearest family had been present. His life could be celebrated , he needed to ritualize his life and death. I would offer him the concert as his funeral. I invited as many of his friends and students as I could remember to the performance, and planned a gathering, to meet and share reminiscences of David's life.

Where to meet afterwards? It must be close by the town hall, where the performance was to be held. It must be intimate, beautiful, close to nature if possible. I talked to Leah, who suggested a tea room in the gardens nearby the city. The next weekend when I was in town for the choir practice, I decided to investigate.

Meanwhile Beth (now sixteen years old) had moved to Melbourne to attend boarding school. I had started that year in Sweden, Mia and Esther were also away. But Sam began healing the loss we had all suffered when Beth had left our family. Being a movie buff, he took her out to the cinema on the weekends, and gradually they became firm friends.

The day I planned to choose a place for David's wake, Beth rang saying that she needed to pick up a bag from her Grandmother's.

"I'll drop it in for you if you like" I answered, "I'm going that way. Would you like to have a coffee with me?"

So Beth and I found ourselves walking through the gardens, amongst the blooms in the conservatory, making our ways through thick bushes, along winding paths, over stone bridges, across the grass to the tea rooms. Beautiful Beth, walking towards her adult life. Just to look at her made my heart leap with joy. A sunny spring day, the rhododendrons shimmering with rich pink and purple blooms. We sat in the tea rooms, ordered coffee and looked about. It didn't seem the ideal place for David's wake. The tables were for four people, in two long rows outside, and a big bare room inside, filled with more impersonal small tables. We asked about hiring a space.

"No the tea room closes at 5 pm" explained the manager, "Then we have weddings booked."

Beth and I walked around the gardens to see if there would be another suitable place. Morton Bay fig trees extended their roots, creeping into the earth, and spreading oak trees cast huge shadows on the grass. We walked towards an embankment planted with hundreds of small bushes, flowering in rich colour. As we turned the corner, I walked into my dream. There in front of me stood the metal dolphins, swimming over rocks the colour of chocolate, water playing over the whole in a fountain of fantasy. A little further on lay a large semicircle of bushes, a vast tree guarding the enclosure from the path winding along up the hill. This was the place.

David's friends began to ring me.

"Where have you been for so long, we haven't seen you, you're singing in it too? I'd love to be there"

Everyone I contacted was interested, almost all would come. I felt events shaping themselves, in the control of those who did things, the powers that mattered. I was not the sort of person who could enthuse people by my own capacity. 'The world's worst sales rep' I had acknowledged myself. Suddenly all these people were ready to pay their respects to David, were indeed pleased to renew contact, were vital and alive, and coming on this journey. I felt surrounded and protected by goodness. I had only to do my own part, all would be well.

"David my friend, thank you!" Today on my birthday I awoke with his good wishes, and the big pink parcel on the end of my bed, tied with rose ribbon. I unwrapped it and found a beautiful bowl inside it.

I had awakened with this vision in my head. It had been many years since David had remembered my birthday, but when we were together we had delighted in surprising each other with gifts. I confided often in David, whilst realizing that he was already aware of what I was doing.

Later I sat in the rose garden, in the quiet semicircle of trees where I often went to meditate. I imagined David sitting beside me. I turned my face towards him, remembering how he had kissed me before. My lips started to tingle. I closed my eyes, giving my feelings to him. Sat enjoying his closeness.

"Hello" a voice intruded.

I struggled back to the physical world, and saw a fat boy on a bicycle ride by.

"Hello" I managed to find my voice.

I remembered previous interruptions to our lovemaking,

"We are still not allowed our privacy!"

I imagined I could hear David laughing at the absurdity of life's situations.

I chose the bowl for my birthday present, Japanese craftsmanship expressed in jade green, a scatter of white cherry blossom petals over the surface, an elegant deep shape.

Tempel Tuttle, the comet's tail through which earth was passing had given a display of meteors in the night sky. I got up at 2am to see a spray of small white lights coming from the constellation Leo. The next night I went outside at 9.30pm, and saw the big green and orange meteor, my birthday gift.

Neptune, the planet of the spiritual life was preparing to leave the sign of Capricorn symbolizing paternalistic structures. The negativity of our earthly systems was being smashed finally, to come into the new life of Aquarius. I considered various problems, where rules and regulations intruded on good sense and honest behaviour. The religions of the world filling souls with fear and guilt when they could have supported people's personal consciences. The education system through which so many students were battling just now, versus education respecting people in their most human context. I had a vision of the arbitrary rules joining with the compassionate approach to life, both being swept upwards to become one, which then exploded in a spray of white lights, like the meteor shower I had seen in the sky. The Christ love burst forth from the reconciliation of opposites, showering the earth in a new consciousness.

*

Whilst the choir were practicing the Requiem on Friday night I tuned in to David, and saw that he was meditating on his future. He was preparing to release his earthly life and step into the life of a freed spirit. I saw that he felt awed, on the brink of the scarcely remembered, stepping into the precipice and trusting there would be some sort of ground under his feet.

On the morning of the performance, I awoke to hear the clock strike forty, highlighting the day. My sanity was not now in question, but there was a riddle in my head. It was a book, 'The Aquinas Man' by Agatha Christie. A mystery story. David of course, the Aquinas man. I had recently read about St Thomas Aquinas. He believed in the 'Natural Law', laws which could be approached validly from either reason or Christian faith. The truth of one approach overlaps with the truths reached from the other. The two ways of reaching a truth complement each other, like greeting a person, seeing their face and hearing their voice. I understood that David and I had found the same spiritual understanding, I coming from earth, and he from the world of spirit.

Before the concert as the choir dressed in their black skirts and white blouses, the men in their dinner jackets and bow ties, I looked into my inner vision to see what David was doing. He stood resplendent in his dinner suit and black tie, putting the final touches to his appearance, adjusting his tie. He nodded to me, saying,

"It's nearly time, good luck!" A touch apprehensive I thought, anticipating the bitter-sweet change.

The choir walked onto the stage, in lines like school children, sat stiffly correct and viewed the audience, slowly finding their places. I looked to the seats I had sold, they were filling up. In the distance the faces were strangely mixed, the features of one seen on the face of another. My mind began to identify each one, and it subtly recalled the influence each one had had on David and me.

*

Suddenly I became Sibyl, my feet on either side of the river of death, holding the energy as the requiem began, evoking our love for God, life and suffering, death and life anew. The music commenced in softness, almost whispered prayers for light and peace, then high drama, resounding trumpets calling the dead, to come and be present, accept their judgement, grovel at the feet of the almighty God. An angry God who has no place these days, bar in the poetry of death. As the four drum beats invoked the *Dies Irae*, I felt my soul respond in magnitude, blending with all the souls there present, in the majesty of the music. The drama giving way to pleas for leniency, 'Grant them eternal rest' over and over.

The music brought all the players of my life into focus. I saw my father, sitting with my brother. My mother was singing with me in the choir. I remembered their unceasing love and loyalty for all their children and saluted them in gratitude.

On the other side of the bridge I acknowledged my grandparents and dearest Paddy. How much she taught me. We will meet again.

Our two families of children, now adults and in their own careers. So much love I have for them. I blessed them, recalling David's devotion and my tenderness. I remembered Beth and Alice. When I saw Beth growing up, talented and determined, I knew I had made a good decision. Two pictures came into my mind. George de la Tour's 'The Newborn'. In it a mother and daughter with serene faces gaze at the sleeping infant. The scene is lit by a single candle, catching expressions and throwing up deep shadows. A world within a world, as the world of spirit within their eyes looks out on the physical reality. The child sleeps on undisturbed. The second is a photograph of David looking down at our newborn daughter. I am impressed by the similarity in the two pictures. Again, timelessness is present in their stillness and the radiance of their faces. Beth will always be a part of us no matter what happens, all I have to do is to stand back and radiate love to her. All the rest she will do herself.

I saw Leah's dear face, calling to mind our lives as we had grown together, friends who always responded to a call, always held out our hands to each other. I gave thanks.

My husband and David's wife. I recalled them to mind and saw that at last I could accept them, their roles, their help to create the situations which now I had mastered. What chaos had resulted from disobeying the conventions of society . I made my peace with them.

I looked out at David's students, always beloved and served. His fellow workers, sitting in front of me in the audience. We had shared our lives for those years, enjoyed academic discussions, had eaten together in pubs and taught our students in turn. I recalled the stories David had told me of each one, and saw them within their context in the scientific life of our city. I acknowledged them. I thought of Professor Bullgate with forgiveness, and knew he would reap an appropriate reward.

The Sanctus marched its rhythmic phrases, bringing lightness and hope.

I focussed once more on David and saw him sitting with his head resting on his hand, in an attitude I knew well of complete concentration on the task in hand. In how many lectures had I seen him sitting so, collecting his thoughts, planning his response?

He was a person of great love. He brought people together, he cared for his family, he fostered his students, assisted his colleagues, and was respected and admired by them. The bridge of love exists between him and them, it is only for those on earth to dare to traverse it. This is the person he was on earth, how much more he is now that he is freed from the body. After David had died we had found each other because of the strands of love which bound us together. It seemed that once two people have loved each other, no matter what has intervened in the physical life, beset with difficulties as it is, that the path is laid, and can always be traversed again. Lovers once are lovers always, all forgiven, all slates wiped clean.

During the '*Lux aeterna*' the music wafted higher, at last at peace. I glanced again at my vision of David. He stood up suddenly and turned to leave. Nostalgia flooded me. In my mind I called to him

"Don't go yet, wait until we are finished" but at the same moment he looked into my eyes and I realized that this was his time. In my heart I released him. I saw his suit of clothes fall on the ground, lying in a crumpled heap as his body disappeared. And in its place I saw his spirit, huge, shining and radiant, copper and bronze. Beaming love, knowledge and joviality, the essence of Jupiter the expansive. David was free.

As the Requiem marched towards its concluding prayer, the town hall altered as my consciousness floated upwards to another sphere. The space became voluptuous in its decoration, and yet spare. Rich simplicity. Spontaneous creativity. Every thought changed the hangings, first a deep blue, then gold, then a gentle turquoise. The white walls arched into a vault above my head. I could see the Angels above me, not painted on the surfaces, but living spirits, now visible to my inner eyes. In the centre of the hall was a soft couch, the carpet led me to it, the colours still changing with my mood, a soft orange now, warm and comforting. I walked up to it and sat down. I saw David enter the hall from the other end, he walked towards me and sat beside me. We smiled at one another as we took each other's hands. I felt waves of peace flow through my veins. I saw that we had begun to merge. I felt the energy rise from my toes, saw our two figures becoming one. The music soared to a crescendo, weaving colours of rose and orange about us, intensifying our bliss. The energy rose, up our legs, thighs, through our bodies, up to our heads. We sat together, the soprano voice intertwining with the choir and forming a cocoon around us allowing our spirits to explore each other. Conscious of every part of life still, but focussing our radiance on love. An experience including dimensions as yet untried, including the known and introducing the unknown. Head and heart functioning as one. Then the Christ light, the electric blue overshadowed us, and as we released each other the blue remained with each. To accompany us through life as a reminder of all possibilities.

And Life continues, its manifest threads searching out the non-manifest, longing for them, as made opposites. These facets in David and I are present in everyone, finding each other for a few precious moments, then drifting apart again to prepare for a new visit to the hall of dreams, uniting then separating, to recreate the joy of union. For ever and ever, finding, losing, seeking, keeping. On earth as it is in heaven.

꩜ EPILOGUE ꩜

DAVID HAS GONE ON to his life of spirit. From now on he seemed more distant, I received no visions of him in my sitting room as I had previously. And yet, sometimes as I sit here writing, delving into a scarcely remembered past, I am visited by a strange quivery feeling, and suddenly the words are pouring out of me, my memory is renewed and the story takes shape. Or I awaken with the knowledge that we have spent time together in a realm which I am unable to reach in my waking state.

David, I remember the bridge you were to help me to build, the bridge over the old ways of living, the duality. The place where good follows bad, or bad follows good. The see-saw of life. Where rich and poor exist side by side, and enormous efforts count for so little. Where war and violence are used in the pretense that they can bring peace. The place where almost all relationships are doomed to failure. Where children are abused, and peoples massacred. We are so tired of duality.

I go into the space in my head where I can see the answers to my questions, and look again at our bridge into oneness. Much of the work is behind us now, there are crowds of us on the bridge, and we are all working towards its completion. I can see it stretching into our new earth, shimmering and shining, light and white, glowing and radiating. Although our journey continues, we now see our destination clearly. The earth whose travail is over, her purification by fire complete, is a world where love rules. Where there is one aim, to honour all life as an expression of God's joy. Each grain of sand and waft of air is valued for the life which springs forth and we cooperate with every being, person, animal, plant and mineral. Where the Garden of Eden returns to earth. My companions and I know that the goal is worth working for, there is no possibility of retreat. It is simply to continue. Already I see amongst my friends the results of openness with each other, honest dealing and direct communication. The new relationships are growing, finding depths which have not been seen here before. The promise is great.

I feel a bond of spirit with Beth that is eternal. When I see her, growing taller, her ideas developing, her essence maturing, I am reminded of her father's temperament. Open and welcoming, a smile and a warm greeting for everyone. Even in her appearance I can see her parents' traits. Her being and mine are at one. And yet here is a young woman whom I hardly know. At her marriage she had long dark hair, defying genetics and choosing her own way of presenting herself. During her teenage years our meetings were few and rarely planned, and yet they were strung like a necklace of jewels, precious at a level way beyond the banalities of physical life. I perceived her soul, creating itself in its own perfection, embracing each stage of life as it came to her, stepping surely forward. Everything is perfect exactly the way it is.

My decision to give Beth to Alice was clear since before she was conceived, and never regretted. The consequences however each took their own time to resolve. The first was the grief of parting which burst upon me and took two years of mourning to take away its rawness. It is still with me. The second consequence was that of unfulfilled motherhood. This has been left hanging, during all the years of Beth's childhood and adolescence until now as a free woman, we meet as equals, and also as mother and daughter. Her life is turning out so like mine, with no prompting from me. She lives her life for love. We understand each other implicitly. Now that she has married her first boyfriend like I did so many years ago, and she lives close to me, we have the opportunity to be friends. We confide in each other, and I find my motherhood reawakening, feelings that I had to suppress in order to survive. I had never been satisfied to let these feelings be, but now the wheel has turned full circle, and all is as it should be.

Beth is also becoming a sister to Mia, Sam and Esther, forming individual friendships with each one. Their tempestuous teenage years have fallen away, and mature relationships are blossoming between all four of my children.

Another mystery solved itself now – Beth, Elizabeth Patricia – every time I meet her now I am so reminded of Paddy, both her looks and her presence feel similar. Paddy's message from the Spiritualist Church suddenly went click inside me, "She knows you well, and even has the same name". Paddy's eyes looked out through Beth's, reminding me of eternity.

Mother's wilful clock struck 225 before it was finally sent for repair. In a sense it approached infinity, as it took 15 minutes to strike so many, and then it was time to strike the next quarter. Afterwards it was back to a sedate earthly rhythm of one to twelve. My own world parallels the clock, it seems as if the exterior is unchanged, whilst I know that my interior also approaches infinity. I live in total surrender to the Creator. The love of all humanity pulses though my veins, and with it an astute person might see the synchronicity of events in my physical life. My daily life is streamlined, shopping made easy, parking places appear where I need them. Even my face seems to grow younger. A new relationship, the white pearl, is growing in my heart, this time unfettered by the rules of society. It is based on the love of self for the Self, ultimately all Life. As we children of the Creator dance in the starlight, our moments of joy are reminders of the universe of love which is our being. A red carpet is laid before us. As we wait for our final days here on earth in silence, we are blessed. Even when we see in compassion the hideous events which burst forth on earth's surface like boils healing, we walk together in acceptance of her process. The physical earth reality is in a different dimension now, the life of love has taken precedence, has divided away and is creating anew. Even though we can still see the greed and selfishness unfolding their world, our world of harmony is still open for anyone to join. For Earth too will soon shed her physical skin, to emerge like a butterfly, cleansed and beautiful, in alignment with her original purpose.

꧁ The Author ꧂

DR KRISTIN SCHNEIDER is an Agricultural Scientist, who has worked for 25 years in teaching and research in universities in Melbourne Australia. After leaving the university, she worked briefly as a consultant, and found herself speaking to people who had an alternative view of Agriculture, often on hobby farms. Her interests broadened to embrace Biodynamic Agriculture and Permaculture, which gave her a clear understanding of ecology, the dependence of all things upon each other. She worked to encourage people to live in harmony with their surroundings. From here it was a small step further to reach into the Oneness of all things, and to know that the smallest acts can have great consequences. After retirement she spent seven years in a community in Sweden where she studied massage and healing, working not only with people and their physical and emotional states, but also in plants, soils and the earth herself. Through her Great Uncle who fought during WW1, she developed an interest in the shattered lives of the soldiers of that time, and has visited many of the old battlefields, seeking out men's stories to bring order into old memories. This the subject of her latest book. Now she lives in Australia, dividing her time between her children and grandchildren, writing and travelling. She can be contacted by email, kris.schneider@iinet.net.au

❖ ❖ ❖